I0877255

Collectanea Celto – Asiatica Cracoviensia

Editors:
Jadwiga Pstrusińska
Andrew Fear

Cracow 2000

Editors:
Jadwiga Pstrusińska
Andrew Fear

Technical editor:
Agnieszka Kuczkiewicz-Fraś

The editors generally respect the author's editorial choices contained in the volume.

The printing of this volume would not have been possible without the financial support of the Philological Faculty and the Institute of Oriental Philology, Jagiellonian University, Cracow.
The Celto-Asiatic Seminar wishes also to express its gratitude to the Jagiellonian University for the 1996 and 1998 research grants.

The cover shows the motives of the Celtic cross and the cross on a cult pilar in the Hindukush region.

ISBN: 83-7188-337-4

© Institute of Oriental Philology
Jagiellonian University, Cracow

KSIĘGARNIA AKADEMICKA
ul. Św. Anny 6, 31-008 Kraków
tel./fax (+48 12) 43 127 43, 422 10 33 ext. 1167
e-mail: ksakadem@cicero.law.uj.edu.pl
http:/www.ch.uj.edu.pl/ksiegarnia.html

Contents

Preface

The articles collected in this volume represent some of those presented by the participants of an interdisciplinary Celto-Asiatic Seminar established in 1995 by Jadwiga Pstrusińska (Department of Iranian Philology) at the Institute of Oriental Philology, Jagiellonian University, Kraków. The basic theme of the seminar is outlined in the paper "Why the Celto-Asiatic Seminar?"*. The following papers represent a wide spectrum of views, including some controversial ones, not all of which support the initial hypotheses of the seminar, and which give the reader a taste of the discussion generated by the project. After the papers, there is a list of the entire programme of Seminar meetings during the four years of its existence.

J. P., A. F.

---

* [in:] *Iranica Cracoviensia. Cracow Iranian Studies in memory of Władysław Dulęba*, ed. A. Krasnowolska, Kraków 1996.

Marzenna Czerniak-Drożdżowicz
(Cracow)

Celto-Indian parallels in art

Indian and Celtic art developed in distant regions, but in the light of present-day research concerning migration and contacts of the nations inhabiting areas of Eurasia the distance between these two cultures is not perceived as barrier which cannot be crossed. While is worth thinking over the possible similarities or connections, it seems that our present level of knowledge does not let us draw any explicit conclusion.
Before I go into the question of possible parallels in Celtic and Indian art, I would like to dwell on these two areas separately.

Indian art is not only that of the Aryan nation, which appeared in India about 1500 B.C., but also the art of the nations inhabiting India long before the arrival of Aryan people. The most interesting non-Aryan art is that of the Mohenjo Daro and Harappa culture, which seems to precede the Aryan invasion. The origin of the nation of Harappa culture has still not been explained. The theory of Dravidian origin is opposed to the theory about the possible Indo-European origin of this nation or, if it was not Indo-European, maybe there were some contacts with the earlier waves of Aryan invaders, which, it is supposed, could have appeared in India before the main wave of the Aryans – creators of the Vedas[1].

The art of Harappa and Mohenjo Daro is represented by a number of exhibits, among which steatite seals are distinguished. On these seals samples of still undeciphered writing are accompanied mainly by representations of animals and also people or rather deities. Apart from the seals, there are the sculptures of human shapes which include two male torsos, one female dancer, and a bearded man (priest?).

---

[1] About *dāsyu* and *paṇi* see: A. Parpola, "The coming of the Aryans to Iran and India", [in:] *Studia Orientalia*, vol. 65, Helsinki 1988, p. 195-302.

Early Aryan art, very probably, developed from the time of the settlement in India, but very few traces of this time, such as ruins or rather foundations of the palaces, remain.

Usually, when speaking about Indian art, one starts with Buddhist art because it is only from this school that many wonderful monuments of architecture, sculpture and painting remain. The survival of these monuments was due to the change in the construction technique from the use of wood to that of stone or bricks. This change is usually attributed to the Iranian influence. Among monuments of this period sanctuaries and monasteries built in rocks, stupas, columns, reliefs, and sculptures should be mentioned. They are connected with the three styles: Gandhara, Mathura, and Amaravati. Painting is represented especially by pictures decorating the caves of Ajanta. Buddhist art is dated between the 3rd century B.C. and 7th century A.D. (in any case, the most representative works belong to this period).

The development of fine art connected with Hinduism started prior to the beginning of the Christian era. Apart from Buddhist works, there appeared Hindu ones which were very often similar to Buddhist art, but usually it is understood that in the Buddhist art peace and calm dominate whereas Hindu works are more dynamic. Hindu sculpture is similar to Buddhist but in architecture discrete styles typical for Hinduism appear. It refers mainly to the architecture of temples which, from about 1000 A.D., were built in several particular styles: nagara, vesara and dravida. The mass of the temple enlarges with time and its construction becomes more complicated, developing from simple, rectangular temples covered with flat roof to the temples topped with a tower very often tens of meters high, having several halls added for devotees. Inside and outside decorations on the walls of the temple are also more and more elaborate. There appear wonderful reliefs which continue the Buddhist tradition of depicting the whole story in following stages of development in one composition. Side by side with monumental sculptures of gods (for example Maheśamūrti) there appear bronze sculptures made by the "a cire perdu" method, speciality of artists particularly in the South of India in the 11th century. But from about the 10th century a slow decline in art begins. This was caused mainly by the final codification of every rule concerning the process of creation of any object of art. The Indian theory of art created many manuals, which artists-artisans had to use and only few of them were able to go outside of the firm frame-works of convention and create original works of art. Wonderful bronze sculpture with time also becomes less valuable. Only in painting did unquestionably valuable works still appear. In India miniatures are mostly connected with Muslim painting. However even before the appearance of the Moghul school in India, there existed original painters' workshops which dealt mainly with the illustrating of Hindu and Buddhist manuscripts. Without doubt the Moghul school had a prevailing influence on the miniatures of, most probably, all local schools of painting in India. So from the 15th century A.D. Indian miniatures develop in several schools: Moghul, Rajput, and Pahari, which survived until the beginning of the 20th century. The Moghul period is the time of the influence of Islamic art in India and this bore fruit not only in the appearance of such a splendid monument of "clean" Islamic art like the Taj Mahal, but also provoked the appearance of a style connecting the elements of both arts which is visible also in architecture. Although Indian art resisted Moghul influence and continued to develop, the period from 3rd century B.C. until the 10th century A.D. is considered as the time of its most significant development. This time is also important for our consideration of Celtic-Indian parallels.

Let us stay for the moment with Celtic art before we start our comparison. The Celts did not leave written sources concerning art, so the whole theory of their art is not clear. The question as to whether, like in India, art was closely connected with religion is also difficult to answer.
It seems that, as opposed to classical art, the Celtic art was not interested in imitating nature or in consummate beauty, but was mainly ornamental[2].
From what we know, on the continent Celtic art was developed in two periods, which bears fruit in works in two styles: Hallstatt (Austria) and La Tène (Switzerland).

The Hallstatt style is the earlier of the two and its beginning is usually dated to about 700 B.C. Paul Jacobsthal mentions several main characteristics of this style: use of geometrical design, the appearance of floral motifs, and the presence of eastern elements about which Jacobsthal writes: *The eastern components offer great difficulties. There was no trade with the east, there are no imports, the employment by Celts of Oriental artisans is doubtful. Yet the Celtic orientalizing style has a firm physiognomy*[3]. According to him the sources of these influences could be found in Italy, Scythia, and Persia. In the early phase Celtic art was dominated by ornaments, masks, and beasts, but devoid of the representation of human beings.

---

[2] L. and J. Lang, *Art of the Celts*, London 1994.

[3] P. Jacobsthal, *Early Celtic Art*, Oxford 1944, p. 160.

The art of La Tène, originating from about 500 B.C., is considered as wholly developed, and representing all the main characteristics of Celtic art. Geometrical-ornamental elements are replaced by human beings and fanciful lines, eliminating straight lines and acute angles for curved lines and curves. Fanciful lines very often covered patterns and pictures invisible on first sight. Among ornaments appear: palmetes, lotus flowers, lyre motifs, and calices calyx of flowers. There are also animal motifs which show many similarities to Oriental art. Part of these animals cannot be identified. La Tène style evolved from an early style which was raw and symmetrical to one which was asymmetrical and restless. Among frequent motifs one can see triskeles, smiling animals ("Cheshire Style"), faces with down-pointed mouths, creepers, bearded heads, adornments in the shape of fish bladders or dots, spirals, and torques. The later La Tène style is sometimes described as a plastic style because there appears a three-dimensional relief; rings, fibulae have convexities and balls adorned with convexities and small, snail-like balls. Another characteristic is the filling of the whole surface with motifs which are mainly floral, but also include stylised figures of animals (*horror vacui*). Eastern Celtic art, which was in contact with Sarmatians and Thracians, had some specific characteristics. Pictures of man and animal showing the traces of Iranian art appeared. Rosen-Przeworska writes: *In the eastern group influence of classical Greek and Roman art was still weak visible, but more distinct was the autochtonic background for example Italian, Illirian, Thracian, Dacian, German, Ligurian, Iberian and general influences called "Oriental" (...)*[4].
One of the most famous works of Eastern Celtic art is the cauldron from Gundestrup which reached Jutland from Danube region.
In the course of time Celtic art on the continent acquired some features of Roman art which dominated considerable areas of Europe, however it continued to develope in the British Isles.

The Insular art of Celts bears the traces of earlier styles (Hallstatt and La Tène) and also of Roman influence, but finally here, on the islands, Celtic art reached its greatest development. The insular style is sometimes called "scroll-work" due to its dominating spiral ornamentation. The plastic style also continued on the islands, but with clear Roman influence. 1st and the 2nd century A.D. are regarded as the climax of insular art. It is during this period that examples of s-shaped ornamentation appear on the reverse sides of the mirrors (as at Birdlip and Desborough).

[4] J. Rosen-Przeworska, *Ikonografia wschodnioceltycka*, Wrocław 1976, p. 22.

In the plastic style of this period enamel and coral were set in the ornament. On the islands the so called neo-Celtic style, which was developed under the influence of Christianity, appeared about the 6th century A.D. This contained elements of the old abstract-ornamental Celtic-style border on figural-plastic elements of German origin. Later, especially in 11th century, works of Celtic art were created for the church, and on reliquaries, bells, and crucifixes one could find Celtic ornaments. This style had been slowly losing its influence and finally was replaced by the style of the Romanesque period.

Do Celtic and Indian art contain any common features? When I started to deal with this problem, it seemed to me that, if I could see any similarities, they were mainly between Celtic and Buddhist art, or, more generally, Indian art of the period from the 3rd century B.C. until the 7th century A.D. I think that this first impression was correct because, as far as I could say something on the basis of the few materials available to me, in this particular period such similarities are visible and possible. Nevertheless I am not able to answer the question about the direction of influence. It is probable that, apart from the Persians and Greeks, a very big role in the transmission of influences could have been played by the Scythians. Tribes, which at the end of previous and at the beginning of this era captured considerable tracts of land in India: Śaka, Yue-zhi, originated from the steppes, and are connected with the Scythians[5]. Esther Jacobson reports the findings of the Russian scholars Rayevski and Bessonova, according to whom the mythology and religion of the Scythians had Iranian and Indo-Iranian sources[6]. The Yue-zhi nation, whose representatives established the Kushan dynasty in India, stimulated a very rich development of mainly Buddhist art. Among the Buddhist transitional styles are two which, in my opinion, are very interesting: the Gandhara and Mathura styles (represented also by the works from the Kushan epoch).

The Gandhara style, represented by the works created in the north-western part of India, but also in modern-day Pakistan and Afghanistan, is characterised by the influence of Mediterranean art which came here together with invaders under Alexander the Great's command. In depictions of the Buddha, which appear here as some of the earliest, after the period in which Buddha was repre-

[5] E. Jacobson, *The Art of the Scythians. The Interpretation of Cultures at the Edge of the Hellenic World*, Leiden 1995, p. 30.

[6] E. Jacobson, *op. cit.*, p. 60.

sented only by his symbols, one could visibly discern the influence of classical art. The Buddha is stylised as the young man with Apollo's beauty and his clothes are also classical. At the same time, in this style Iranian elements appear, especially in the pictures of boddhisattvas, who are shown as Parthian or Scythian warriors. Similarly, as in Celtic art, one can see here elements of classical art.

In case of the art of the second school – the Mathura foreign influences seem to be clearly visible. One can see the influence of the nomads from the Asian steppes, who are connected with the Scythians. Figures are often dressed in clothes typical for nomads and have "Scythians caps". Similarly, some parallels can be seen when looking at Celtic numismatics and also at the coins from the North of India dating from the beginning of our era (especially of the Kushana period). Evidently both were under the influence of classical numismatics but there appeared motifs which one can find among the Celts and in India: the circle (*cakra*), the swastika, animal figures, especially of horses, and also of deities. The swastika is a very frequent motif in India, but it is interesting that it can also be seen on the seals from Mohenjo Daro, and Harappa. This fact could also speak for the universality of this motif or for its Indo-European origin, or only for earlier contacts of the nation of Mohenjo Daro with Indo-Europeans (possibly with an earlier wave of invasion). In any case, this motif, very typical for Indian art, was found at Mohenjo Daro and also among the Celts in Europe.

One more discovery from Mohenjo Daro is worth noticing: the seal representing the so-called proto-Śiva surrounded by animals[7]. A human figure with its head crowned with horns is sometimes identified with Śiva in his form called Paśupati – the Lord of Animals. It is difficult to say how correct this supposition is, especially on the basis of present-day research. It is worth noticing the pose in which the presumed deity sits – it reminds one of the yoga postures and from this appeared theories about yoga's pre-Aryan origins. This seems probable, if one considers that Śiva himself has non-Aryan lineage (it is supposed that Śiva was, at the beginning, one of the local deities of the South of India, worshipped among non-Aryan tribes). Asko Parpola in the preface to the *Corpus of Indus Seals and Inscriptions*[8], draws attention to the identification of this figure with Mahisha made

[7] Asko Parpola in the preface to the *Corpus of Indus Seals and Inscriptions* noticed that the language of the seals is sometimes considered to be proto-Dravidian, but sometimes also proto-Indo-European, proto-Indo-Iranian etc.

[8] *Corpus of Indus Seals and Inscripions*, ed. J. P. Joshi and A. Parpola, Helsinki 1987, p. XVII.

by Alf Hiltebeitel. The Mahisha demon is very often represented as a sinister bull or man-bull and is identified with the sinister (*bhairava*) aspect of Śiva. Parpola writes: *Sir John Marshall's identification of a "Proto-Śiva" in the buffalo-horned deity of a famous seal from Mohenjo-daro (M-304) may well be correct, and so may be Alf Hiltebeitel's even more convincing identification of this figure as "Proto-Mahisa", although this deity and his "yogic posture" have close counterparts in the earlier glyptic art of the proto-Elamits. Comparative studies thus suggest that the Indus civilisation may have been an integral if marginal part of the West Asian cultural area and that there is an unbroken cultural continuity in South Asia from the Harappan times until the present day.*

The posture in which the proto-Śiva appears can be found in many works of Celtic art (figures from Roquepertuse, the figure from Gundestrup cauldron, and sculpture depicting Cernunnos). This posture, in the literature concerning Celts, is described as the "Buddha posture", but in my opinion, the authors of *The Oxford Illustrated Prehistory of Europe* are right when they described it as a yogic posture. They refer specifically to the picture of the deity from the Gundestrup cauldron, one of the most splendid monuments of continental Celtic art. It is difficult to resist the impression that this figure reminds one of the horned deity from Mohenjo Daro: it has the same posture, head with horns, and is surrounded by animals figures. The torque which the deity holds in his hand reminds us of the bracelets which one can find in India. It is, possibly, one of the most spectacular examples of the probable similarities in both arts, however one cannot speak about proved parallels. As for the posture of the deity, there are also some sceptical opinions concerning the connection of this posture with yoga. J. Rosen-Przeworska, for example, quotes S. Muller's opinion that: *Sitting in the Buddha pose is characteristic for pastorals (shepherd's) nations which, due to their nomadic style of life, did not use tables and stools on high legs which were difficult to be carried*[9].

One feature of Celtic art was an aversion to empty space, so it was covered with ornaments or was filled with reliefs representing scenes with human and animal figures. As J. Rosen-Przeworska describes it: *(...) on the stelas of the graves we have the scenery which is laid in the square frames. They close in a particular area the particular plot*[10]. The typical monuments of insular art – crosses – were decorated in the same way. A very similar style can be found in

[9] J. Rosen-Przeworska, *op. cit.*, p. 75 ff. 3.

[10] *Ibidem*, p. 176.

some Buddhist monuments. In Sanchi the gates leading to the stupas were covered with narrative reliefs which represent scenes from the life of the Buddha. Monuments from Gandhara, Bharhut, and Amaravati are ornamented in a similar way. Also in case of Indian art one can see predilection for filling space.

In both arts we meet androgynic figures and deities with many heads. This should be connected with the belief in the many aspects of the deity and his omnipotence. Rosen-Przeworska writes: *It seems however that doubling of the faces, multiplication of their number to three or four had the aim to show to simple people the omnipotence of the deity in such an evident way, because the initiated (like Druids) understood the deity rather abstractively*[11]. Androgynic figures showing the union of the male and female elements in one figure appear among Celts and in India. It is worth noticing that in both arts the method "a cire perdu", which I have mentioned as one of the most important techniques of sculpture in India, was present.

Very probably one could find many more similarities between both arts (as one of the few examples of the influence of Celtic art on the art of Asia is considered, for example, the head of the Celt from Hadda in Afghanistan), but more detailed studies are necessary and such research, and the development of the knowledge in this field will enable us to answer unanimously whether such similarities are accidental or the result of a common origin or only contacts of both cultures.

On the basis of the materials which were available to me not much more can be said, but I would like to draw attention to one more domain of art – religious literature – or rather the way it is passed down. Anne Ross writes: *All these traditional disciplines, then, were required to be handed on orally from master to pupil, from generation to generation. A Druid-elect, we know now, took some 20 years to master and fully assimilate the secret of his calling. Likewise, in Ireland, a fili ("poet", "seer"), was required to study for from 7 to 12 years in order to master orally the complex disciplines with which he was concerned.*

The oral tradition and its persistence is one of the most striking characteristics of the culture of the Celts[12].

The whole religious-philosophical literature of ancient India was handed down to the next generations in the same way, and the transmission demanded the same

---

[11] *Ibidem*, p. 80-81.

[12] A. Ross, *Everyday Life of the Pagan Celts*, London 1970, p. 135.

discipline from pupil and priest. What is treated by the scholars working on the culture of Celts as the characteristic feature of this particular culture could also be treated as the characteristics of the Indian culture, so the search for common places and parallels seems to be justifiable.

Bibliography

Chakraborty S., *Socio-Religious and Cultural Study of the Ancient Indian Coins*, Delhi 1986

Corpus of Indus Seals and Inscriptions, ed. Joshi J. P., Parpola A., Helsinki 1987

Czuma S. J., *Kushan Sculpture: Images from Early India*, Cleveland 1985

Gąssowski J., *Mitologia Celtów*, Warszawa 1979

Green M. J., *Dictionary of Celtic Myth and Legend*, London 1992

Jacobson E., *The Art of the Scythians. The Interpretation of Cultures at the Edge of the Hellenic World*, Leiden 1995

Jacobsthal P., *Early Celtic Art*, Oxford 1944, vol. I

Lang L., Lang J., *Art of the Celts*, London 1994

Maier B., *Lexikon der keltischen Religion und Kultur*, Stuttgart 1994

Lengyel L., *Le secret des Celtes*, Paris 1969

Megaw J. V. S., "The orientalizing theme in early Celtic art: East or West", [in:] *The Celts in Central Europe*, ed. Fitz J., Székesféhérvar 1975

Morgan J. D., *Manuel de Numismatique Orientale*, Paris 1923

The Oxford Illustrated Prehistory of Europe, ed. Cunliffe B., Oxford 1994

Pugachenkova G. A., *Iskusstvo Gandhari*, Moskva 1982

Rosen-Przeworska J., *Ikonografia wschodniceltycka*, Wrocław 1976

Ross A., *Everyday Life of the Pagan Celts*, London 1970

Schlette F., *Celtowie*, Łódź 1987

Schmidt K. H., "The Celtic Problem", [in:] *Zeitschrift für Celtische Philologie*, Tubingen 1992

Seaborne M., *Celtic Crosses of Britain and Ireland*, 1994

Andrew Fear
(Keele)

Solum litera scripta manet?

Any consideration of Eastern influence on Western culture needs also to take into account possible occurences of the reverse process – the potential impact of the colonists from the West on their host Eastern cultures. This paper will attempt to analyse the potential impact of settlement from the Greek-speaking world in the Classical and Hellenistic periods on the peoples and cultures of modern-day Afghanistan.

During his advance to India in 329 B.C., Alexander the Great's troops found a useful source of firewood – cedar boxes scattered over a hillside. Unfortunately these boxes turned out to be coffins and the local inhabitants of the region were less than impressed at the novel use Alexander's men found for their ancestors' tombs. For once in Alexander's career however his encounter with foreigners was to have a happy ending. After they had surrended, these natives revealed to their conqueror that their town was named Nysa and that they were descendants of the army of Dionysus who had been settled by the god in a colony on his return from the East[1]. Proof was forthcoming in the fact that the Nysaeans' holy hill was called 'meros', happily showing recognition of the myth that Dionysus had been born from his father's thigh (the Greek for thigh is *meros*). Moreover, alone of all the hills Alexander had passed, this one was covered by ivy, the god's plant. What more proof could be wanting? Arrian tells us that Alexander accepted these claims to the mythological past and his army gave itself over to *Bacchanalia* which lasted for over a week[2]. Arrian is

[1] For Dionysus' connection with Nysus see Homer, *Iliad* 6.130-140 where the god is chased by Lycurgus the Edonian over Nysus. The location is clearly envisaged as being in Thrace. The tradition of his invasion of the East is mentioned by Euripides, *Bacchae* 13.

[2] Arrian 5.1.1-3.

more than a little edgy about this tale and notes that several sceptical commentators, such as Eratosthenes, were inclined to reject the whole story out of hand[3]. He himself remains ambivalent, noting in his *Indica* that the Nysaeans were not Indians and might have been Greeks[4]. Some modern commentators however have shown far less scepticism than Eratosthenes or even Arrian: George Woodcock in his *Greeks in India* is inclined to deduce that the Nysaeans were in fact a settlement of Greeks[5].

This incident encapsulates many of the problems which any modern historian asking how Western cultures influenced the East is forced to confront. The classical world was ruthlessly parochial in its approach to radically different cultures which means that the statement about Dionysus cannot be taken in the same way as one made, for example, by a missionary in the last century suddenly happening upon a group of Christian natives. The Classical mind rapidly assimilated new Gods to familiar models: the Roman historian Tacitus tells us that Isis was worshipped by the native Germans[6]. Few now would take these words to suggest that a cult of this Egyptian goddess had in reality sprung up among Germans or feel the need to speculate, as Tacitus did, whether there had been an importation of this Egyptian goddess to strange Northern climes. It seems clear that in the tale of Nysa we are dealing with a similar phenomenon. The native god Shiva and his devotees' ecstatic rites have been assimilated by Alexander, quite possibly sincerely, despite the fact that he had much to gain in terms of morale-rising, to the classical God Dionysus. Dionysus was believed in classical antiquity, albeit probably falsely, to be a late Eastern newcomer to the Greek pantheon and the name of the settlement chimed in nicely with one of the God's standard titles, 'Nysaeus'. The thigh, meros, is likely to have been a misunderstanding for 'Meru', the holy mountain of Hindu cosmology. The Greek author Megasthenes similarly argued that all the hill-dwellers of this area worshipped Dionysus, whereas the plain-dwellers worshipped Heracles. He is taken to task for this rash statement by the geographer Strabo, but Strabo's gro-

[3] The Geographer Strabo writing in the Augustan period minces no words at all stating that 'It is clear that these stories have been made up by flatters of Alexander'. Strabo 15.1.9.

[4] Arrian, *Indica* (=*Anabasis* bk 8) 1.4.

[5] G. Woodcock, *The Greeks in India*, London 1966, p. 21 ff.

[6] Tacitus, *Germania* 9.

unds for complaint are inaccuracies in Megasthenes' account of where vines grow – he has no difficulty in assimilating Greek and non-Greek deities under a Greek umbrella[7].

The whole tale of the Nysaeans, therefore, seems at first sight entirely fanciful. Yet in the Swat hills there is a Kafir tribe who bury their dead in such coffins and cultivate, alone out of their neighbours, the vine. Like many unlikely tale from ancient sources, it is not the facts of the matter, but rather their interpretation that has gone awry.

Quite apart from the methodological problems this incident raises, it also poses obliquely another question. Were there settlements of Greeks in Central Asia prior to Alexander's expedition? Such a question is of importance as clearly if there was a long-standing tradition of settlement in this area the possibility that Greek culture made a lasting and deep impact on its host communities is increased.

Evidence for such settlements is however extremely sparse. There are stories which are mythological parallels to the tale of the Nysaeans. Eratosthenes mentions the discovery of a cave in the Hindu Kush which with the aid of a local legend was interpreted as the cave where Prometheus was chained by Zeus[8]. Another example is the assertion that the Sibae tribe living round the rock of Aornus in Sogdiana were followers of Heracles[9]. Here we are probably confronted with more pieces of religious rationalisation similar to that discussed above and quite possibly in the latter instance simply with a narrative doublet. The Indian Heracles is most likely to be an interpretation of the Hindu god Krishna. Apart from such accounts, our only evidence for Greek settlement in the story of Alexander's encounter with the Branchidae. This group is said to have been the descendants of the priestly clan of Apollo Didymus at Miletus who had been accused of stealing temple treasure and handing it over to the Persian king, Xerxes. The Great King therefore deported them to Sogdiana in 480 B.C. to prevent them suffering reprisals at the hands of local population.

[7] Strabo 15.1.58.

[8] Strabo 15.1.8.

[9] The 'proof' of this is that the Sibae wore skins like Heracles, carried clubs and branded their cattle with the mark of a club, Strabo 15.1.8.

The Branchidae greeted Alexander with enthusiasm: he ordered the preemptory extermination of these 'traitors'. It is difficult to know what to make of this story. The fact that it does not appear in Arrian, our best account of Alexander's campaigns, makes it immediately open to suspicion[10]. The notion of Panhellenic vengeance on 'collaborators' with the Persian fits perhaps a little to easily with Alexander's official reason for first launching his Persian venture and provides a convenient justification for continuing it beyond the death of the Great King. There is no account of the treachery of the Branchidae in Herodotus' account of the siege and sack of Miletus during the Ionian revolt (indeed he imputes a desire to sack the treasury to the initiators of the rebellion rather than the Persians or their supporters[11]) or of the Persian Wars and, while *argumenta ex silentio* are always problematic, this omission is certainly striking. The Branchidae's location is also suspicious. Bactria and Sogdiana, far from being a desirable residence, appear to have been a Persian equivalent of Siberia, and hence an odd place to move a favoured group asking for protection[12]. Transportation of Ionian women to Bactria had been a Persian threat at the beginning of the Ionian revolt[13]. Deportation, though not to Bactria, was certainly the fate of the other Milesians who survived the sack of their city in 494 B.C. Darius resettled them at Ampe by the Tigris[14]. We are told that the Persians retained the area of Miletus itself for their own use and settled the mountainous areas of its *chora* with Carians. These groups are most unlikely to have nursed grievances against the Branchidae. However, Darius' deportation may not have been as thorough as Herodotus implies (the Branchidae at least must have survived it) as the Milesians appear in the later Persian Wars and as members of the Delian League. Neverthless, as noted above, the choice of Sogdiana by Xerxes as a safe haven for the Branchidae out of all the Persian Empire seems remarkably odd. One way round some of these problems would be to suggest that the Branchidae were in fact deported by Persians because of their anti-Persian activities and

[10] It is rejected for these reasons by How and Wells *ad HDT* 6.19.3 and by Tarn, *Alexander* vol. 2, app 13. The story, probably deriving from Callisthenes, is found in Plutarch, *Moralia* 557b, Quintus Curtius 7.5.28-35, Diodorus Siculus 17.20, and Strabo 11.11.4.

[11] Hdt 5.36.

[12] Hdt 4.204.

[13] Hdt 6.9.

[14] Hdt 6.20.

that reports of their treachery were devised to justify Alexander's actions or as a *post eventum* excuse to hide his inability to control his army[15].

Supposing for a moment the improbable – that the Branchidae had indeed by whatever means arrived in Bactria – what is to be made of the story detailing their fate?

Given the lack of Greek scruples about close interbreeding[16], and that according to the tale their entire *genos* was deported, the Branchidae probably could have survived as a distinctive group in their new home for the four or so generations before Alexander exterminated them. Nevertheless Quintus Curtius states that they were already degenerating by the time of Alexander's arrival and had become bi-lingual[17]. Bilingualism is, at first sight, a very useful phenomenon by which to judge a community's cultural survival. It could suggest at least a degree of assimilation into the surrounding peoples, but at the same time we must remember that a community can easily shed its native tongue and still remain substantially distinct from its host. A fine example in the ancient world is the Greek-speaking Jewish diaspora The modern Irish form an equally good example from the present-day.

Again, the important question is how would such a group have survived. Did they interact with the local population or hold themselves aloof from it? Even if there was such a detached attitude, there would still have been some reaction by the host community to the new group's presence. This could have been one of contempt and disdain, of simply ignoring the newcomers, of fear, or of a wish to imitate and join the new community.

Whatever seeds the Branchidae may or may not have planted, there can be no doubt that it was Alexander who was responsible for the widespread implantation of Hellenistic settlement in the area. He seems to have been determined to secure his Northern frontiers against the steppe nomads of Sogdiana and

---

[15] A cynical suggestion could be that the Branchidae were indeed deported for this reason and Alexander's wrath was provoked by their not accepting him as a Macedonian as a leader of Panhellenic anti-Persian crusade.

[16] Cornelius Nepos, *Praef.*

[17] 7.5.29.

perhaps also to ensure the loyalty of the satrapy of Bactria itself whence had come his only serious challenger to the title of Great King, Bessus[18].

Alexander's settlements do not seem to have been popular either with the native population or his intended settlers. The local population had been only lukewarm supports of Bessus, but a furious revolt broke out after the planting of the city *Alexandria Eschate*. The best reason for the revolt is to see it as a reaction against the disruption of local patterns of allegiance and life. While it is a commonplace that Alexander founded cities in Sogdiana and Bactria, it is less often remembered that he is said to have destroyed others[19]. Moreover, settlers need to make a living and there can be no doubt that land which had already been worked and irrigated was taken from the locals to create suitable territorial enclaves to ensure the survival of Alexander's new foundations[20]. Those unlucky enough to be captured by Alexander in battle were allocated to work the land for the new settlers as their serfs[21]. In other words, the indigenous population found that a much stricter and more intrusive form of rule was being devised for them than of the old Persian satraps. It is little wonder that, if this was the case, the Sogdians and Bactrians rebelled against these new and unfamiliar restrictions. On advancing into India, Alexander left Bactria an armed camp, stationing no fewer than 13,500 men there to hold the area[22]. On his withdrawal west, at least 23,000 settlers were left in the region. To these settlers, mainly Greek mercenaries from Alexander's army, their presence in Bactria was no more welcome than it was to the natives. Black Cleitus, prior to his murder by Alexander, complained bitterly that he had been made satrap of Sogdiana, describing his new position as 'being sent among wild beasts'[23]. Cleitus was, of course, a Macedonian rather than a Greek and hence accustomed to a harsher more northerly climate. His views would have struck a loud cord in the minds of the Greek mercenaries who composed a substantial number of the

[18] On Darius' death Bessus proclaimed himself Artaxerxes V.

[19] Strabo 11.11.4, cf. 11.11.5 for the imposition of new toponyms by the Macedonians.

[20] This was definitely the case at Aï Khanum, see A. B. Bosworth, *Conquest and Empire*, Cambridge 1988, p. 248 'The new Foundations'.

[21] Arrian, 4.16.10.

[22] Arrian, 4.22.

[23] Quintus Curtius, 8.1.35 'You give me Sogdiana, ever-rebellious, which is not merely an unconquered land, but one that can't be conquered. I am being sent among wild beasts'.

settlers placed in Bactria. Mutiny broke out and after the death of Alexander an army of 23,000 settlers led by Philo of Aeniania attempted to march away from the new foundations and back to the west. Diodorus tells us their motives: 'they were sick for Greek culture and the Greek way of life'[24]. This desperate migratory army was faced down by a force despatched from Babylon by Perdiccas and, after considerable slaughter, the remaining settlers were forced back to their Eastern homes. Actions speak louder than words and the revolt of the settlers should in itself be sufficient to rule out the notion of large-scale Greek settlement or the diffusion of a semi-Greek way of life in Bactria prior to the arrival of Alexander. In fact, it seems that Bactria had retained its 'Siberian' reputation which it had possessed under the Persians. Racial tension may also have played a role in the rebellion. While the commanders of these new settlements were Macedonians, the majority of the settlers were Greeks. There appears to have been little love lost between these two groups in Alexander's army[25]. It may well be significant that by 320 B.C. the satrap despatched to this area was a Greek, not a Macedonian, the Cypriote Stasanor of Soli[26]. Alexander therefore appears to have laid not the foundations of civilisation, but the Eastern satrapies was continued by Seleucus Nicator with, it appears, little in the way of change in how they were regarded by all parties involved.

What is known of the settlements placed in the area? By far the most important is Aï Khanum, the city which was discovered by King Zahir Shah of Afghanistan in 1961 while hunting by the Oxus. Judging by its buildings, Aï Khanum ought to have been the satrapal capital of Bactria and then that of the new independent kingdom established in the region[27]. The changing interpretations of the site by its principal excavator, Bernard, encapsulate the drift of scholarship towards Alexander's activities in the East over this century. Bernard started by asserting that Aï Khanum was a completely Hellenistic city[28]. In this he echoes the notion of 'Alexander the civiliser' – a theme popularised by Plutarch in antiquity[29] and by Tarn in

[24] DS 18.7.1 ff.

[25] See: Arrian 2.10.

[26] DS 18.39.6.

[27] The ancient name is unknown.

[28] "Aï Khanum on the Oxus: a Hellenistic city in central Asia", *Proceedings of the British Academy*, 1967.

[29] Plutarch *Moralia* 328D says that Gedrosian children chanted the plays of Sophocles and Euripides because of Alexander.

modern scholarship. By the time he published a later commentary in the Scientific American[30], this enthusiasm had waned somewhat and the city had taken on important Eastern features.

Aï Khanum is clearly built in a defensive position and divided into a lower town and an upper citadel. The lower town is dominated by a palace complex 20 acres in size. The plan of this palace is Persian in conception containing living quarters, state offices, and a treasury. The building techniques of mud brick and use of flat roofs is also Oriental. Nevertheless the central courtyard had a colonnade with 118 columns surmounted by Corinthian capitals, albeit with Persian-style torus bases, and was adorned with Greek style terracotta ornaments.

The lower town also held a store-complex or arsenal, again of non-Hellenistic design. The plans of private houses also deviate from Hellenistic norms. Instead of a courtyard as the central focus, this is relegated to the front of the building and a large hall becomes the main feature.

A Greek visitor to Aï Khanum would therefore find himself in somewhat unfamiliar surroundings. Other aspects of the town, however, would have been very familiar. Aï Khanum sported two archetypal features of a Greek polis: a theatre whose radius was greater than that of the theatre in Babylon, the Seleucids' capital, and an equally impressive *gymnasium*.

The Greek language also survived. Traces of Greek poetry and even more surprisingly a post-Aristotlean philosophical treatise bearing a strong resemblance to Aristotle's *Physics*[31] have been found in the treasury. Another striking testimony to the survival of Greek is the inscription found near the *Heroön* of Cineas. This is a partially surviving list of 150 admonitory maxims found at Delphi, and copied down by a certain Clearchus. It has been assumed that Clearchus went to Delphi to discover his maxims, but copies of them have been found elsewhere such as Miletopolis in Turkey. Neverthless the reference to the site regarded in classical Greece as the 'navel of the world' and the implied claim by Clearchus to be part of the wider Greek-speaking world is striking.

[30] 246, 1982.

[31] Ar *Phys* 224-226b. See: C. Rapin, "Les Textes Litteraires Grecs de la Tresoserie d'Aï Khanoum", *B.C.H* 111 (1987).

Given this testimonia, perhaps Plutarch's statement that Gedrosian children chanted the poems of Sophocles and Euripides gains a little plausibility[32]. However, it is important to ask which children might have done this. The Greekness of Aï Khanum seems, like its site, embattled. The children involved would surely have been those of the local settler community and not those of the population who surrounded them and made their life possible. There was no civilising mission to Hellenistic culture and if anything the Hellenistic element in mixed settlements, as can be seen most graphically from Ptolemaic Egypt[33], tended to be exclusive and to emphasise its difference from those who lived around them. As Peter Green has put it, 'In all instances what the Successors set up were enclaves of Graeco-Macedonian culture in an alien world, Governmental ghettoes for a ruling elite'[34]. The plays at Aï Khanum would have been performed not to inculate Hellenistic Culture into the people by the Oxus, but to underline, probably for the colonists' own comfort, how different the settler population was from their host community. The *gymnasium*, always an exclusive cultural marker, as can be seen from Egypt or Palestine, would have performed the same function[35]. If anything the tension between native and settler in Bactria is likely to have been worse than in the more Mediterranean areas of the Hellenistic World. It is unlikely that many women were among those originally settled in Bactria. Although there may have been some camp followers, prostitutes, etc, it is inconceivable that there would have been enough to go round the number of settlers planted in the region. Unlike other areas of settlement, such as Egypt, Bactria was too far away to receive a continuous stream of new immigrants. The settler community would therefore have taken native wives hence making the status of their offspring ambiguous. This in turn should warn us against tales of enclaves of racially pure Macedonians or Greeks surviving in Afghanistan[36]. There simply would not have been enough women to go round to make this even a theoretical possibility. In such circumstances the status markers which differentiated

[32] Plutarch, *Moralia* 328d.

[33] See: N. Lewis, *Greeks in Ptolemaic Egypt*, Oxford 1986, passim.

[34] P. Green, *From Alexander to Actium: The Hellenistic Age*, London 1990, p. 319.

[35] See: M. Avi-Yonah, *Hellenism and the East*, Jerusalem 1978, p. 129. On the whole the *gymnasia* did little to further an understanding between the Greek settlers and the native population and did a lot to keep them apart.

[36] For a modern and somewhat fanciful attempt of this sort see: M. A. Dimitri, *In search of the Macedonians in Pakistan*, Fort Wayne 1995.

the two groups and the *paideia* that they encapsulated would have been all the more jealously guarded.

The culture so stubbornly clung to also seems to be dated. Pebble mosaics appear at Aï Khanum (including a star resembling those found on the *larnaces* of Tomb 2 at Kutlush in Macedonia, though this design was itself an old Near Eastern one). But the technique, already dated when the town was first built, never develops. While Hellenistic mosaics moved on from pebbles to tesserae, the Aï Khanum mosaics do not even show signs of developing the pebble mosaic style. Hellenistic culture appears frozen – probably because of the isolation of these communities from the rest of the Hellenistic World, an isolation which would have intensified after the area broke away from the Seleucid Kingdom and declared its independence in 256 B.C.: an event closely followed by the intrusion of the Parthians into Sogdiana in c.248 B.C. Some later finds such as those at Begram, the probable site of Alexandria-in-the-Caucasus, might at first sight to contradict this view. Here plaster casts of high-quality classical metal working have been found. However, this material was found in the ruins of Kapisa, the summer palace of the Kushan King Kanishka, and probably reflects the Kushan enthusiasm for imported foreign goods rather than any native tradition of classical work[37]. The Kushans certainly seemed to have had a taste for material from the classical world, but such a taste could have been catered for by imports and the hiring of workmen from the West rather than relying on a continuing Hellenistic tradition in Afghanistan itself. The presence of a mosaicist in Miram with the Roman name Titus certainly shows that such itinerant workmen did exist[38].

Despite an inbuilt tendency towards separation, some interaction between settlers and natives was inevitable. The onomastics of Aï Khanum reveal substantial numbers of Greek and Macedonian names such as Lysanias. Howe-

[37] The treasure is normally dated to the late first, or early second, century A. D. Attempts to date it back the pieces to the Hellenistic period, e.g. G. M. A. Richter, "Ancient Plaster Casts of Greek Metalware", *AJA* 62 (1958) appear to rely on nothing more than snobbery against Roman art and a uniformly 'progressive' interpretation of classical art. Moreover, the cast could substantially postdate the manufacture of the original item upon which the dating is based.

[38] See: B. Rowland, *The Art and Architecture of India*, London 1953, p. 186.

ver, we know of two palace accountants called Oxeboakes and Oxebazes whose names appear to refer to the local divinity of the Oxus (cf Oxyartes, the name of Roxane's father[39]). These two individuals and their names open up two possible ways of looking at the social dynamics of Aï Khanum. If they are members of the indigenous population, it appears that even natives who were closely associated with the ruling palace bureaucracy and hence its Greek-speaking masters saw no need, or perhaps possessed no incentive, to change their names to assimilate to a Greek-speaking norms. On the other hand, if the two were part of the settler community, we see a degree of acculturation away from the Hellenistic norms that the settlers appear to have been endeavouring to protect. It is not clear what language our scribes used to carry out their duties. The Seleucid Empire used both Greek and Aramaic as official languages[40]. The use of several official languages has the tendency to allow the majority of the population to remain monoglottal. It perhaps would not be surprising if at Aï Khanum there were descendants of settlers who knew nothing but Greek, save a few native words[41], surrounded by a native population who, even if working in the administration of the kingdom, were their linguistic mirror-image. That administration itself was probably Persian in style. This was almost inevitable. Running an empire was a novel experience to the settlers and the old Persian apparatus was probably adopted as much as was practicable.

The best way of looking at Aï Khanum therefore is a community determined to preserve intact, possibly to the degree of fossilisation, areas which were thought important as community status-markers, while displaying indifference to (or perhaps an inability to halt) change in other areas. There is likely to have been no desire on the settlers' part to export their culture to others, indeed, on the contrary, they probably possessed a wish firmly to restrict the use of such elements as they thought important to that culture for themselves.

Such an interpretation of the evidence would explain the dilemma posed by Bernard's 1982 article of why some areas of Hellenistic culture at Aï Kha-

[39] Inter alia Strabo 11.11.4.

[40] See: S. Sherwin-White, "Seleucid Babylonia", in: A. Kuhrt, S. Sherwin-White, *Hellenism in the East*, London 1987.

[41] Cf Plutarch's statement that Cleopatra, the last ruler of Ptolemaic Egypt, was the first of the Ptolemies to learn Egyptian (*Life of Antony* 27).

num were preserved and other acculturated to a native norm. This model can easily accomodate a shift away from Hellenistic religious practices. The heroön of Cineas is a product of a Greek manner of thought (cf the Tomb of Brasidas at Amphipolis), but the style of the building in which this thought is physically embodied is non-Greek. Bernard notes that the general nature of temple architecture and religious idols in the city display substantial native elements. Given the polytheistic nature of ancient Classical society and its tolerance of new forms of religious worship, this should come as no surprise. Indeed, it is possible that native cults were actively patronised by the settler elite both as a safety measure – the gods of any area needed placating – and to make their rule more acceptable to the native population[42], On the other hand, the coins struck by the Bactrian Greeks cling firmly to Greek models. Coins were regarded very much as a cultural defining mark, and here, where communal identity was thought to be at stake, religious iconography remained much more firmly Greek. Perhaps this makes it of interest that the coins we possess emphasize more than those of the other Successors the *causia*, or characteristic Macedonian hat. The *causia* in fact poses a strong methodological problem for us. It has normally been assumed to be Macedonian in origin, but a reçent revisionist view has asserted that it is a cultural borrowing from the tribesmen of the Chitrali region[43]. But even if we accept this new view (which we probably shouldn't[44]), we need not see its adoption as necessarily either expressing a wish to accept and integrate with native culture or simply an inability to resist the native customs of the area. Rather it may merely be a sign of marking the area where the king's writ ran, similar to the depictions of rulers wearing elephant skins. An alternative would be to see the borrowing in reverse and the Chitrali hat as a product of native imitation of the new settlers' community. Strabo mentions Indians borrowing Macedonian practices[45]. Even so, such a borrowing need not imply that any form of acculturation to a Hellenistic mode of life followed. Items, or whole practices, can be taken over and incorporated into another culture without that culture changing. Few people, I suspect, would argue that the popularity of football in Poland is evidence of a wish on the part of the Poles, either now or in the past, to adopt the English way of life, despite football indubitably being an

[42] This was certainly the practice of the Seleucid rulers.

[43] B. M. Kingsley, "The cap that survived Alexander", *AJA* 85.1 (1981).

[44] Herodian 1.3.3 seems an insuperable obstacle to the theory.

[45] Strabo 15.1.67.

English invention. Similarly the Chitrali hat, if it is the Macedonian *causia*, need be no more than a useful artefact that it was found convenient to borrow and was then subsumed into its new environment with no further cultural consequences.

This interpretation of Hellenistic culture at Aï Khanum is probably the way to look at other settlements in the area too. Kandahar (possibly Alexandria-in-Arachosia and preserving its name via the Arabic Iskander) and Herat (Alexandria-in-Areia?) have both produced Greek inscriptions, but the use of a language in a formal context is no guarantee of its everyday and extensive use in a community. A plethora of Latin inscriptions are found throughout Europe in areas where it had long since ceased to be a language understood by any but a small elite such as Britain or had only ever been so used such as Poland. We find the Indian ruler Asoka publishing decrees in Aramaic and Greek[46], but this implies nothing more than a wish to command respect in an area and certainly need net imply anything about the literacy or linguistic loyalties of the communities among whom such inscriptions were erected[47].

Looking at later period of Oriental history, perhaps the strongest parallel with the Hellenistic community of Bactria is with the Anglo-Indians of British India. This group again fell across a racial divide and clung aggresively to the cultural markers, this time including religion, which they believed marked out their privileged status. Their impact on Indian culture *in toto* however has been minimal, albeit the wish to preserve notions of Englishry has led to Indian English being far more conservative and grammaticaly pure than the version spoken in England[48]. If we are to look for an ancient parallel, Levick's Roman settlers in Asia who tried to keep their culture and the status which went with it alive but in the end were overwhelmed by the local population may well provide the best analogy to Aï Khanum and Bactria's fate[49].

---

[46] The most notable example is to be found at Kandahar.

[47] It certainly does not imply as Lane Fox asserts that Kandahar was a 'lively site of Hellenism', *Alexander the Great*, London 1982, p. 533, n. 33.

[48] This is often the sign of a language not in common use. See: K. Jackson, *Language and History in Early Britain* (Edinburgh 1953), on the Latin of Roman Britain. Jackson's conclusions have been challenged, but his methodology which is what concerns us here has not.

[49] B. M. Levick, *Roman Colonies in Southern Asia Minor*, Oxford 1967, ch. s 12-13.

If the cultural impact of the Hellenistic Bactria withered away, its genetic contribution to the area was at best minimal. As noted above, the Hellenistic settler population would have been racially mixed from the start and no doubt became more so as time went on. Moreover the vast bulk of settlers would have lived in the cities and not have survived their demise. While claims of descendent from Alexander and the Macedonians are found, for example amongst the Afridi[50], in the area to this day, these should not come as a surprise given that Alexander was the one Westerner to make a profound impact on the East[51]. They are even more to be expected, if those making them thought they would impress Western anthropologists and travellers making such inquiries. The majority of ancestry claims found in the region appear to be based on Biblical lineages rather than those concerned with Classical history[52]. This leaves us with the mystery of the light skinned tribesmen of Nuristan. A variety of proposals have been made linking them to fair-skinned Turkic tribes, the bastard offspring produced during the British occupation of Afghanistan, and, via linguistics, to a migration of Indo-European peoples into the area which substantially predated Alexander's adventure[53].

Some relics did survive the Bactrian Kingdom. Greek lettering persists, albeit in an increasingly degenerate form, on local coins for a period of time. A specifically Macedonian month, Artemisius, turns up on a late inscription from Kabul. According to the writer Philostratus, the pagan philosopher and wonder-worker Apollonius of Tyana was able to speak Greek all the way to Taxila in the first century A.D. But Philostratus is a dangerous source upon which to rely and, as part of the 'second sophistic' movement which embodied a recrudescent pride in Hellenistic achievement, one with an axe to grind too. Even if he was right, this need only imply that some native aristocrats continued to have dealings with the classical world and found learning some koine Greek useful for this purpose. It does not imply that substantial communities of Greek-speakers

---

[50] See: O. Caroe, *The Pathans*, London 1958, p. 44-45. Caroe is loathe to dismiss the link but eventually concedes that he must.

[51] He is the only Westerner mentioned in the *Koran*, sura 18 'The Cave', 83-98.

[52] See: O. Caroe, *The Pathans* ch. 1.

[53] The latter is the favoured solution of Robin Lane Fox, *Alexander the Great* (1973) chapter 24, though he is inclined to think that 'the enterprising ladies of the British Empire' may also have had something to do with this. While attractive, modern linguistic theories which see the movement of language happening without the migration of people make this theory too problematic.

were left in the area. Most Greek-speakers would have been located in the cities of Bactria and these, and presumably their populations, suffered heavily at the end of the period of Hellenistic rule. Some would have survived and may well have wished to cling on to what was left of their cultural heritage. But it would have been an uphill struggle. Tacitus tells us of a Greek-speaking community in Asia Minor which lasted for at least 100 years after Parthian rule was imposed over it and it is common knowledge that Greek-speaking communities survived in Italy into the medieval period. Nevertheless, we must remember that Tacitus' group had the incentive of vibrant Greek-speaking communities nearby and that similiarly in Italy such a group would have been sustained by a sympathetic environment. Without such support, and little would have been forthcoming in Central Asia, Greek may well have withered away much more rapidly as it did, for example, in Ottoman Anatolia. A much more eroded Greek community, the Posidonians of Tyrrhenia (i.e. Paestum in Italy), are mentioned by the fourth-century philosopher Aristoxenus[54]. According to Aristoxenus, in his day the Posidonians, whose colony was a sixth-century foundation, kept a solitary Greek festival and had preserved the vocabulary associated with it, but no more. No doubt the Bactrian Greeks moved through both these stages and then on to complete forgetfulness.

In the end, therefore, we must agree with Narain that the Alexander came and saw but India conquered. While it is true that now mute ruins as well as the written word tell us about the Bactrian Greeks, in the end their culture was Western sand thrown into the gale of Central Asia.

[54] *Apud* Athenaeus 14.632.

Tadeusz Majda
(Warsaw)

The Celts, the Scythians, and the Turks. Parallels in the visual arts and in literature

The present consideration of the mutual impact and similarities of the Celtic, Scythian, and Turkish peoples of Central Asia pertains to two important aspects of the lives of peoples inhabiting a vast stretch of Eurasia – art and literature. Attempts at finding any direct cultural relationships between the Celts and the Turkish peoples – the Huns, the Protobulgarians, the Avars, and the Orkhon Turks – are, as of yet, foiled by insufficient historical knowledge and a dearth of archaeological material. A discussion of parallels between the Celts, the Scythians, and the Turks, meanwhile, seems to be in order given that the Scythians constituted, without doubt, a connecting link between the Celtic and the Turkish tribes.

Turkish peoples inhabited large areas of Eurasia as early as the 3rd century A.D.; they gradually shifted westward from Siberia, taking over lands which were largely inhabited or controlled by the Scythians (a general name for the East Iranian tribes). In the process, the Turks adopted many Scythian traditions, particularly with regard to the arts and to ceremonies; these mutual relations are corroborated both by accounts of neighbouring peoples as well as by numerous artefacts. It is worth mentioning here that many scholars, particularly Turkish ones, still subscribe to the theory whereby the Altai burial mounds are of Turkish origin, as a point of difference from those who ascribe them to the Altai Scythians. There are certain elements among the various archaeological findings, such as Mongoloid types in Scythian graves, which give us plenty food for thought as regards the complexity of the Scythian – or, should we say, Eurasian – culture.

The cultures of the Celts and Scythians and, subsequently, of the Turks were influenced by the ancient cultural centres of Greece, Akhemenid Persia, and China; this impact took different forms and manifested itself at various periods. Influences were also exchanged between these centres - the Greek (Greco-Bactrian) influence on the Scythians, the Iranian influence on the Greeks, that of the Greeks on Italy and the Etruscans as well as the Celts and the Scythians, and the Chinese impact on Central Asia and Iran (the silk route).

The Celtic Culture

The presence of the Celts in Central and Western Europe dates to the first millennium B.C., and some researchers place it even further back[1]. Greek sources dealing with the Scythians refer to the 6th century B.C.; by the same token, most archaeological materials originate from the time spanning the 6th century B.C. to the 2nd century A.D. and are divided into two periods, that of the Hallstatt culture and of the La Tène culture. The heartland of the area inhabited by the Celts is generally believed to have been located north of the Alps in what is now Switzerland, Bavaria, and western Austria. But as early as the 14th century B.C., a culture characterised by traits such as the building of mounds over graves, ornamentation of weapons and decorative items, and ceramic crafts – all of which are associated with the Celts – begins to make its presence known in Central Europe. It is not clear where the Celts came from when they settled the area referred to as their cradle. To go by the theory whereby the original settlements of the Indo-Europeans were located in Eastern Europe and Western Asia, one would have to assume that the Celts broke off from the Protoarians and wandered westwards, much in the same way as the Italic peoples, Ionians, and Germans or, alternately, in which the Iranian tribes migrated eastwards to present-day Iran and in which the Indo-Arian tribes headed for India.

The Celtic migrations eastward along the Danube are dated to pre-historic times, and the westward ones to the Bronze Age. As far as the Celtic presence in South-Eastern Europe is concerned, it is known that they reached Thrace, made occasional armed ventures into Greece, and established a state in present-day Bulgaria; some of these Celts eventually settled in Asia Minor (the Galatians). In the east, the Celts made it as far as Dobruja and the coast of the Black Sea, where they encountered the Scythians and, according to some scholars, even established a single Scythian-Celtic group; these contacts are testified to by artefacts found in western Scythia.

---

[1] M. Dillon, N. K. Chadwick, *Ze świata Celtów*, Warszawa 1975.

According to Z. Woźniak[2], the eastward penetration of the Celtic culture into the Scythian lands during the La Tène period was rather short-lived. There is, however, a considerably larger amount of Scythian artefacts from Celtic areas or from their outer reaches, such as Hungary and Zakarpacie. As regards similarities between the Celtic and Scythian culture and the Scythian-Turkish (or, to adopt a wider perspective, the Turkish-Mongolian one), I have distinguished the general headings of (1) art, (2) literature, (3) ceremonies, customs, and (4) mythology, cosmogony, and beliefs.

Celtic Art

Numerous artefacts indicate that the Celts maintained contacts with the Scythians, especially the Eastern ones from the steppes by the Black Sea. Celtic items have been found in Scythian areas and in the Dniepr region as far afield as the Crimea (according to Jacobstahl, the peoples inhabiting this region were, so to speak, in the *avant garde* among the Eurasians)[3]. Scythian artefacts, in turn, have been found in Hungary, Podole, and Zakarpacie. During the migrations set off in the 9th – 8th centuries B.C. by the Chinese invasion led by Emperor Süan (827-781 B.C.), the Goths brought the Eurasian (Scythian) style to the lands populated by Celts, principally with regard to the animal style and to decorative motifs.

Another route of Scythian influence led through Scandinavia to northern Germany, Great Britain, and Ireland; the main factor here were the Scandinavians and Varegs who ventured as far as the Black and Caspian Seas. The Viking invaders of the British Isles brought with them certain elements of the Scytho-Sarmatian style, as seen in Celtic, and even Saxon, sculpture and jewellery. Scytho-Sarmatian influences are also discernible in the final stage of the Hallstatt culture and the early one of the La Tène culture (approximately 500 years before Christ). It is likely that the lifestyle of the Hallstatt Celts was similar to that found across Eurasia, thus creating a link with Scythian art (the richly decorated trousers from the Hallstatt period[4] are executed in the same way as Scythian garments seen on the Chertomlyk vase, and Scythian capes are similar to those from the Katanda grave in the Altai).

[2] Z. Woźniak, *Wschodnie pogranicze kultury lateńskiej*, Wrocław 1974.

[3] P. Jacobstahl, *Early Celtic Art*, Oxford 1944.

[4] The trousers are kept in the Naturhistorisches Museum in Vienna.

Some of the characteristic traits of Celtic art could have developed under the influence of the Scythians; at any rate, there are clear parallels, although some of the derivations are limited to selected motifs or inspirations. Some of the "borrowed" elements are used for a long time and passed on to neighbouring peoples; others are rather superficial and comprise the taking up of a certain detail or motif and placing it in a new context or formula within the Celtic culture.

I believe that the list of these common characteristics includes the following:

- the use of zoomorphic figures (deer, horses, boars, birds) for decorative purposes;
- the use of animal and bird figures in bands, one atop the other, or in single file;
- during the La Tène period, the use of mystical, imaginary animals (griffins, various winged creatures) and of oriental plants (possibly derived from Scythian art, although these motifs could also have come from Greece or Etruria);
- ornamentation which takes precedence over narration;
- sumptuous designs, rich drawings, full utilisation of the material and of the decorated surface;
- linear style of sculpture, especially as regards wood (branch ornament, S curves).

On the other hand, many oriental-style elements in Celtic art were derived from Greek art by way of the Balkans (the Greek influence is particularly conspicuous in the art of the Thracians); the Oriental-style "Greek" elements were adopted from the Near East, usually from Persia.

Similarities can also be observed in stone sculpture. Thus, we have stone figures reminiscent of the Scythian and Siberian stone matrons, some of them with Mongoloid features, as is the case with Scythian sculpture. One of the princely tombs at Reinheim was decorated with sculpted anthropomorphic figures similar to those made by the Scythians; the same is true of the post in Pfalzfeld, Wittenberg as well as of the Tarasque sculpture in Noves, southern France. A Celtic sculpture found in Afghanistan likewise has Mongoloid features[5].

5 J. Rosen-Przeworska, *Ikonografia wschodnio-celtycka*, Wrocław 1976, p. 194.

While Scythian art (including that of the Sakas and Sarmatians) was influenced by Greek art (in the Pont) and by Akhemenid art (in Central Asia and the Caucasus), as we move further east we see Chinese influences such as frontal views of animals. Scythian influences, meanwhile, can be observed in Chinese art from the Shu period.

As regards similarities in Scythian-Turkish art, it is certain that they go back to the Hiung-nu (Hun) period in Ordos. The animal style and branch decorative patterns spread across Eurasia to Panonia and the Balkans; it is seen in the art of the Orkhon Turks, the Avars, Khazars, Pechengs, Kumans, and the Kirgiz (as well as of the early Russian peoples!). In Siberia, their use continued to the 20th century. The Seljuks took it from Central Asia to Iran and Asia Minor, Mesopotamia, and Egypt.

The illumination of manuscripts from the neo-Celtic period in Ireland (5th – 7th century) merits separate mention. The pages of the Burrow and Kells manuscripts feature a distinct framing which relies on a continuos design of intertwining bands; there are also spirals and what is known as the tapestry pattern, an abstract geometric design. F. Schlette believes that this style of illumination has close similarities to the Syrian gospels and to Coptic art from the 6th century[6]; T. T. Rice, meanwhile, sees the Irish illuminations as being indicative of the Scythian influences coming in by way of Scandinavia[7].

Literature

While there are some written accounts of Celtic literature as well as original Celtic texts from more recent periods, very little is known about the literary work of the Scythians; while they probably had works which were passed on orally, we know nothing of their characteristics.

There are, however, striking similarities between the literary works of the Celts and the Turks; it could be, therefore, that similar convergence existed as regards Scythian literature. One should bear in mind here that, albeit the earliest written works – known as Orkhon – date back to the 7th – 8th century, oral works had been thriving centuries earlier, as indicated by the well-developed form of the earliest transcriptions. For example, Chinese accounts from the 3rd – 2nd century B.C. refer to stories of the Turks (Huns?); the Chinese authors clearly believed them to be unique, somehow different from other works known to

[6] F. Schlette, *Celtowie*, Łódź 1987 (transl. by S. Lisiecka, B. Wierzbicka).

[7] T. T. Rice, *Les Scythes*, Paris 1958.

them. They were translated into Chinese, and the translation of the Chinese versions into contemporary Turkish produced by Muhaddere Özerdim[8] shows them to carry the most characteristic traits of the poetry of the Turkish peoples, as subsequently corroborated by the dictionary of Mahmud of Kashgar (11th century)[9], the *Codex Cumanicus*[10], and by Uygur texts from Eastern Turkestan[11]. The poems are of lyrical content, describing the landscapes of steppes and of Northern China, dwelling on the skies above them, and pondering life, both of free men and those in captivity; there are also *ağit* – laments. The dominating form is the quatrain, and there are also two- and three-lined poems and nine-syllable pieces, all notable for their use of alliteration and parallelism.

For centuries, the literary works of the Celts lived on in the oral tradition only; they were first written down in Ireland during the 6th – 7th century A.D. and, by that time, they had yielded to certain Christian influences. They did, however, retain many of the traditional characteristics of epic poetry. They are alliterated syllabic poems telling heroic stories in lyrical form; elegiac literature is popular. The old prosody was syllabic and unrhymed (much like Turkish poetry); in the earliest period, there were some quatrains as well as lines of alternating length (as in the works from the Orkhon inscriptions). Some British researchers have been trying to prove that Irish heroic poetry shares common roots with the Greek and Vedic meters! Kuno Meyer[12], meanwhile, believes that, on account of their form and content, Irish lyrical poems are unique (sic) in world literature. Finally, Watkins[13] has advanced the theory that the seven-sylla-

[8] M. N. Özerdim, *Çin'in şimalinde hanedan kuran Türklerin şiirleri*, Ankara 1943.

[9] Mahmud of Kashgar, *Divan lughat at-Turk* (Divan of Turkish language) – an Arabic-Turkish dictionary written in the 11th century which contains a great number of examples of the poetry of the Turkish peoples of Central Asia.

[10] *Codex Cumanicus* (Codex of the Kumans) – a unique manuscript containing texts in Kuman-Turkish composed in the 13th century for the catholic missionaries active among the Kumans.

[11] Uygur texts come from Eastern Turkestan, where, after the defeat of the Uygur state (Kaganate) in the Altai region in 840, many Uygur tribes settled down. They established a kingdom which existed to the 14th century. The Uygurs were adherents of the Mani religion, but Buddhism and Nestorianism were also popular. Litterary texts in Uygur language, although deal with new religions and beliefs, preserved many characteristics of the old Turkish poetry.

[12] K. Meyer, after M. Dillon, N. K. Chadwick, *op. cit.*

[13] Watkins, after M. Dillon, N. K. Chadwick, *op. cit.*

ble verse is the basic form of an indigenous poetic tradition hearkening back to Indo-European times!

Many of the changes affecting Irish poetry were introduced by monks. In the 8th century, the old system of versification was substituted with rhymes, and alliteration was improved. Poetry was brought out to listeners by bards/lyrical poets who would recite verses to the accompaniment of their *crottas*, instruments similar to lyres. These bards were also known as musicians/poets (like the Turkish *ozan* or *bakhshi*); in their work, they lauded bravery and the exploits of famous men, relying more on their own poetic imaginations than on the principles of the learned literature with which the *file* (authors of epic works) worked. The body of epic literature consists of many pieces – primarily legends – of uneven length. The oldest among them have been written down in prose augmented with the occasional verse or two and are divided into three cycles – mythological (dealing with the origin of gods and men), heroic (about the feats of Conchobar and Aihulain), and about Finn and Arossin (a type of *chanson de gestes*). As Dillon-Chadwick put it,

> "It appears that the prose narrative with dialogues in verse was the oldest literary form in the Indo-European tradition. The poem was metrically arranged while the prose narrative was entrusted to the creative memory of the storyteller. This was the oldest form in India; it was also used in Ireland. It even surfaces in a few oral epic works in Central Asia. ..... The complete absence of narrative poetry is a noteworthy characteristic of the early Irish tradition. The earliest Irish poetry comprised the songs of praise, satirical pieces, and dirges composed by court poets; stories, meanwhile, were told in prose. ..... No other folk has been blessed with the ability of discovering nature so early and to such an extent, of observing it and loving it (sic) both in its most minute and most grandiose forms."[14]

Uar ind adaig i Moin Móir
ferdaid dertain, ni deróil
dorddán fris-tib in gaeth glan
géssid ós chaille clithar[15].

[14] M. Dillon, N. K. Chadwick, *op. cit.*

[15] I. V. Stebleva, *Razvitie tyurkskich poeticheskikh form v XI veke*, Moskva 1971, p.119.

While there is no final rhyme, every line contains alliteration.

Cold is the night at Moin Móir
the rain flows in streams, a deep rumble
answered with the loud laughter of the wind
is sounding out above the trees.

The following examples show how the alliteration was developed in Old Turkish poetry.

Kültegin inscription (1st half of the 8th century, verses 147-150)

Qaγan at **b**unta **b**iz **b**irtimiz	We gave (him) the title of kaqan
siŋlim **q**unculyγ **b**irtimiz	we gave (him) our younger sister – the princess, as wife
özi janylty **q**aγany **ö**lti	he commited a blunder, his kagan died
buduny **k**ün **q**ul **b**olty	his people became slaves

Mahmud of Kashgar (11th century), "The battle with the Tanguts" (15)

Käčä turub joryr ärdim	Getting up at night I wandered
qara **q**yzyl böri **k**ördüm	I saw black and red-haired wolves
qatyγ jany **q**ura **k**ördüm	I looked – a strained bow
qaja körüb baqu aγdy	looking back the wolves moved on to a mountain range

Mani Hymn in Uygur language (16)

Tang **t**engri **k**elti	The God Tang came
Tang **t**engri özi **k**elti	the God Tang came himself
Tang **t**engri **k**elti	the God Tang came
Tang **t**engri özi **k**elti	the God Tang came himself
Turung **k**amuγ begler **k**ada(r)šlar	get up all lords (begs) and brothers
Tang **t**engrig ögelim	let us praise the God Tang
körügme **k**ün **t**engri	the God-Sun, who is seen
sizi bizi **k**üzeding	protect you and us
körünügme ay tengri	the God-Moon, who appeared
sizi bizi **k**urtgaryng	save you and us

Bibliography

M. Artamanov, *Goldschatz der Skythen in der Ermitage*, Prag 1970

R. Bleichsteiner, "Zum euroasiatischen Tierstiel", *Berichte des Asien-Arbeite Kreises*, H. 2, 1939, p. 9-64

I. Brashinskiy, *Sokrovishcha skifskikh tsarei. Poiski i nakhodki*, Moskva 1967

B. Brentjes," Zur Westtrift ost-und zentralasiatischer Motive in skythischer Zeit", [in:] *Schriften zur Geschichte und Kultur des Alten Orients*, Bd. 5, Berlin 1974, p. 153-159

B. Brentjes, *Der Tierstiel in Eurasien*, Leipzig 1982

G. Charrière, *L'art barbare scythe – de la Siberie à la Mer noire*, Paris 1971

N. L. Chlenova, *Proiskhozhdeniye i rannaya istoriya tagarovskoy kul'tury*, Moskva 1967

H. D'Arbois de Jubainville, *Introduction à l'étude de la litterature celtique*, Paris 1883, t. I

M. Dillon, N. K. Chadwick, *Ze świata Celtów*, Warszawa 1975

J. Filip, *Celtic Civilization and its Heritage*, Praha 1976, II wyd.

F. Henry, *Irish Art in the Early Christian Period to A.D. 800*, London 1965

P. Jacobstahl, *Early Celtic Art*, Oxford 1944

N. G. Jalagin, "*Skifskie antropomorfnye stely*", *Sovetskaya Arkheologiya*, (2) 1952, p. 187-196

K. Jettmar, "The Altai Before the Turks", *The Museum of Far Eastern Antiquities Bulletin*, No 23, 1951, p. 135-22

K. Jettmar, *L'art des steppes. Le style animalier eurasiatique – genèse et arrière-plan social*, Paris 1965

T. D. Kendrick, *The Druids*, London 1928

A. N. Kirpichnikov, G. S. Lebedev, B. A. Bulkin, S. V. Dobov, V. A. Nazarenko, "Rusko-skandinavskie svyazi v epokhu obrazovaniya drevneruskogo gosudarstva (IX-X v.)", *Scando-Slavia*, t. 24, 1978

P. Meyer, *Historia sztuki europejskiej*, t. I, Sztuka celtycka, Warszawa 1973

M. N. Özerdim, *Çin'in şimalinde hanedan kuran Türklerin şiirleri*, AUDTCF Dergisi, sayi 1, Ankara 1943

T. G. E. Powell, *The Celts*, London 1958

T. T. Rice, *Les Scythes*, Paris 1958

J. Rosen-Przeworska, *Ikonografia wschodnio-celtycka*, Wrocław, 1976

A. Ross, *Everyday Life of the Pagan Celts*, London-New York 1970

S. I. Rudenko, N. M. Rudenko, *Iskusstvo skifov Altaya*, Moskva 1948

S. I. Rudenko, *Iskusstvo Altaya i Peredney Azii*, Moskva 1961

N. K. D. Sanders, *Orient and Orientalizing in Early Celtic Art*, "Antiquity", vol. XLV,178, London 1971, p. 103-112

F. Schlette, *Celtowie*, Łódź 1987

Skifosibirskiy zverniy stil' v iskusstve narodov Evrazii, Moskva 1976

Z. Woźniak, *Wschodnie pogranicze kultury lateńskiej*, Wrocław 1974

L. K. Galanina, L. L. Barkova, *Złoto scytyjskie*, Katalog wystawy, Muzeum Narodowe w Warszawie, Warszawa 1976

1) Neolithic stone "menhir" of a woman, found in France, Celtic art (G. Charrière, *L'art barbare scythe*, Paris, 1971).

2) Stone figure of a Turkic "baba", Volga region, 10th century (G. Charrière, *L'art barabare scythe*, Paris, 1971).

3) A so-called "deer stone", Mongolia, 8th century B. C. (E. Novgorodova, *Alte Kunst der Mongolei*, Leipzig, 1980).

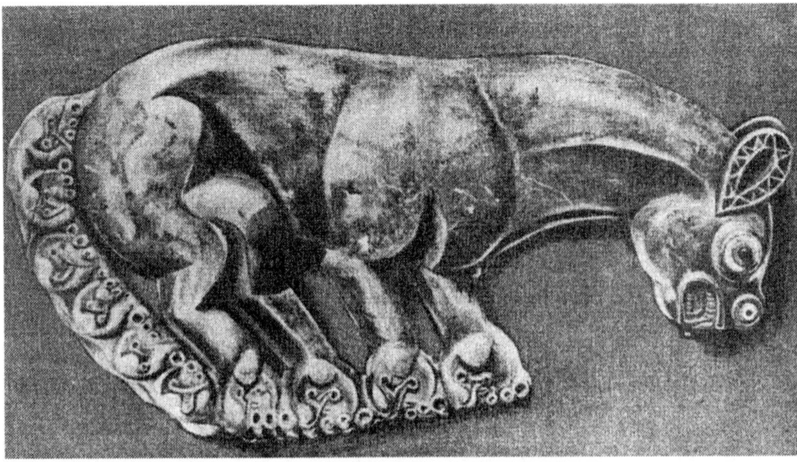

4) Metal plate depicting a panther, found in the kurhan Kelermes, Scythian art, beginning of the 6th century B. C. (G. Charrière, *L'art barbare scythe*, Paris, 1971).

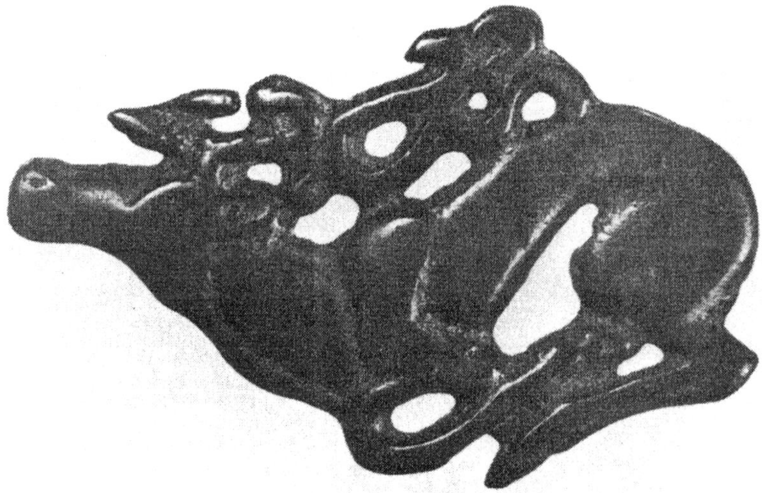

5) Figure of a bronze stag, Tagar culture, 5th century B. C. (G. Charrière, *L'art barbare scythe*, Paris, 1971).

6) Repoussé metal sheet depicting a characteristic "Scythian" deer motif. From the foundings in Ziwiye in Iran, capital of the Caucasian Scythes (G. Charrière, *L'art barbare scythe*, Paris, 1971).

7) Felt, caparison, with appliqué technique. These motifs are popular in Central Asia down to present day. From the finds at Pazyryk, Altai, tumulus 5 (G. Charrière, *L'art barbare scythe*, Paris, 1971).

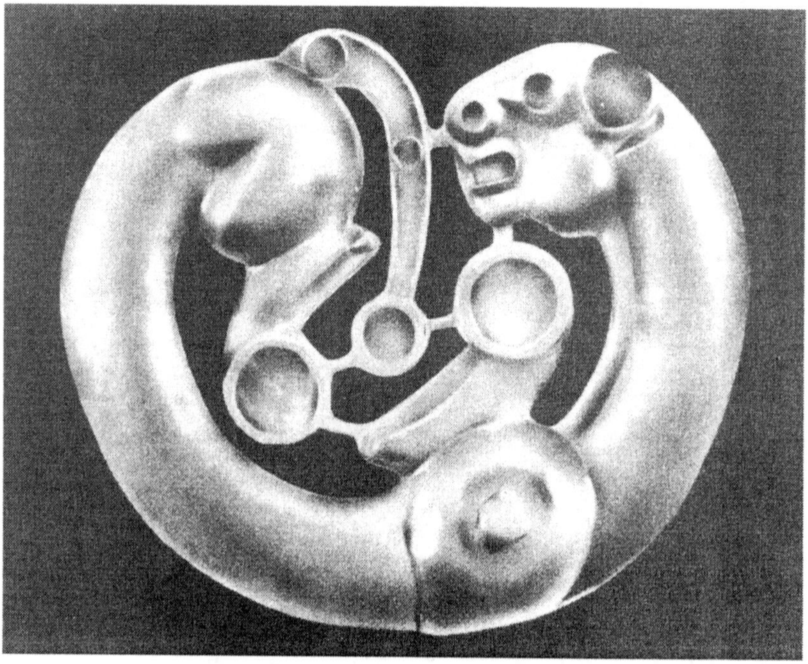

8) Ornamental gold plate representing a bend lion, Scythian art. From the foundings at Pazyryk, Altai (K. Jettmar, *L'art des steppes*, Paris. 1965).

9) Ornamental belt plates. Stag motif and stylized bird head, Tagar culture II (K. Jettmar, *L'art des steppes*, Paris, 1965).

10) Ornamental bronze harness plate depicting a gryphon, art of the Avars, 5th-6th century (K. Jettmar, *L'art des steppes*, Paris, 1965).

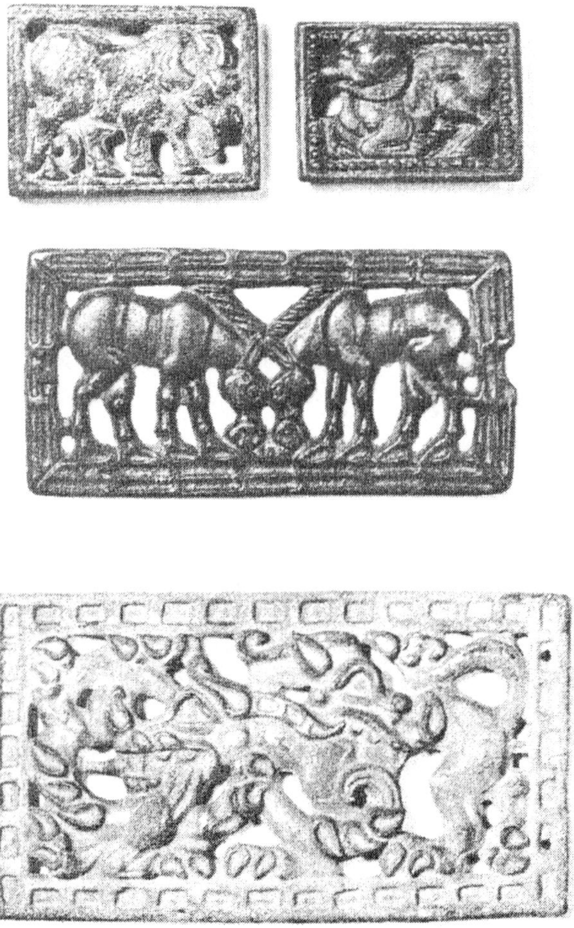

11) Ornamental bronze plates, art of the Ordos region, 3rd century B. C. (K. Jettmar, *L'art des steppes*, Paris, 1965).

12) Ornamental bronze plates, art of the Ordos region (?), Zhou period, 5th century B. C. (K. Jettmar, *L'art des steppes*, Paris, 1965).

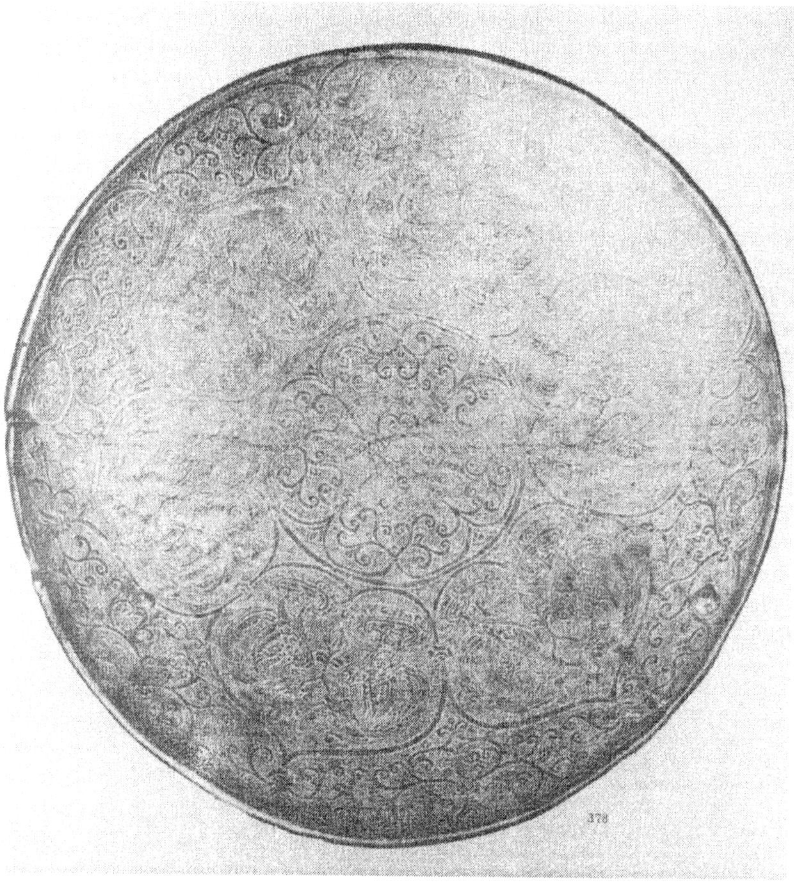

13) Metal plate showing pairs of confronted birds in medalions. From the tumulus Chaatas near the Yenissei River, Kirghiz art, 8th century (G. Charrière, *L'art barbare scythe*, Paris, 1971).

14) Metal jug showing animal and floral motifs common to the Eurasian style. From the tumulus Chaatas near the Yenissei River, Kirghiz art, 8th century (G. Charrière, *L'art barbare scythe*, Paris, 1971).

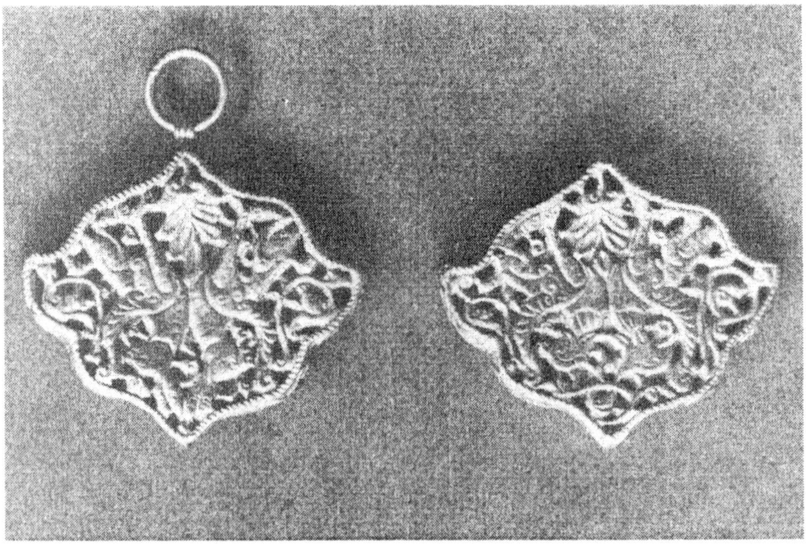

15) Gold plates depicting a motif of pairs of animals, early Russian art, 11th-12th century (?) (B. Brentjes, *Der Tierstiel in Eurasien*, Leipzig, 1982).

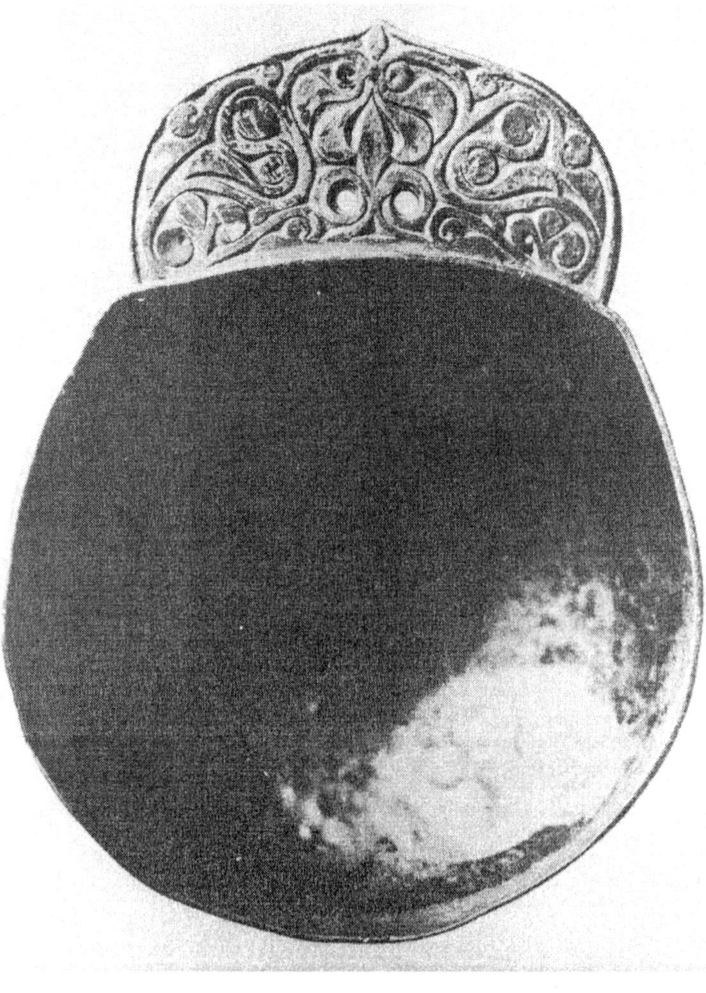

16)Gold cup showing a characteristic Eurasian motif. From finds in Albania , 6th century (?) (J. Strzygowski, *Alati-Iran und Völkerwan-derung*, Leipzig, 1917).

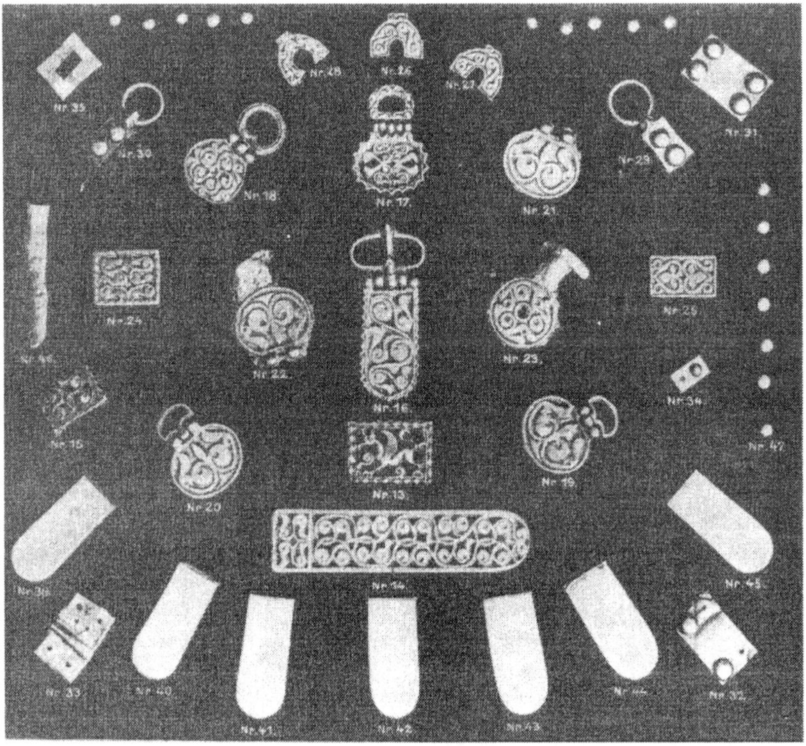

17) Ornamental gold objects showing various Eurasian motifs. From finds in Albania, 6th century (?) (J. Strzygowski, *Altai-Iran und Völkerwanderung*, Leipzig, 1917).

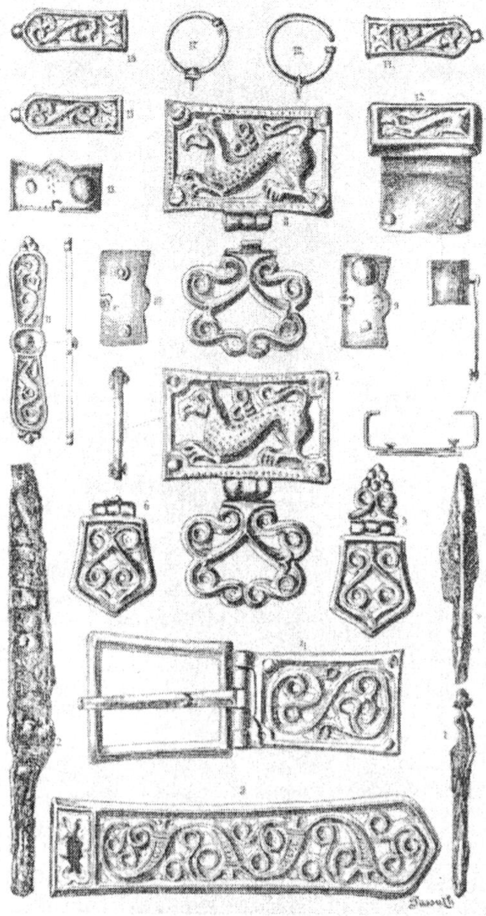

18) Bronze ornaments showing Eurasian ornaments, art of the Avars, 5th-6th century. From the finds at Csuny (Hungary) (J. Strzygowski, *Altai--Iran und Völkerwanderung*, Leipzig, 1917).

Iwona Milewska
(Cracow)

Sandhi in Sanskrit and in Celtic languages

Similarities between Sanskrit and Celtic languages were noticed as early as 1786 when William Jones, a prominent Welshman and one of the fathers of European Sanskrit studies, announced the affinities of these languages in one of his famous Anniversary Discourses at the meeting of the Asiatic Society of Bengal. His observations were of general nature but inspired later linguists to continue the search in this direction.

One of the phenomena where we may notice similarities is sandhi. For years this term covered a wide range of meanings, which sometimes led to confusion. However, this term comes from the Sanskrit word sandhi and its original meaning is as follows: *euphonic junction of final and initial letters in grammar (every sentence in Sanskrit being regarded as a euphonic chain, a break in which occurs at the end of a sentence and is denoted by a Virama or Avasana, stop; this euphonic coalition causing modifications of the final and the initial letters of roots and stems when combined with terminations to form such words).* Sandhi defined in such a way is a phenomenon in Sanskrit and it is described precisely in Sanskrit grammar. It is divided into two main groups: external sandhi and internal sandhi. In this article we treat sandhi in the sense defined above and we focus on external sandhi rules.

The comparison concerns Sanskrit and Breton languages, where we have found several direct similarities. Both in Sanskrit and in Breton we observe the phenomena of external sandhi and both languages follow the general rule of assimilation of final and initial sounds. Sanskrit external sandhi rules can be formulated in a corpus of about 50. For Breton I have not found the source discussing all the rules in the form of rules. Anyhow, all the authors whose works on the Breton language I have scrutinized (Jean Le Du, Elmar Ternes,

Donald Macaulay, Paul Russell, Janig Stephens) are unanimous in describing general tendencies.

In both languages changes happen for:

- single final consonants
- final consonants followed by initial vowels
- final consonants followed by initial consonants

There are several dominant rules:

- backward similarity of voiceness
- single final voiced consonants become voiceless
- reduction of final consonant cluster to a single consonant
- final voiceless consonant become voiced before vowels and voiced consonants.

Sandhi w sanskrycie i w językach celtyckich

The Sanskrit language, whatever be its antiquity, is of a wonderful structure; more perfect than the Greek, more copious than the Latin, and more exquisitely refined than either, yet bearing to both of them a stronger affinity, both in the roots of verbs and in the forms of grammar, than could possibly have been produced by accident; so strong indeed, that no philologer could examine them all three, without believing them to have sprung from some common source, which, perhaps, no longer exists: there is a similar reason, though no quite so forcible, for supposing that both the Gothick and the Celtick, though blended with a very different idiom, had the same origin with the Sanscrit; and the Old Persian might be added to the same family, if this were the place for discussing any question concerning the antiquities of Persia. („Sanskryt, jakakolwiek byłaby jego starożytność, posiada wspaniałą strukturę; doskonalszy niż greka, bogatszy niż łacina, subtelniej wyrafinowany niż jedna i druga, ale pokrewny im obu; podobieństwo to wyraża się i w rdzeniach czasownikowych, i w określonych formach gramatycznych, nie mogąc być dziełem jedynie przypadku; pokrewieństwo jest tak duże, iż filolog nie może badać tej trójki bez wiary w ich wspólne pochodzenie ze źródła, które być może już nie istnieje. Podobny, choć nie tak niewątpliwy powód sprawia, że można przypuszczać, iż również język gocki i celtycki, mimo że nasycone innymi idiomami, mają wspólne z sanskrytem pochodzenie; do tej rodziny może być również dodany staroperski, jeśli tu właśnie byłoby miejsce na rozważanie pytań odnośnie perskich starożytności.") – tak właśnie mówił William Jones w swoim słynnym w późniejszych dziejach językoznawstwa porównawczego trzecim wykładzie z cyklu "Anniversary Discourse" już w 1786 roku, 2 lutego, na odbywającym się w Kalkucie posiedzeniu Asiatic Society of Bengal[1]. William Jones to jeden z ojców indologii europejskiej, a jednocześnie człowiek o celtyckim pochodzeniu, badacz i znawca kultury indyjskiej, Walijczyk, żyjący w latach 1746-1794. Spostrzeżenia jego oraz wielu innych badaczy sprawiły, iż podobieństwa pomiędzy językami zaliczanymi do rodziny indoeuropejskiej, oraz pomiędzy szczególnie nas tutaj interesującymi językami celtyckimi i świętym językiem Indii, sanskrytem, stały się polem badań porównawczych trwających nieprzerwanie do tej pory.

Tutaj szczególnie interesować nas będzie zjawisko określane w językoznawstwie mianem sandhi, w kontekście jego ewentualnych paraleli bądź ich braku, jakie można zaobserwować pomiędzy sanskrytem i językami celtyckimi.

Sam wyraz sandhi używany w pracach językoznawczych zaczerpnięty został z sanskrytu. Monier Monier-Williams w swoim *Sanskrit-English Dictionary* podaje gamę jego możliwych znaczeń. Znaczeniem powtarzającym się, sensem dominującym jest „połączenie, zestawienie, przejście, kombinacja". I znaczenie to odnosi się do najrozmaitszych sfer rzeczywistości, np. kosmologii – tu oznacza przestrzeń pomiędzy niebem a ziemią; czasu – sandhi to świt jako przejście pomiędzy nocą a dniem; w kosmogonii oznacza okres zwieńczający poszczególne Jugi, wielkie okresy w rozwoju świata, przejście do kolejnych; w polityce sandhi oznacza porozumienie, układ, zawarcie pokoju; jako rzeczownik femininum jest imieniem Bogini Połączenia. Analogiczne znaczenie słowo sandhi ma również w gramatyce sanskrytu. Słownikowo bowiem sandhi to: *euphonic junction of final and initial letters in grammar (every sentence in Sanskrit being regarded as an euphonic chain, a break in which occurs at the end of a sentence and is denoted by a Virāma or Avasāna, "stop"; this euphonic coalition causing modifications of the final and initial letters of the separate words of a sentence and in the final letters of roots and stems when*

[1] Pierwszy raz tekst ten został opublikowany [w:] *Asiatic Researches*, vol. 1, s. 442-443; cytat ten podaję za: F. Edgerton, "Sir William Jones", [w:] T. A. Sebeok, *Portraits of Linguists. A Biographical Source Book for the History of Western Linguistics, 1746-1963*, Bloomington and London, 1966, vol. 1, s. 5-6.

combined with terminations to form such words)[2]. (Rzeczownik ten pochodzi od rdzenia *dhā* z prefiksem *sam* I PĀ, którego znaczenie podawane jest we wzmiankowanym słowniku następująco – *to place or hold or put or draw or join or fasten or fix or sew together, unite*)[3].

Zgodnie z jego słownikowym znaczeniem przyjmuje się zatem, iż w gramatyce sanskrytu sandhi to wzajemne oddziaływanie na siebie sąsiadujących dźwięków ich „zestawienie, połączenie, uzgodnienie". Polski badacz Franciszek Malinowski, autor napisanej w 1872 roku gramatyki sanskrytu przełożył to pojęcie na pięknie brzmiący po polsku i oddający istotę sprawy termin „miłodźwięk"[4].

W gramatyce sanskrytu dzieli się oddziaływania typu sandhi na dwie duże grupy: sandhi wewnętrzne, które zachodzi w częściach składowych wyrazów – pierwiastek, temat, sufiks, końcówka oraz w złożeniach, a także na sandhi zewnętrzne – tu chodzi o oddziaływania w zdaniu, pomiędzy poszczególnymi wyrazami[5]. Przy czym dla osiągnięcia biegłości w rozumieniu tekstu podstawowe znaczenie ma zrozumienie i opanowanie reguł sandhi zewnętrznego.

Przy omawianiu sandhi zewnętrznego pojawia się pierwsze podobieństwo z językami celtyckimi. Jak pisze bowiem Myles Dillon w swej książce *Celts and Aryans* powołując się w swych spostrzeżeniach na wielu swoich poprzedników, językoznawców, to właśnie cechą mowy Indo-Europejczyków był fakt traktowania zdania, czy przynajmniej frazy jako najmniejszej jednostki mowy. To nie słowo, czy pojedynczy dźwięk (fonem) były za taką najmniejszą jednostkę uważane, ale właśnie frazy czy wręcz zdania. Stąd wynika zachowanie tak w sanskrycie jak i w wielu innych językach indo-europejskich sandhi w wypowiedziach i to nawet w zapisie. Dillon tym uzasadnia też np. zjawisko mutacji w językach celtyckich[6].

Wracając do sandhi w samym sanskrycie. Działają tu dwie główne zasady: unikanie rozziewu i asymilacja. Jako regułę trzecią można dodać jeszcze

[2] M. Monier-Williams, *A Sanskrit-English Dictionary etymologically and philologically arranged with special reference to cognate Indo-European languages*, Oxford 1899, s. 1144.

[3] M. Monier-Williams, *op. cit.*, s. 1144.

[4] F. Malinowski, *Gramatyka sanskrytu*, Poznań 1872.

[5] Patrz np. A. Gawroński, *Podręcznik sanskrytu. Gramatyka, wypisy, objaśnienia, słownik*, Kraków 1932 (II wyd. Lublin 1985); M. Coulson, *Teach Yourself Sanskrit. An Introduction to the Classical Language*, London 1976.

[6] M. Dillon, *Celts and Aryans*, Simla 1949, s. 33.

deaspirację – aspirowane tracą przydech w każdej pozycji, wyjąwszy przed samogłoską, półsamogłoską i nosówką.

W sandhi zewnętrznym zmiany najczęściej występujące dotyczą przede wszystkim stojących na sąsiadujących pozycjach samogłosek, kończących wyraz: wisargi, *t* lub *n* zębowego – zmiany zachodzą w zależności od dźwięków jakie następują po nich.

Sandhi zewnętrzne w sanskrycie da się ująć w system liczący około 50 reguł (przy czym około 1/3 dotyczy reguł sandhi samogłosek i dwugłosek – 15 reguł, 11 reguł opisuje zachowanie się kończącej wyraz wisargi, pozostałe dotyczą końcowych spółgłosek.) Wygłosowe spółgłoski zmieniają się według ściśle określonych reguł gdy: stoją w izolowanym wygłosie, następują po nich samogłoski lub określone spółgłoski. Najczęściej następuje upodobnienie wsteczne (udźwięcznienie bądź upodobnienie pod względem miejsca artykulacji danej głoski).

Termin sandhi używany jest w pracach językoznawczych nie tylko w znaczeniu jakie posiada w gramatyce sanskrytu. Pierwszym, który wprowadził ten termin na określenie całej gamy zjawisk do językoznawstwa ogólnego był najprawdopodobniej Georg von der Gabelentz. Uczynił to w pracy *Die Sprachwissenschaft. Ihre Aufgaben, Methoden und bisheringen Ergebnisse* wydanej w Lipsku w 1891 roku. Uczynił tak, mimo że już wcześniej bo w 1881 roku Mikołaj Kruszewski, a w 1895 roku Jan Baudouin de Courtenay wykazali, że termin ten odchodzi od znaczenia pierwotnego i zaczyna denotować całą gamę znaczeń, nieraz bardzo odległych. Od końca XIX wieku słowo sandhi stało się mimo to ogólnym, poręcznym semi-terminem na określenie całej gamy zjawisk, które pojedynczo wymagają bardziej ścisłego zdefiniowania. Na ten fakt mylących nieścisłości terminologicznych zwrócił uwagę np. Henning Andersen we wstępie do zbioru tekstów zatytułowanego *Sandhi phenomena in the languages of Europe*[7]. Teksty zamieszczone w tym zbiorze opisują właśnie szereg rozmaitych zjawisk określanych w językoznawstwie zbiorczym terminem sandhi. Z pracy tej wynika, iż używa się w pracach językoznawczych terminu sandhi nie tylko na określenie zmian ściśle fonetycznych ale również termin ten obejmuje inne co do swej istoty zjawiska w rodzaju występujących w językach celtyckich mutacji początkowych, wyrażających zmiany gramatyczne raczej niż czysto fonetyczne.

---

[7] *Sandhi Phenomena in the Languages of Europe*, red. H. Andersen, Berlin-New York-Amsterdam 1986, s. 1-10.

Używanie terminu sandhi na określanie zjawisk tak różnych co do swej przyczyny i istoty, prowadzi czasem do nieporozumień np. przy pobieżnym porównywaniu, bez dogłębnej znajomości wybranych, porównywanych języków czy zjawisk. W tak szerokim rozumieniu obejmującym zjawiska od czysto fonetycznych, przez morfologiczne do deklinacyjnych termin sandhi używany był np. w słynnej pracy Leonarda Bloomfielda *Language*, wydanej w Londynie w 1935 roku[8].

Niektórzy językoznawcy, np. wybitny znawca jednego z języków celtyckich, języka bretońskiego, prof. Elmar Ternes, postulują ograniczenie rozumienia terminu sandhi w językoznawstwie ogólnym do zjawisk ściśle fonetycznych, porównywalnych z rozumieniem jakie termin sandhi ma w gramatyce sanskrytu. Definicja, którą proponuje Ternes jest następująca: sandhi to *phonetically motivated alternations, occuring at word boundaries* czyli sandhi to jego zdaniem „zmiany umotywowane fonetycznie, pojawiające się na granicy słów"[9].

Inny, zajmujacy się tym problemem językoznawca Rene Jongen podaje następującą definicję: *all phonological modifications associated with combination of signs and localized at their boundaries* czyli uważa on, że sandhi to „wszystkie modyfikacje fonologiczne związane z kombinacją znaków, zlokalizowane na granicy pomiędzy nimi"[10]. Obaj uczeni expressis verbis wykluczają zatem z zakresu zjawisk określanych mianem sandhi modyfikacje, które następują nie ze względu na współwystępowanie dźwięków obok siebie.

W celu uniknięcia nieporozumień mogących wyniknąć z powodu porównywania ze sobą zjawisk nieporównywalnych, starałam się na tyle na ile to było możliwe, skupić się na obserwacji zjawiska sandhi w językach celtyckich tylko w tym zawężonym, ale ściśle zdefiniowanym rozumieniu. Przy takim założeniu wstępnym, i przy ograniczonych możliwościach czasowych, udało mi się stwierdzić, iż zjawisko z pewnością analogiczne, czy wręcz identyczne co do istoty z sandhi występującym w sanskrycie zachodzi w języku bretońskim, zaliczanym łącznie z językiem walijskim i kornickim do grupy brytańskiej języków celtyckich. Skupiłam się zatem wyłącznie na teoretycznym przestudiowaniu sformułowanych przez znawców tego języka zasad i reguł sandhi rozumianego tak jak w sanskrycie. Język bretoński używany był i jest w Bretanii, w północno-

---

[8] L. Bloomfield, *Language*, London 1935.

[9] E. Ternes, "A grammatical hierarchy of joining", [w:] H. Andersen, *op. cit.*, s. 18.

[10] R. Jongen, "Les phenomenes de sandhi dans un dialecte bas-francique meridional", [w:] H. Andersen, *op. cit.* s. 121.

zachodniej Francji. W jego rozwoju wyróżnia się 4 podstawowe fazy: od V-VI wieku, kiedy używany był *Archaic Bretonian*, przez występujący pomiędzy VI, a XI wiekiem *Old Bretonian*, do używanego od XI do połowy XVII wieku *Middle Bretonian* po trwający do czasów nam współczesnych *Modern Bretonian*[11]. W obrębie języka bretońskiego występuje również zróżnicowanie dialektologiczne, mające wpływ także na szczegółowe reguły sandhi, oddziaływania międzywyrazowego. W literaturze fachowej podaje się pewne cechy stałe, charakterystyczne dla języka określanego mianem *standard Bretonian*, należy jednak pamiętać o różnicach tak diachronicznych jak i dialektologicznych. Nasza analiza porównawcza dotyczyć będzie zatem cech ogólnych raczej niż szczegółowych, a informacje pochodzić będą głównie z prac kilku autorów zajmujących się ogólnie i szczegółowo językiem bretońskim, na których to pracach opieram moją wiedzę o języku bretońskim. Co do charakterystycznych cech podstawowych zgodni są bowiem autorzy tacy jak: Jean Le Du, Elmar Ternes, Donald Macaulay, Paul Russell, Janig Stephens[12]. Chciałabym przywołać tu na wstępie stwierdzenie Donalda Macaulaya, iż znajomość reguł sandhi jest bardzo ważna tak dla standardowego bretońskiego jak i dla dialektów bretońskich[13]. Bretoński nie ma bowiem w zasadzie jasnej fonetycznej precyzacji granic poszczególnych słów. Cecha ta zachowywana bywa też w piśmie. Tu mamy kolejną analogię z sanskrytem, którego poprawne zrozumienie jest niemożliwe bez znajomości reguł sandhi, jako że zapis zachowuje zmiany powstałe pod wpływem oddziaływań typu sandhi.

Sandhi zewnętrzne zachodzi zatem w języku bretońskim i można je podzielić na grupy analogiczne do opisanych powyżej dla sanskrytu. Będą to odpowiednio: izolowane spółgłoski wygłosowe, spółgłoski wygłosowe przed samogłoskami i wreszcie spółgłoski wygłosowe przed spółgłoskami nagłosowymi. Jeśli idzie o grupę pierwszą, izolowanych spółgłosek wygłosowych to zwykle ulegają one, podobnie jak w sanskrycie – ubezdźwięcznieniu. Końcowe zbitki spółgłoskowe są redukowane, również analogicznie do końcowych zbitek

[11] Klasyfikacja wg: P. Russell, *An Introduction to the Celtic Languages*, London and New York 1995.

[12] J. Le Du, "A sandhi survey of the Breton language", [w:] H. Andersen *op. cit.* s. 435-452; E. Ternes, "The Breton language", [w:] *The Celtic Languages*, red. D. Macaulay, Cambridge 1992, s. 419-451; D. Macaulay, *op. cit.*; P. Russell, *op. cit.*; J. Stephens, "Breton", [w:] *The Celtic Languages*, red. M. J. Ball, London-New York 1993, s. 349-409.

[13] *The Celtic Languages*, red. D. Macaulay, *op. cit.*, s. 435.

w sanskrycie, do pojedynczych spółgłosek. Różnice dotyczą konkretnych fonemów, jako że bretoński i sanskryt różnią się co do swoich zasobów fonologicznych. Reguły ogólne są jednak całkowicie analogiczne. Jeśli idzie o grupę drugą – wygłosowych spółgłosek stojących przed samogłoskami to zachodzi tu identycznie jak w sanskrycie udźwięcznienie spółgłosek wygłosowych. Przy czym w bretońskim wyjątkiem jest sytuacja, gdy końcową spółgłoskę poprzedza *s* – wtedy udźwięcznienie nie zachodzi (np. *klask a zo*, gdzie końcowe bezdźwięczne *k* pierwszego wyrazu pozostaje takim mimo następującej po nim samogłoski). W grupie trzeciej przy współwystępowaniu spółgłosek na granicach wyrazów zasadą dominującą jest, znowu podobnie jak w sanskrycie, upodobnienie wsteczne, czyli dźwięczne początkowe udźwięczniają bezdźwięczne wygłosowe, a bezdźwięczne nagłosowe ubezdźwięczniają dźwięczne końcowe. W bretońskim zachodzi jeszcze inne zjawisko, nie występujące w sanskrycie, mianowicie gdy sąsiadują ze sobą dwie identyczne spółgłoski np. *-n* i *n-* to stają się one jedną, w tym wypadku jest to *n*. Od tych reguł ogólnych pojawiają się sporadyczne wyjątki.

W opracowaniach do których miałam dostęp nie znalazłam kompletnego zestawu reguł sandhi dla wszystkich możliwych współwystępowań dźwięków w bretońskim. Zastanawia mnie też brak informacji na temat ewentualnych oddziaływań współwystępujących samogłosek. W sanskrycie reguły sandhi samogłoskowego stanowią, jak wspominałam wyżej 1/3 wszystkich reguł. Ciekawe mogłoby zatem być zestawienie dotyczące właśnie samogłosek . We wszystkich opracowaniach powtarzają się jednak omówione powyżej, dominujące reguły ogólne, wspólne dla języka bretońskiego i sanskrytu a mianowicie:

1. pomiędzywyrazowe oddziaływanie dźwięków – sandhi zewnętrzne
2. dominująca reguła upodobnienia wstecznego pod względem dźwięczności
3. ubezdźwięcznianie się izolowanych spółgłosek wygłosowych
4. redukcja wygłosowych, izolowanych zbitek spółgłoskowych do pojedynczych spółgłosek
5. udźwięcznianie wygłosowych spółgłosek pod wpływem nagłosowych samogłosek bądź spółgłosek dźwięcznych

Można zatem stwierdzić, na zakończenie, iż wspomniany na początku fragment wykładu walijskiego indologa Williama Jonesa znajduje potwierdzenie w toku badań szczegółowych, a dalsze poszukiwania z pewnością przyniosą inne jeszcze potwierdzenia wspólnoty języków celtyckich z sanskrytem.

Bibliografia

W. S. Allen, *Phonetics in ancient India*, Oxford 1953

W. S. Allen, *Sandhi. The theoretical, phonetic, and historical bases of word-junction in Sanskrit*, The Hague and Paris 1972

H. Andersen ed. by, *Sandhi phenomena in the languages of Europe*, Berlin 1986

M. J. Ball with J. Fife ed. by, *The Celtic Languages*, London and New York 1993

M. J. Ball, G. E. Jones ed. by, *Welsh Phonology. Selected Readings*, Cardiff 1984

L. Bednarczuk ed. by, *Języki indoeuropejskie*, Warszawa 1988

M. Bloomfield, *Language*, London 1935

M. Coulson, *Teach Yourself Sanskrit. An Introduction to the Classical Language*, London 1976

D. Crystal, *A first dictionary of linguistics and phonetics*, London 1980

M. Dillon, *Celts and Aryans. Survivals of Indo-European Speech and Society*, Simla 1949

A. Gawroński, *Podręcznik sanskrytu. Gramatyka, wypisy, objaśnienia, słownik*, Kraków 1932, II wyd. Lublin 1985

D. B. Gregor, *Celtic. A Comparative Study (of the six languages: Irish, Gaelic Manx, Welsh, Cornish, Breton seen against the background of their history, literature, and destiny)*, Cambridge 1980

K. Jackson, *A historical phonology of Breton*, Dublin 1967

W. P. Lehmann, *Historical Linguistics*, London 1992, III wyd.

W. P. Lehmann, *Theoretical Bases of Indo-European Linguistics*, London and New York 1993

H. Lewis, H. Pedersen, *A Concise Comparative Celtic Grammar*, Gottingen 1937

D. Macaulay ed. by, *The Celtic Languages*, Cambridge 1992

E. Majewicz, A. F. Majewicz, *Języki celtyckie na Wyspach Brytyjskich*, Wrocław 1983

F. Malinowski, *Gramatyka sanskrytu*, Poznań 1872

A. T. E. Matonis and D. F. Melia ed. by, *Celtic Language, Celtic Culture: A Festschrift for Eric P. Hamp*, California 1990

M. Monier-Williams, *A Sanskrit-English Dictionary etymologically and philologically arranged with special reference to cognate Indo-European languages*, Oxford 1899

P. Russel, *An Introduction to the Celtic Languages*, London and New York 1995

T. A. Sebeok ed. by, *Portraits of Linguists. A Biographical Source Book for the History of Western Linguistics 1746-1963*, Bloomington and London 1966

E. Ternes, *Grammaire structurale du breton de l'Ile de Groix*, Heidelberg 1970

E. Ternes, "Konsonantische Anlautveränderungen in den keltischen und romanischen Sprachen", [w:] *Romanistisches Jahrbuch* 28, s. 19-53

Marek J. Olbrycht
(Cracow)

The Cimmerian problem re-examined: the evidence of the Classical sources[1]

1. Introduction

Of all the nomadic peoples who were present in the Caspian steppes and in Western Asia in the 1st millenium B.C. none has probably caused historians and archaeologists so much trouble than the Cimmerians. The history of the Cimmerians is still being discussed and reconstructed in different ways[2]. The whole problem contains lots of misunderstandings mainly due to the fact that the most important source groups, i.e. literary and archaeological evidences, have been examined on the basis of some aprioric assumptions not all of which are immidiately obvious.

In the following paper an attempt will be made to discuss the problem of the Cimmerian presence in Southeastern Europe and related aspects as seen in the light of Classical testimonies. One of these questions, the problem of an alleged migration of the Cimmerians from the North Pontic steppes into Central and Western Europe, requires consideration. The thesis about western movements of the Cimmerians has also had wide repercussions in historical, archaeologi-

[1] The present article is an extended version of a paper presented in February 1998 at the Celto-Asiatic Seminar, Jagiellonian University, Institute of Oriental Philology, Kraków.

[2] During the last decade more than ten articles and monographs on the Cimmerians have been published. General histories of the Cimmerians are: Kristensen 1988; Lanfranchi 1990; Ivantchik 1993; Tokhtas'ev 1993; Ivančik 1996; D'iakonov 1994; Parker 1995. Amongst recent archaeological works we should mention: Dudarev 1991; Pogrebova/Raevskii 1992; Kačalova/Alekseev 1993; Chochorowski 1993; Makhortych 1994; Dudarev 1995.

cal and philological studies[3]. The well documented history of the Cimmerians in Western Asia is not the topic of this paper, but it provides important fixing points for a reconstruction of the whole development of that people. In exploring the Classical testimonies related to the Cimmerians, it is hoped that a greater insight into the complex history of the earliest known ethnic entities of South-eastern Europe may be achieved.

The history of the Cimmerians in Europe can be discussed mainly from the point of view of Classical sources, for the basic evidence for the study of this people are testimonies of Greek and Roman authors[4]. On the other hand, valuable evidence for the Cimmerians in Western Asia is provided by Oriental, mainly Assyrian, records[5]. The written evidence can be to some extent supplemented by archaeological data from the Ponto-Caspian steppes, the Caucasus area and Western Asia[6]. However, the presently available archaeological materials do not allow any convincing hypothesis about the character of genuine Cimmerian culture. It is due to the fact that archaeological interpretations depend on historical premises and the latter, relying on fragmentary and contradictory testimonies, still do not enable us to give definitive answers to certain important questions about Cimmerian history.

2. Homer and the Cimmerians of fable

The name of the Cimmerians appears in the *Odyssey* of Homer. The vague notion of that people entertained by Homer has often been commented both in antiquity and at present. Homer says the following about the Cimmerians: "She (i.e. the ship of Odysseus, M.J.O.) came to deep-flowing Oceanus, that bounds the Earth, where is the land and city of the Cimmerians, wrapped in mist

---

[3] Cf. Sulimirski 1959; Bouzek 1983; Pstrusińska 1996.

[4] For detailed studies of the available literary classical sources, see Lehmann-Haupt 1921 and Tokhtas'ev 1993.

[5] These sources have been already sufficiently analysed, cf. Lanfranchi 1990; Ivantchik 1993; Ivančik 1996.

[6] Cf. Samokvasov 1908; Sulimirski 1959; Terenožkin 1976; Leskov 1981; Bouzek 1983; Meliukova 1989; Melyukova 1990; Dudarev 1991; Kačalova/Alekseev 1993; Makhortych 1994; Dudarev 1995. See, especially, the excellent analysis of archaeological materials relating to the nomads of the Pre-Scythian period, as being identified with the historical Cimmerians, given by Chochorowski 1993.

and cloud. Never does the bright sun look down on them with his rays either when he mounts the starry heaven or when he turns again to earth from heaven, but baneful night is spread over wretched mortals. Thither we came and beached our ship, and took out the sheep, and ourselves went beside the stream of Oceanus until we came to the place of which Circe had told us"[7].

There is an intense debate over the interpretation of this passage. Homer lived in the second half of the 8th century B.C.[8], and his outstanding *Odyssey* was probably written in the last quarter of that century. On the basis of the long nights the Cimmerians of Homer are placed in the far North, even in Britain and in Jutland[9]. The majority of modern authorities try to locate the Homeric Cimmerians in the North Pontic steppes[10]. However, some circumstances could contradict such assumptions. Firstly, it is necessary to recognize that the *Odyssey* is a poem and combines fantasy with naturalism, supernatural elements with echoes of real events. On the whole, the aura of fantasy surrounds even the most realistic topics of the Homeric poem. This factor must be taken into account when attempting to locate the Cimmerians. Secondly, the above quoted description of the Cimmerians is placed in the *Nekyia*, the most difficult and mysterious part of the Odysseus saga[11]. Thirdly, the mysterious country of the Cimmerians is situated in the dark western edge of the Ocean; in this region Helios sets[12]. The entrance to the Underworld is to be placed also there[13]. The quoted passage of the *Odyssey* permits the statement that in the context of the Homeric poem the Cimmerians lived in the westernmost edge of the Ocean floundering in thick mists and cloud. It is obvious that the Homeric Cimmerians

---

[7] Translation quoted after: Homer, *The Odyssey*, vol. I, transl. by A. T. Murray, London/ Cambridge (Mass.) 1953 (LCL). In the present paper, translations – unless otherwise stated – will be drawn from Loeb editions (with some improvements).

[8] Lesky 1967, 693.

[9] For a discussion of this problem, see Lehman-Haupt 1921, 428ff.; Huebeck/ Hoekstra 1989, 78.

[10] Chochorowski 1993, 9f. Similarly Parker 1995, 31.

[11] The *Nekyia*, the eleventh book of the *Odyssey*, tells the story of Odysseus' journey into Hades and describes the magic rites by which the ghosts of the dead were called up, cf. Lesky 1967, 811ff.

[12] Od. 24.12.

[13] Cf. Od. 24.11-14. Odysseus leaves Aiaia, the island of Circe, and travels to the entrance of the Underworld (Od. 12.3-4). Cf. also Od. 10.490-515.

and their country belong the the world of legend[14]. In such circumstances, it is not difficult to accept the opinion of Huebeck/Hoekstra: "The mythological location of the Homeric Cimmerians' country at the entry to the Underworld in fact exclude any possibility of connecting them with the historical Cimmerians"[15].

It is worth noting that the idea of a people in the dark West, which is never penetrated by the sun, was apparently created to be in complete contrast to the location of the peoples of the Laestrygonians and the Ethiopians who inhabited the eastern borders of the world and lived in perpetual light[16]. Modern authorities overlook the fact that Homer mentions the city (*polis*) of the Cimmerians. Assuming that Homer's description is reliable, it is hardly possible to understand the existence of a city in the homeland of a people which was unanimously treated in the ancient tradition as a nomadic tribe.

To sum up: The testimony given by Homer is actually a poetic one and does not provide any reliable location of the Cimmerians in the real world. It should be considered a *licentia poetica*. However, the Homeric idea of the Cimmerians living near the entrance to the Underworld exerted a strong influence on the treatment of Cimmerian history in antiquity, and especially on the location of that tribe.

What might actually the source for the Homeric knowledge of the Cimmerians have been? To pursue this issue the discussion has to turn to the Argonautic saga. Some modern authorities maintain that the *Odyssey* took some themes, especially the notion of Cimmerians, from the Argonautic tale[17]. This story was a favourite subject for Greek poetry already before Homer and the poet knew it[18]. The saga of the Argonauts was connected with the Black Sea and

[14] Cf. the valid arguments of Huebeck/Hoekstra 1989, 78: "Both the people (of the Cimmerians, M.J.O.) and their country do, of course, belong to the realm of folk-tale; they are part of irrational world which lies beyond the confines of the real world and surrounds it, itself being bordered by the circumambient Oceanus".

[15] Huebeck/Hoekstra 1989, 78.

[16] See Il. 1.423; 23.205; Od. 1.22. Cf. Huebeck 1963, 491.

[17] See Meuli 1921 and Willamowitz-Moelendorf 1920, 362ff. For a convincing discussion of this issue, see Tokhtas'ev 1993, 47ff.

[18] In the *Odyssey* 12.70 the good ship Argo is said to be of interest to all.

Colchis, the land on the river Phasis in modern Georgia[19]. On the other hand, the Cimmerians are placed in Transcaucasia according to Assyrian sources of the last quarter of the 8th century B.C., i.e. in Homeric times. Assyrian records locate the first known country of the Cimmerians in Asia, Gamir, in the Gori area (Georgia) on the eastern borders of Colchis[20]. Based upon this evidence, then, one can assume that Homer was indebted to the Argonautic saga for information recording the mysterious people of the Cimmerians.

3. Aristeas of Proconnesus and Hecataeus of Miletus on Cimmerian history

Alongside the *Odyssey* the earliest Classical source for the Cimmerians in Europe seems to be the *Arimaspea*, a poem written by Aristeas of Proconnesus. Aristeas lived in all probability in the first half of the 6th century B.C., anyway not earlier than circa 650 B.C.[21]. Consequently, his activities cannot be dated earlier than the establishment of the first Greek colonies in the northern shores of the Black Sea. This circumstance permits the supposition that Aristeas could not have witnessed Cimmerian tribal movements north of the Caucasus or get any reliable current information on the Cimmerians in the North Pontic area, for that people – if we believe Herodotus' account – migrated into Western Asia, and this happened prior to 715 B.C. in the light of Assyrian records. On the other hand, Aristeas must have known the Cimmerian movements in Asia Minor[22]. In his *Arimaspea*, which we know only from few fragments transmitted by other authors, he describes some tribes of the Eurasian steppe area such as the Issedones, the Arimaspi, and the Hyperboreans. There can be little doubt that those accounts, with their speculative (Pythagorean) and mythological tendencies, did not intend to provide strictly documentary evidence on ethnography and geography of the Eurasian tribes[23]. Nevertheless, they were of primary

[19] In the poem *Korinthiaka*, written by Eumelus of Corinth, in the related writings of Epimenides of Creta and in the Hesiodic *Catalogue of women* the aim of the Argonauts' journey is Colchis, cf. Tokhtas'ev 1993, 22f. See also Easterling/Knox 1989a, 65ff.

[20] Diakonoff/Kashkai 1981, 71; Tokhtas'ev 1993, 49; Ivančik 1996, 30.

[21] Suda (Suidas) dates Aristeas' akme circa 547-546 B.C. and such a date appears to be reliable, cf. Tokhtas'ev 1993, 28f. There are, however, other proposals, and Bolton (1962, 179) dates the activities of Aristeas in the third quarter of the 7th century B.C..

[22] Tokhtas'ev 1993, 26f.

[23] Bolton 1962, 74ff.

importance for the further development of ancient investigations on the peoples of central Eurasia. The *Arimaspea* was used by Hecateaus of Miletus[24]. Furthermore, in his description of Scythia, Herodotus quotes some versions on the origins of the Scythians. One of those accounts comes from Aristeas: "But Aristeas, son of Caystrobius, a man of Proconnesus, says in his poetry that he was transported by the god Phoebus to the land of the Issedones (...). The Issedones were driven of their country by the Arimaspians and the Scythians were driven out of theirs by the Issedones; and the Cimmerians, who lived by the southern sea, were hard pressed by the Scythians, and left their country. So Aristeas also differs from the Scythians about these regions"[25].

Aristeas of Proconnesus seems to have used the earliest knowledge of the Ponto-Caspian steppes drawn from the first Greek colonists in the region. Thus, according to Aristeas, the Cimmerians originally inhabited some lands on the "southern sea". Then, the Scythians, under the pressure of the Issedones, supplanted the Cimmerians from their country. Aristeas' account on the "chain" nature of steppe migrations is fully correct. But where did the Cimmerians live? To answer this question, attention should be drawn to the expression: "dwelling by the southern sea" (οἰκέοντας ἐπὶ τῇ νοτίῃ θαλάσσῃ). Bolton identifies the sea as the Black Sea and locates the Cimmerians in the North Pontic area[26]. However, the term "southern sea" cannot be interpreted as a reference to the Black Sea which is elsewhere never mentioned under this name. It is hardly possible that Aristeas considered the well known to the Greeks Black Sea a "southern sea". The context makes it clear that the Cimmerians dwelt on the shores of a sea which was actually beyond the sphere of common Greek knowledge for it bears no specific name. At the same time the passage implicates that the "southern sea" was located to the south of the Cimmerian country. The account of Aristeas permits thus the following statement: The "southern sea" should be identified as the Caspian Sea; its notion was really poor under the Greeks in Aristeas' times, i.e. before Hecataeus and Herodotus and before the establishment of the Persian Empire[27]. Consequently, the country of the Cimmerians mentioned by Aristeas should be located in the Northern Caspian steppes.

---

[24] Cf. Jacoby 1912, 2717; Tokhtas'ev 1993, 24f.

[25] Hdt. 4.13 (Bolton frg. 1). Quoted after: Herodotus, *Historiai*, with an English translation by A. D. Goodley, vol. 1-4, London 1946-1957 (LCL).

[26] Bolton 1962, 75.

[27] On this issue see Herrmann 1914, 36; idem 1919.

When attempting to show the origins of the Scythians, Herodotus quotes not only Aristeas but also other sources. It was Hecataeus of Miletus who seems to be largely responsible for Herodotus' picture of Scythia[28]. Hecataeus (circa 540-480 B.C.)[29] was an outstanding Ionian exponent of scientific geography who composed the *Ges Periodos*, a description of the Mediterranean and Black Seas, and the *Genealogiae* (*Historiae*), both preserved only in fragments. Hecataeus wrote the first extensive description of Scythians and neighbouring tribes of the steppes[30]. This was mainly due to the fact that he had a plenty of new information acquired by the army of Darius I during its campaign against the Scythians in the North Pontic area[31]. Hecataeus' starting points in his description of the Cimmerians were: the location of the Homeric Cimmerians in the Ponto-Caspian region[32] and the existence of the so-called "Cimmerian" toponyms in the North Pontic Bosporus area[33]. Moreover, Hecataeus knew Aristeas' work on the peoples of the steppes[34]. The above facts serve to confirme the statement elaborated by some modern scholars that Hecataeus placed the Cimmerians in the North Pontic area[35].

4. Herodotus, the Cimmerians, and the origins of the Scythians

The most extensive and important information on the Cimmerians in Europe is contained in the *Histories* of Herodotus of Halicarnassus (circa 485-425 B.C.), the founder of ancient historiography. Herodotus' work is composed of longer accounts which may be designated as *logoi*; they in turn comprise smaller *logoi*. His "Scythian" logos is connected with the genealogy of the Scythians. Herodotus quotes three versions of the origins of the Scythians[36].

[28] Herodotus was heavily influenced by Hecataeus not only in his description of Scythia but also in other accounts, see Easterling/Knox 1989b, 18f. Cf. also Herrmann 1914, 12ff.; Junge 1939, 20ff.

[29] Cf. Aly 1921, 122ff.; Junge 1939, 21ff.; Lendle 1992, 44; Tokhtas'ev 1993, 22.

[30] FGrHist 1 F 184-195 with Jacoby's commentary.

[31] Cf. Jacoby 1912, 2717ff.; Plezia 1959/1960.

[32] See the excellent analysis if this issue by Tokhtas'ev 1993, 22f.

[33] Hecateaus in Strabo (7.3.6) mentions a "Cimmerian polis" in that region.

[34] Cf. Jacoby 1912, 2717.

[35] For a convincing discussion of this problem, see Tokhtas'ev 1993, 22ff.

[36] Cf. Sulimirski 1985, 165ff. On the sources of this passage Jacoby 1913, 431f.; Fehling 1971, 33ff.

According to the first version, taken from the Scythians, their origins stemmed from a hero named Targitaos[37]. In the second account, given by the Pontic Greeks, Heracles entered the inhabited land, now called Scythia, and met a monster, half serpent, half maiden, who bore him three sons. One of them, Scythes, became the first Scythian king[38]. In both accounts there is no mention of the Cimmerians. Undoubtedly, these accounts reflect local traditions of the inhabitants of the North Pontic area. It is striking that the two accounts considered the Scythians to be autochthons in their country[39]. The stories are historically not credible, but they contain valuable details attested in other sources[40]. They differ from the third version of the descendance of the Scythians (given as ἄλλος λόγος), which Herodotus considers the most probable as resting on the authority of the "barbarians and Greeks"[41]. This account combines the migration of the Cimmerians and the establishment of the Scythians in the Pontic steppes. Herodotus writes:

"There is yet another tale (ἄλλος λόγος), to the tradition whereof I myself do especially incline. It is to this purport: the nomad Scythians inhabiting Asia, being hard pressed in war by the Massagetae, fled away across the river Araxes to the Cimmerian country (for the country which the Scythians now inhabit is said to have belonged of old to the Cimmerians), and the Cimmerians, at the advance of the Scythians, took such counsel as behoved men threatened by a great host. Their opinions were divided; both were strongly held, but that of the princes was the more honourable; for the commonalty deemed that their business was to withdraw themselves and that there was no need to risk their lives for the dust of the earth; but the princes were for fighting to defend their country against the attackers. Neither side would be persuaded by the other, neither the people by the princes nor the princes by the people; the one part planned to depart without fighting and deliver the country to their enemies, but the princes were resolved to lie slain in the own country and not to flee with the people, for they considered how happy their state had been and what ills were like to come upon them if they fled from their native land. Being thus resolved they parted asunder into two equal bands and fought with each other

[37] Hdt. 4.5-7.

[38] Hdt. 4.8-10.

[39] See Tokhtas'ev 1993, 19 with further references.

[40] Fehling 1971, 33-37.

[41] Cf. Fehling 1971, 37f.

till they were all slain by their own hands; then the commonalty of the Cimmerians buried them by the river Tyras, where their tombs are still to be seen, and having buried them departed out of the land; and the country being empty, the Scythians came and took possessions of it" (*Histories* 4.11)

"And to this day there are in Scythia Cimmerian walls, and a Cimmerian ferry, and there is a country Cimmeria and the Cimmerian Bosphorus. Moreover, it is clearly seen that the Cimmerians in their flight from the Scythians into Asia did also make a colony on the peninsula where now the Greek city of Sinope has been founded; and it is manifest that the Scythians pursued after them and invaded Media, missing the way; for the Cimmerians ever fled by the way of the coast, and the Scythians pursued with the Caucasus on their right till where they came into the Median land, turning inland on their way. I have now related this other tale (ἄλλος λόγος), which is told alike by Greeks and barbarians" (*Histories* 4.12).

Herodotus' description of Scythia, as mentioned above, is based on some specific sources. He defined his informants by the words: "there is yet another tale (ἄλλος λόγος), to the tradition whereof I myself do especially incline"[42], and: "I have now related this other tale (ἄλλος λόγος), which is told alike by Greeks and barbarians"[43]. What were the sources of Herodotus with respect to his most important Scythian account[44]? Firstly, he used Oriental sources, especially from Lydia and Persia (the informants are named *barbarians*) for the history of the Scythians in the Near East and related affairs[45]. Secondly, as to the mentioned Greek informants, Herodotus' main authority for the Scythian, Cimmerian and Median matters was surely Hecataeus of Miletus (circa 540-480)[46]. The expression "Greeks" ("Ἕλληνες) suggests that Herodotus used, besides Hecataeus, other sources of Greek origin, such as relations from Greek settlements of the North Pontic area (e.g. Tyras, see be-

[42] Hdt. 4.11.

[43] Hdt. 4.12.

[44] On the problem of the sources see Jacoby 1913, 419ff.; Tokhtas'ev 1993, 21.

[45] Müllenhoff 1896, 23; Jacoby 1913, 419ff.

[46] Cf. Aly 1921, 122ff.; Junge 1939, 21ff.; Lendle 1992, 44; Tokhtas'ev 1993, 22. Herodotus may have taken some details also from other writers such as Pherekydes of Syros or Damastes, cf. Tokhtas'ev 1993, 24.

low). Herodotus also reports a story related to the Cimmerians written by Aristeas of Proconnesus (see above, *Histories* 4.13).

Herodotus' logos about the Cimmerians, given in the *Histories* 4.11-12, appears to be partially not historical. Moreover, Herodotus is clearly wrong in many details. The fratricidal battle of the Cimmerian "kings", i.e. of the aristocracy, seems to be a creature of northern Pontic Greek folklore. In Assyrian records, the Cimmerians are said to be a powerful nation. How could we explain the dominating position of a tribe immediately after a shattering defeat and self-annihilation of its ruling class? It is striking that Herodotus knows no names of Cimmerian rulers. Furthermore, it is surely false if Herodotus claims that the Cimmerians, supplanted by Scythians to the west, escaped from the Scythian pressure... to the east and to the Caucasus, into the regions which were already under Scythian control! The natural way of retreat before invaders would be to the west.

Herodotus expressively mentions the river Tyras as the place where the Cimmerian aristocracy fought and was buried. Herodotus says also that the "tombs (θάψαι) are still to be seen". The fragment seems to represent some first-hand acquaintance with the region. But who was buried in the graves? Apparently, we have to do in this case with a folk-tale which should explain the origin of certain remarkable monuments; similar stories are widely attested in the Near East and in the Greek world, where old tombs or buildings were connected with a previous race or with a great mythical hero[47]. Based upon the above mentioned remarks, the assumption can be brought forward that the whole story about the Cimmerians in the Tyras region is not genuine and was created by the local Greek colonists to explain the existence of some ancient tombs.

Herodotus' mention of the river Araxes is very important. According to his statement, it was once the border between the Scythians and the Cimmerians. The Araxes of this passage should be identified with the Volga[48]. This piece of information is surely drawn from Hecataeus of Miletus whose

[47] As to this issue it may be noted that in Greece there were many local traditions in which Pelasgi or Cyclops were credited with lots of mythical achievements, see, e.g. Grimal 1987, 282 and 64f. Cf. also Hdt. 6.137ff.

[48] Herrmann 1914, 13, note 1.

acquaintance with the region is well attested[49]. Herodotus could find a more certain attestation of the existence of the Araxes amongst the merchants of Olbia who must have travelled in the Ponto-Caspian steppes[50]. In the passage under discussion Herodotus makes the pressure of the Massagetae responsible for the retreat of the Scythians from beyond the Araxes. This statement is very significant for the issue under discussion. In the 6th-4th centuries B.C., the northwestern parts of Central Asia were dominated by a powerful tribal confederation named Massagetae in Greek sources. Cyrus the Great, the founder of the Achaemenid Empire, met his death while fighting against this group. The earliest description of the Massagetaeis provided by Hecataus of Miletus transmitted by Herodotus[51]. Hecataeus was familiar with the peoples living in the Transcaspian plains of Turkestan. Consequently, he may be expected to know of the tribal struggles in the region. This assumption can be supported by the quoted above fragment describing a conflict between the Massagetae and Scythians. We should not overlook the fact that in Aristeas, who probably had no knowledge of the Massagetae, the people pressing on the Cimmerians are Issedones (perhaps a "Sarmatian" tribe?).

Herodotus (4.12) gives further evidence for the Cimmerian presence in Scythia and lists toponyms containing the term "Cimmerian" and coming from the region of Bosphorus (see below). At the same time, Herodotus claims that the starting point for the Cimmerians' escape from the Scythian country was the Tyras (Dniester). This circumstance allows us to suggest that Herodotus tried to combine two different local traditions on the Cimmerians which were created in Tyras and in the Greek settlements of the Bosphorus area.

It might then be concluded that Herodotus transmits the best known story of the origins of the Scythians. As to this issue, he rejects the traditions originated amongst the Scythians and the Pontic Greeks which claimed autochthony for the Scythians. Another account, which he considers the most probable, combines the appeareance of the Scythians with the withdrawal of the Cimmerians from the steppes. According to this view, the Scythians, being har-

[49] Hecataeus knew the Caspian/Hyrcanian Sea and the river Araxes which is differently identified by modern scholars, cf. P'yankov 1975, 50.

[50] On the informants from Olbia see Herrmann 1914, 13.

[51] P'yankov 1975, *passim*.

assed by the Massagetae, went across the river Araxes and drove out the Cimmerians of their country. In this story, Herodotus apparently followed Hecataeus of Miletus.

It is of particular importance that Herodotus vindicates his own view against the "mythological" traditions by a reference to Aristeas and the statement that "Aristeas also differs from the Scythians about these regions". The version given by Aristeas on the Cimmerian beginnings coincides in the most important details with that of Herodotus 4.12. Firstly, both versions locate the original Cimmerian country in the same area in the Caspian steppes and recognize the earlier occupation of the region by that nation; secondly, they explain the Cimmerian migration by the pressure of the Scythians. The only difference, as to the tribe which drove the Scythians into the Cimmerian country, is of secondary importance for it is connected with poorly known Innerasian movements east of the Volga.

The Herodotean way of working is clearly visible in the account of the Cimmerian activities in Asia. Herodotus writes that the Cimmerians constantly moved along the coast (of the Black Sea) in their flight from Scythia to Asia (*Histories* 4.12). However, it is hardly possible for a relatively numerous tribe to go along the eastern shores of the Black Sea (next to the western fringes of the Caucasus) owing to its precipitous nature[52]. Moreover, the Assyrian records document a long Cimmerian presence in Transcaucasia and then mainly in the interior of Asia Minor (Tabal, Phrygia, Lydia) as well as of northwestern Iran (Manna, Media). Cimmerian activities in the coastal regions were quite sporadical, and just for the Greeks were certainly of particular importance for the Cimmerian raids devastated Sinope, Magnesia and Ephesus[53]. Based upon those observations, therefore, it is impossible to accept Herodotus' statement that the Cimmerians "constantly fled by the way of the coast". The version of the Cimmerian migration given by Herodotus appears to have followed primarily some traditions of Greek coastal cities in Asia Minor, such as Sinope, a colony mentioned explicit in the passage under question. At the same time, however, he is capable of referring only to few episodes concerning the Cimmerian activities

[52] See Strab. 11.2.12ff.

[53] Such a raid aginst Ionia is referred to in Hdt. 1.6.

in the interior of Asia Minor[54]. We may assume, on the whole, that Herodotus – when describing the Cimmerian migration – combined some different local traditions taken from Greek cities in the North Pontic area and from Asia Minor and those tales constituted one of his chief sources for his "Cimmerian logos"[55].

The history of the Cimmerians in Western Asia is briefly presented by Herodotus in chapter 12 of the 4th book. That account can be verified by Assyrian records and the Greek tradition of Asia Minor. Thus, Herodotus maintains the Scythians pursuited the Cimmerians and entered the Median country[56]. However, the Scythians in the Near East are attested at least 40 years after the first appearance of the Cimmerians. Consequently, it is hardly possible to accept Herodotus' claims about a pursuit as reality. As regards the problem of the Cimmerian and Scythian migrations into Asia, there is a striking contradistinction in Herodotus' account. Herodotus maintains that the Scythians, following the retreating Cimmerians, moved into Asia with the Caucasus on their right[57]. Apparently, the Scythians took the way between the Caucasus and the Caspian Sea, similarly as several later nomadic tribes invading Asia (Sarmatian peoples, Alans and Huns). The Cimmerians, on the contrary, moved southwards probably by way of the Darial pass (also used by nomads of antiquity) for their first documented appearance in Asia is to be located in Georgia. If so, it may be confidently stated that the Scythians and the Cimmerians migrated into Asia choosing two quite different routes. Again, this conclusion contradicts the picture given by Herodotus as regards the nature of the Cimmerian migration into Western Asia.

To sum up, Herodotus' account of the Scythian and Cimmerian movements as conducted through the Caucasus is generally true. However, as to the accuracy of details, there is much unreliability; the Cimmerian and Scythian invasions were different in direction and date. Both processes were wrongly associated by Herodotus himself or by his sources.

---

[54] Cf. Hdt. 1.15-16 on the Cimmerians in Lydia and their decline. See, also, Hdt. 1.102.

[55] Such a combination was assumed by Ali 1921, 122f. Cf. also Tokhtas'ev 1993, 31f.

[56] Hdt. 4.12. The same also in 1.103.

[57] Hdt. 4.12. The same in 1.104.

Modern scholars often omit one important tradition of the Scythian origins. Diodorus of Sicily[58] speaks of the Scythians living originally on the Araxes as a small nation. Afterwards, they created a mighty kingdom between the Caucasus, Oceanus, Lake Maeotis, and the Tanais. It seems that this account, drawing many valuable details from much earlier sources, is exceptionally convincing in showing early Scythian history. If we accept the identification of the Araxes with the Volga (as in Herodotus 4.11[59]), the Tanais with the Don, and Lake Maeotis with the Sea of Azov, we could define quite precisely the Scythian country before their migration further to the west in the Pontic steppes and before the Scythian invasions into Western Asia. Moreover, the picture drawn by Diodorus corresponds with archaeological evidence concerning the location of the early Scythian culture between the Caucasus, the Caspian Sea, the Don and the Volga[60].

In classical sources relating to the Bosphorus region, several toponyms are attested which contain the designation "Cimmerian". Herodotus treats such names as evidence for the presence of the Cimmerians in Scythia. Thus, he enumerates: Cimmerian walls (Κιμμέρια τείχεα), Cimmerian ferry (πορθμήια Κιμμέρια), a region (χώρη) named Cimmeria (Κιμμέρια) and the Cimmerian Bosporus (Βόσπορος Κιμμέριος). All these toponyms are situated in the Bosporus region[61]. Besides Herodotus, several classical authors enumerate "Cimmerian" toponyms[62]. Hecateaus in Strabo mentions a "Cimmerian" city (polis)[63]. Aeschylus knows a "Cimmerian isthmus"[64]. Such names are frequently attested in Strabo who mostly followed older traditions. He writes: "Cimmericum (Κιμμερικόν) was in earlier times a city situated on a peninsula, and it closed the isthmus by means of a trench and a mound. The Cimmerians possessed great power in the Bosporus, and this is why it was named Cimmerian Bosporus"[65]. Somewhere in the Crimea region Strabo seems to lo-

[58] Diod. 2.43.1-5.

[59] I am following here Herrmann 1914, 21, note 5.

[60] Cf. Pogrebova-Raevskii 1992, 21f. Main early Scythian complexes come from that area (ibid. 185) and to the south beyond the Caucasus up to Urmia Lake (ibid., map on p. 197).

[61] On these names see Tokhtas'ev 1993, 30.

[62] Tokhtas'ev 1993, 34ff.

[63] Strab. 7.3.6.

[64] Aesch. Prom. 730.

[65] Strab. 11.2.5. See Tokhtas'ev 1993, 35.

cate the mountain Cimmerius, so called "because the Cimmerians once held sway in the Bosporus; and it is because of this fact that the whole of the strait which extends to the mouth of Lake Maeotis is called the Cimmerian Bosporus"[66]. Posidonius in Strabo maintains that the Cimmerian Bosporus in the region of Lake Maeotis was named after the Cimbri for the Greeks named the Cimbri "Cimmerians"[67].

As to the validity of the "Cimmerian" toponymy for historical research there is much controversy. V. Parker considers that the Cimmerian names confirm the Cimmerian presence in the North Pontic area[68]. G. B. Lanfranchi believes that the names were merely invented to reconcile the well-known Homeric reference to the Cimmerians in the *Odyssey* with the Greek concepts which placed the Cimmerian country in the North Pontic area[69]. J. Chochorowski accepts the view that the names, besides the older designation "Cimmerian Bosporus", were employed in the 6th century B.C.[70], i.e. in the period of Scythian domination in the steppes. The whole issue has recently been reexamined by S. R. Tokhtas'ev. His conclusion is that – as far as the toponyms under dicsussion are discernible in the available evidence – the Cimmerian toponymy of the Pontic region had for the most part nothing common with the historical Cimmerians[71]. I do not intend in this place to reexamine such a complicated problem in its totality. However, some observations should be taken into account. The term Cimmerian walls (Κιμμέρια τείχεα) cannot be associated with a nomadic people and was apparently a conventional name for a fortification line[72]. The town of Cimmeris on the Taman peninsula, mentioned by Ps. Scymnus[73] was surely established in the 4th century B.C., clearly too late to connect its name with the historical Cimmerians[74]. To the "Cimmerian" toponyms belongs also a

66 Strab. 7.4.3.

67 Strab. 7.2.2.

68 Parker 1995, 10f.

69 Lanfranchi 1990, 142.

70 Chochorowski 1993, 19f.

71 Tokhtas'ev 1993, 37f.

72 Cf. Tokhtas'ev 1993, 34.

73 Ps. Scymnus 896ff.

74 Tokhtas'ev 1993, 35. According to Rohde 1901, 92, note 2, the name was invented "in gelehrter Reminiszenz" of Homeric traditions.

Cimmerium oppidum, located by Strabo (after Ephorus, see below) and by Pliny[75] in Italy in the vicinity of Avernium Lake. On the whole, it would seem probable that the evidence of "Cimmerian" toponyms is of secondary importance for a discussion on the homeland of the Cimmerians. Classical sources reflect the deep dependance of the Cimmerians' location upon the Homeric idea of that people.

The first Greek colonists could not meet the alleged Cimmerians in the Bosporus and Tyras region. The earliest Greek settlements in the north Pontic area are datable to the period after about 650 B.C.[76] On the other hand, the Cimmerians are attested in Transcaucasia prior to 715 B.C. We have really no indications of encounters or contacts between Greek colonists and Cimmerians in the North Pontic region. On the contrary, as the earliest neighbours of the Pontic Greeks appear merely Scythian tribes. At present, the Scythian period in the region can be evidently detected up to the middle of the 7th century B.C.[77]

The Greek colonists of the North Pontic region came primarily from Miletus in Asia Minor[78]. The Oriental Greeks knew the Cimmerians in Asia and that is why the existing settings of the Cimmerians in the west, e.g. in Italy, were for them not acceptable. This circumstance and the nomadic nature of the invaders in Asia stimulated attempts to locate their homeland north of the Caucasus in the colonized Pontic areas[79].

To sum up: documentary evidence of the Cimmerian toponyms is extremely scarce. Therefore, we cannot exclude the possibility that some "Cimmerian" names of the Bosporus region were created after the people living in the North Caspian steppes, whose members might have penetrated the Kuban steppes as far as the Bosporus region. Some names were, however, created without connection with the historical Cimmerians.

---

[75] Plin. NH 3.61: *lacus Lucrinus et Avernus iuxta quem Cimmerium oppidum quondam.*

[76] For the Greek settlement in Tyras on the Dniester (as established circa 600-550 B.C.), see Karyškowskii/Kleyman 1985, 40ff. Cf. Tokhtas'ev 1993, 32. For the Bosporus region, colonized by the Greeks from about 600 B.C., see Tokhtas'ev 1993, 18. A small settlement was founded on Berezan island in the second half of the 7th century B.C., see Vinogradov/Marčenko 1989, 541. Istria, the oldest colony in the northwestern part of the Pontic shore, was established also in the second half of the 7th century.

[77] Vinogradov/Marčenko 1989.

[78] Ehrhardt 1988.

[79] So Tokhtas'ev 1993, 42ff.

5.The later accounts of the Cimmerians

Some Classical authors treat the Homeric wanderings of Odysseus as having been in the western Mediterranean and, consequently, located the Cimmerians there[80]. Ephorus of Cumae, a historian of the 4th century B.C. quoted in Strabo, places the Cimmerians in southern Italy in the Avernus area near Cumae (Campania)[81]. Thus, Strabo writes after Ephorus: "The people prior to my time were wont to make Avernus the setting of the fabulous story of the Homeric Necyia; and, what is more, writers tell us that there actually was an oracle of the dead here and that Odysseus visited it. (...) Ephorus, in the passage where he claims the locality in question for the Cimmerians, says: They live in underground houses, which they call argillae, and it is through tunnels that they visit one another, back and forth, and also admit strangers to the oracle, which is situated far beneath the earth (...). Those who lived about the oracle have an ancestral custom, that no one should see the sun, but should go outside the caverns only during the night; and it is for this reason that the poet (sc. Homer, M.J.O.) speaks of them as follows: "And never does the shining sun look upon them; but later on the Cimmerians were destroyed by a certain king"[82].

Strabo's account of the Cimmerians in the Avernus region, following Ephorus of Cumae, testify to the fact that the geographical location of the people in question depended primarily upon its description by Homer. The poet associated Cimmerians with the entrance into the nether world. Based upon that assumption, Ephorus placed the Cimmerians in the vicinity of Cumae[83]. Obviously, Ephorus' claims have no relation to the historical Cimmerians from the steppes. In antiquity, there were also other locations of the Cimmerians strictly depending on the tradition of Homer. Thus, Hecataeus of Abdera (who flourished in the second half of the 4th century B.C.) placed the Cimmerians in a "Cimmerian city" (Κιμμερὶς πόλις) amongst fantastic Hyperboreans in the north[84].

[80] Cf. Eustathios, *Commentarii in Odysseam*, 1379, 29-31. Eustathios remarks that the Cimmerians in reality lived in the north, cf. 1667, 43; 1704, 57; 1670-1671, 1705.

[81] On Ephorus of Cumae see Lendle 1992, 136ff.

[82] Strab. 5.4.5; FGrHist 70 F 134a with a commentary.

[83] Cf. Grimal 1987, 184.

[84] Bolton 1962, 24. On the location of the Cimmerians as seen by Classical commentators see also Lehmann-Haupt 1921, 425f.

It is striking, as pointed out by S. R. Tokhtas'ev, that the name of the Cimmerians is preserved in the Greek literary tradition practically in one form which is first attested in Homer, i.e. as Κιμμέριοι[85]. This fact stresses the importance of Homer's picture of the Cimmerians for the further development of their treatment in antiquity.

To examine the later classical concepts of the Cimmerians which developed after Herodotus discussion might turn to the account given by Plutarch (*Horuit* about A.D. 50-120).

"Others, however, say that the Cimmerians who were first known to the ancient Greeks were not a large part of the entire people, but merely a body of exiles or a faction which was driven away by the Scythians and passed from the Maeotic Lake into Asia under the lead of Lygdamis; whereas the largest and most warlike part of the people dwelt at the confines of the earth along the outer sea, occupying a land that is shaded, wooded, and wholly sunless by reason of the height and thickness of the trees, which reach inland as far as the Hercynii; and as regards the heavens, they are under that portion of them where the pole gets a great elevation by reason of the declination of the parallels, and appears to have a position not far removed from the spectator's zenith, and a day and a night divide the year into two equal parts; which was of advantage to Homer in his story of Odysseus consulting the shades of the dead. From these regions, then, these Barbarians sallied forth against Italy, being called at first Cimmerians, and then, not inappropriately, Cimbri (...)"[86].

This description was taken from the *Histories* written by Posidonius of Apamea (circa 135-50 B.C.)[87]. Posidonius had a superior knowledge of the Cimbri, a nation which attacked Italy in his times (103-102 B.C.[88]). However, his sources for Northern Europe, where the Cimbrian homeland was to be located, appear to have been partially blundering or scanty. Therefore, Posidonius

---

[85] Tokhtas'ev 1993, 38ff.

[86] Plut. Caius Marius 11.5-7. (Translation quoted after: Plutarch's Lives, transl. by B. Perrin, London/Cambridge (Mass.) 1959, LCL).

[87] Plutarch's use of Posidonius has been shown by Malitz 1983, 57f.

[88] On the value of Posidonius' work, see Malitz 1983, 198ff.

formed some speculative interpretations and, moreover, attempted to account for certain legendary traditions concerning the peoples of the North[89].

Posidonius collected and combined different accounts of the Cimmerians. At first sight, a resemblance with the Herodotean description of the Cimmerians is discernible. Posidonius' intention was also to rationalize the Homeric *Nekyia* in an attempt to identify the Cimmerians with the Cimbri, a nation well-known in his times. The quoted passage offers also etymological and astronomical considerations. On the whole, Posidonius created an artificial account and conceived of the northernmost areas of Europe as the homeland of the Cimmerians. This surprising theory is based on the identification of the names Cimmerians and Cimbri (Κίμβροι). In fact, all interpretations given in the fragment are subordinated to this equation, and the whole account, in comparison with earlier sources, does not provide new reliable details[90]. Plutarch attacked the credibility of Posidonius' account and said: "But all this is based on conjecture rather than on sure historical evidence". Posidonius provides us the name of a Cimmerian king given as Lygdamis and at this point he seems to have followed a good source tradition. At the same time he maintains that Lygdamis led the Cimmerians from Maeotic Lake into Asia; the statement is clearly wrong for Lygdamis (attested in Strabo and in Assyrian records) was a Cimmerian leader *in Asia* in the second half of the 7th century B.C.[91] This fragment exhibits the selective and speculative technique used by Posidonius to clear the origins of the Cimbri by their connecting with the old people of the Cimmerians.

Posidonius' picture of the Cimmerians is preserved also in Strabo. It contains the statement that the Cimmerian Bosporus in the region of Lake Maeotis was named after the Cimbri for the Greeks named the Cimbri "Cimmerii"[92]. The same concept of identifying of the Cimmerians and Cimbri gives Diodorus of Sicily[93].

---

[89] Thus, he tried to rationalize the accounts of the Hyperboreans, cf. Schol. Apoll. Rhod. 2.675.

[90] For the passage see Tokhtas'ev 1993, 13f.

[91] According to Strabo (1.3.21) Lygdamis captured Sardes but lost his life in Cilicia.

[92] Strab. 7.2.1-2. Cf. Malitz 1983, 206f.

[93] Diod. 5.32.3. Cf. Malitz 1983, 210.

The Homeric picture of the Cimmerians had a profound effect on the way Hellenistic writers conceived of that people. To that tradition some other authors, besides Posidonius, belong. Thus, Crates of Mallos (lived in the 2nd century B.C.), the author of a commentary on the *Iliad* and *Odyssey*, employed the conception that Homer was not acquainted with the name of the Cimmerians. Next to the entrance to the Underworld, Crates placed Cerberos and, accordingly, "improved" the *Odyssey* by using the expression "the land of the *Cerberians*" (ἔθνα δὲ Κερβερίων) instead of "the land of the *Cimmerians*"[94]. Such attempst at reinterpretation and improvement of the Homeric picture of the Cimmerians emerged quite often in antiquity[95]. In Proteus of Zeugma, the Cimmerians are transferred into *Heimerioi* (Χειμέριοι), i.e. "winter-people"[96]. Most writers of antiquity conceived of the Cimmerians as a nation of the Homeric poem[97].

As to the Cimmerians in Europe, Strabo of Amasia (68 B.C.-A.D. 26), one of the best geographers of antiquity, provides no new evidence and relies on older accounts. He writes: "The Cimmerians once possessed great power in the Bosporus, and this is why it was named Cimmerian Bosporus. These are the people who overran the country of those who lived in the interior on the right side of the Pontus as far as Ionia. However, these were driven out of the region by the Scythians; and the Scythians were driven out by the Greeks who founded Panticapaeum and the other cities on the Bosporus"[98]. This account is based on the tradition attested already in Herodotus and in his sources.

7. The Cimmerians in Western Asia

The Cimmerians may have appeared south of the Caucasus already in the 720s B.C. This may be supposed on the basis of the fact that the attacks conducted by Urartian kings against Colchis and the adjacent regions in the north were defeated at that time[99]. The first direct references to the Cimmerians in

[94] Tokhtas'ev 1993, 13.

[95] Already Sophocles and Aeschylus seem to have employed the term Κερβέριοι as related to the Cimmerians, see Lehmann-Haupt 1921, 426.

[96] *Etymologicum Magnum* 513.44 Gaisford. Cf. Ivančik 1996, 134.

[97] Tokhtas'ev 1993, 15ff.

[98] Strab. 11.2.5.

[99] Dudarev 1991, 25, similarly Chochorowski 1993, 12.

Western Asia are on Assyrian cuneiform records coming from the reign of Sargon (722-705 B.C.). This testimony mentions a Cimmerian attack against Urartu conducted probably from the Manna region shortly before 714 B.C.[100] In 714 B.C., the Assyrian records describe an Urartian expedition against the country of Gamir inhabited by the Cimmerians[101]. The most probable location of this region is the area to the north and northwest of Sevan Lake in southern Georgia[102]. Other locations are more debatable[103]. The incident's setting in southern Georgia seems to be supported by some archaeological materials testifying to a nomadic presence in the region in the second half of the 8th century B.C.[104]

The location of the earliest well documented Cimmerian seat in southern Georgia on the river Cyrus is very convincing. In the course of steppe migrations taking place north of the Caucasus, many nomadic groups infiltrated Transcaucasia, notably Georgia (Iberia)[105]. The Cimmerians might have taken the route through the Darial Pass which was followed by Sarmatian detachments in the Arsacid period. The material traces of the nomadic presence in Transcaucasia are very abundant. For Cimmerian history, it is necessary to take into consideration close parallels with the movements of some nomadic tribes invading Transcaucasia and Western Asia, e.g. Scythians, Alans, and Huns. It was a natural direction of nomadic migrations by way of the Caucasus.

On the whole, the Cimmerians appear in the Assyrian records circa 715-714 B.C. From the 70s of the 7th century B.C. up to the end of that century, they were involved in wars against Phrygia, Lydia and Assyria. In addition to those struggles with the Near Eastern states, the Cimmerians came into contact with the Greek cities of western Asia Minor. The earliest Greek testimony of this fact is to be found in a poem by Callinus. He recalls an invasion of the Cimmerians against Ionia[106].

---

[100] Ivančik 1996, 50ff.

[101] Ivančik 1996, 21ff.

[102] Ivančik 1996, 29f.

[103] Cf. Parker 1995, 8, who sets the Gamir country near Urmia Lake.

[104] Dudarev 1991, 27.

[105] Olbrycht 1998, 150f.

[106] Fr. 3 Gentili-Prato; cited by Strabo 14.1.40. Cf. Lehmann-Haupt 1921, 419.

During their movements in Western Asia, the Cimmerians acted as allies of various peoples. In the first half of the 7th century B.C., they are mentioned as allies of Hilakku, Tabal, Mushku (Phrygia), and even of Urartu[107]. The movements of the Cimmerians are not easy to determine, but they destroyed the Phrygian state in the first half of the 7th century B.C. From about 675 B.C., Cimmerian detachments invaded the eastern borders of Assyria alongside the Medes and Manneans. To the west, the Cimmerians attacked Lydia from the 660s and about 644 B.C. killed the Lydian king Gyges. At the same time they carried out devastating raids against Greek cities of Ionia[108]. In the second half of the 7th century B.C., the Cimmerians, as stated by Strabo, roamed alongside the Thracian Treres[109]. In two passages Strabo calls the Treres a Cimmerian tribe[110]. This claim is surely wrong. Strabo, using different sources, makes some striking mistakes in his account on the late history of the Cimmerians, Treres and Scythians in Asia. His claim that Madyes was a Cimmerian king is wrong[111]. A little earlier in the same passage he calls Madyes a Scythian ruler, something attested in other sources[112]. The Cimmerians were finally defeated by the Lydian king Alyattes[113]. Their remnants were assimilated by the local populations of Asia Minor[114].

8. On the ethnogenesis of the Cimmerians

As to the genesis of the Cimmerians and their ethnic and cultural identity we have just few indications. On the basis that the Treres, a Cimmerian ally in Anatolia, came from Thracia, the Cimmerians are believed to have been a Thracian people[115]. This opinion has in fact no foundation[116]. According to

[107] On this issue Dudarev 1991, 68.
[108] For sources see Lehmann-Haupt 1921, 419ff.
[109] Strab. 1.3.21. On the Treres see Strab. 1.3.21; 13.1.8; 14.1.10. See also Keil 1937.
[110] Strab. 14.1.40; similarly 1.3.21.
[111] Strab. 1.3.21.
[112] Hdt. 1.103.
[113] Hdt. 1.16; Polyaenus 7.2.1. Cf. Ivančik 1996, 131f. and Parker 1995, 32.
[114] It is possible that Cappadocia was named "Gamirk" after the Cimmerians, see Lehmann-Haupt 1921, 421 and Ivančik 1996, 155f.
[115] Lehmann-Haupt 1921, 397 and 421; Chochorowski 1993, 19.
[116] There is no reason to believe that the Cimmerians and Thracian Treres were ethnically related. Strabo speaks just of a temporary alliance between the Cimmerians and

some scholars, the Cimmerians were of Iranian stock[117]. In his current study, A. Ivančik supports this hypothesis, but at the same time he stresses that the known Cimmerian kings' names have much in common with Luwian, a language from Asia Minor. Although the hypothesis ascribing Iranian origins to the Cimmerians is the most probable at the present stage of research, it cannot be confirmed without further evidence. In fact, it is highly probable that the term Cimmerians designated a tribal entity which was not homogenous[118]. In a similar way, Herodotus called different steppe peoples *Scythians* for they were dominated by a tribe designated by this name[119]. As mentioned above, the scholars of antiquity were very interested in the name of the Cimmerians[120]. At present too, there is much debate on this issue. According to I. M. Diakonoff, the name of the Cimmerians was an autonym and the Assyrian form *Gimirrāia* is the most credible[121].

In Neo-Babylonian and Babylonian texts of Persian times mention is made of Cimmerian arrows, bows, and horse equipment. Such elements, given as characteristic tokens of Cimmerian culture, are common features for nomadic tribes[122]. That factor provides a more certain attestation of the assumption that the Cimmerians were actually a nomadic nation from beyond the Caucasus. This view can be vindicated by the fact that the nomadic Saka peoples of Achaemenid times were designated as Cimmerians (Gimirrāia), an identification made of course in an anachronistic manner but obviously on the basis of similar nomadic ways of life represented by both tribes[123].

The problem of the archaeological materials as ascribed to the Cimmerians is outside the scope of this paper. Therefore, only some characteristic views are referred to here. Actually, there is a fundamental controversy in

Treres. As mentioned above, attested are Cimmerian alliances with several different peoples of Western Asia.

[117] Harmatta 1970, 7; Trubačev 1976; Grantovskii 1970, 81.

[118] As correctly stated by Chochorowski 1993, 17.

[119] Cf. Hdt. 4.6-7; 17-20.

[120] Ivančik 1996, 133ff.

[121] Diakonoff 1981, 125f.; Ivančik 1996, 138f. In the most Assyrian texts the Cimmerians are designated as *Gimirrāia*.

[122] Ivančik 1996, 159f.

[123] Dandamayev 1992, *passim*, esp. 169ff.

archaeological research. Some scholars are inclined to connect the Cimmerians with the so-called "Cimmerian" archaeological finds of the 8th-7th centuries B.C. attested in Ukraina and Central Europe[124]. Such theories rely on historical interpretations claiming that the Cimmerians migrated into Central Europe[125]. There are, however, other conceptions of that problem. Some archaeologists believe that it is impossible to identify the Cimmerians with archaeological cultures of the North Pontic area[126]. It seems that the presently available archaeological materials from the North Pontic area and Central Europe do not allow any substantiated identification with the ethnic Cimmerians.

9. Conclusions

1. Homer's single reference to the Cimmerians goes back to the Argonautic saga. Clearly, any historically argued and credible location of that people in the poetic framework of the *Odyssey* is impossible. Homer's testimony, linking the Cimmerians with the mythical entrance to the land of the dead, had a profound impact on the Classical notions of the Cimmerians and their location[127].

2. Aristeas of Proconnesus is known to have written a work named *Arimaspea*, in which he dealt also with the Scythians and Cimmerians. As far as we can judge at the present state of research, it was Aristeas who combined the appeareance of the Cimmerians with the pressure of the Scythians and other tribes from the steppes. Historically, Aristeas' account of the migrating movements in the steppes is convincing. In Aristeas, the Cimmerians are not linked with the North Pontic area but with the Caspian steppes.

---

[124] Terenožkin 1976; Bouzek 1983; Chochorowski 1993, esp. 22. It is evident, in the light of archaeological relics, that there were nomadic migrations from the Ponto-Caspian steppes into Central Europe in the pre-Scythian period.

[125] Thus, according to J. Harmatta, the Cimmerians penetrated Central Europe in the 8th century B.C. They were "the first people who introduced to Europe a nomadic type of warfare" (Harmatta 1970, 8).

[126] Kačalova/Alekseev 1993.

[127] All in all, Homer's pictures of many peoples were of the greatest importance for the studies of them in antiquity, cf. Ivančik 1996a (for the Homeric Abioi and their treatment in antiquity).

3. Hecataeus of Miletus located the Cimmerian country between the Araxes (Volga) and the Bosporus area in the North Pontic steppes. He did so apparently on the basis of the "Cimmerian" toponymy from the Bosphorus region and the assumption that the Homeric Cimmerians should be sought in the North Pontic area. Herodotus' description and location of the Cimmerians as associated with the Scythians are derived mainly from Hecataeus.

4. The most influential account of the Cimmerians was constructed by Herodotus. He wrote a relatively brief Cimmerian logos combining different sources: Aristeas, Hecataeus, the local legendary Greek traditions from Bosphorus and Tyras, and finally Oriental (mainly Lydian) testimonies.

5. The reliability of the so-called Cimmerian toponymy of the Bosphorus region as evidence for the Cimmerian presence in the region is doubtful. For the most part this toponymy had no historical links with the Cimmerian presence in the North Pontic area. The main body of the Cimmerians had migrated into Western Asia prior to 715 B.C., i.e. a long time before the establishment of the first Greek colonies in the North Pontic region. On the other side, it is not impossible that some parts of the Cimmerians roamed the area east of the Sea of Azov in the Kuban steppelands. Some of them could have been in touch with the Greek of Bosphorus.

6. The Assyrian sources at our disposal locate the first known Cimmerian seat in Transcaucasia. The Cimmerians entered this area in all probability from the steppes to the north of the Caucasus. Additionally, we may assume that the Cimmerians were supplanted by the Scythians from the Volga region.

7. Aristeas of Proconnesus appears to be correct when he shows the movements of Cimmerians from their homeland on the "southern" sea under the pressure of other tribes as a chain reaction which would repeat several times in the history of the Caspian steppes. Thus, the Scythians were supplanted by the Sarmatians, the Jazygs and Roxolanoi by the Aorsoi, the Aorsoi by the Alans, the latter by the Huns. It seems that the Cimmerians originally occupied the steppes on the Araxes/Volga (as related by Hecataeus and Herodotus) and from there they moved further to the south to the Caucasus and into Western Asia.

There, they conducted plundering raids against the rich Oriental states. The same can be said of the Scythians who entered Asia several decades after the Cimmerians.

8. There is no reliable written Classical testimony of any Cimmerian movements into the North Pontic area to the west of the Don or of a Cimmerian migration into Central Europe.

Bibliography

Alekseev A. Ju./Kačalova N. K./Tokhtas'ev S. R. 1993: *Kimmeriycy: etnokul'turnaya prinadležnost'*, Sankt-Peterburg.

Aly W. 1921: *Volksmärchen, Sage und Novelle bei Herodot und seinen Zeitgenossen*, Göttingen.

Bolton J. D. P. 1962: *Aristeas of Proconnesus*, Oxford.

Bouzek J. 1983: "Caucasus and Europe and the Cimmerian Problem", *Sborník Národního Muzea v Praze* 37, 177-240.

Chochorowski J. 1993: *Ekspansja kimmeryjska na tereny Europy Środkowej*, Kraków.

"Cimmerians" in: *The New Encyclopadeia Britannica*, Chicago 1990, Vol. 3, p. 321.

Cozzoli U. 1968: *I Cimmeri*, Roma.

Dandamayev M. A. 1992: *Iranians in Achaemenid Babylonia* (Columbia Lectures on Iranian Studies 6), Costa Mesa/New York.

Diakonoff I. M. 1981: "The Cimmerians", in: *Acta Iranica* 21.

Diakonoff I. M./Kashkai S. M. 1981: *Geographical Names according to Urartian Texts* (Repertoire géographique des textes cunéiformes 9), Wiesbaden.

D'iakonov I. M. 1994: "Kimmeriicy i skify na drevnem Vostoke", *Rossiyskaya Archeologiya* 1994, Nr. 1.

Dudarev S. L. 1991: *Iz istorii sviazey naseleniya Kavkaza s kimmeriysko-skifskim mirom*, Groznyi.

Dudarev S. L. 1995: *K probleme vzaimodeistviya plemeni Severnogo Kavkaza s rannimi kočevnikami v predskifskuiu epokhu*, Armavir.

Easterling P. E./Knox B. M. W. (eds.) 1989a: *The Cambridge History of Classical Literature*, Vol. I, P. 1.

Easterling P. E./Knox B. M. W. (eds.) 1989b: *The Cambridge History of Classical Literature*, Vol. I, P. 3.

Ehrhardt N. 1988: *Milet und seine Kolonien*, Frankfurt am Main.

Fehling D. 1971: *Die Quellenangaben bei Herodot. Studien zur Erzählkunst Herodots*, Berlin/New York.

Grantovskii E. A. 1970: *Ranniaia istoriya iranskich plemen Perednei Azii*, Moskva.

Grimal P. 1987: *Słownik mitologii greckiej i rzymskiej*, Wrocław (*Dictionnaire de la mythologie grecque et romaine*, Paris 1951).

Harmatta J. 1970: *Studies in the History and Language of the Sarmatians*, Szeged.

Herrmann A. 1914: *Alte Geographie des unteren Oxusgebietes*, (Abh. der Königl. Ges. der Wiss. zu Göttingen, Phil.-Hist. Klasse, N.F., Bd. XV, Nr. 4).

Herrmann A. 1919: "Kaspisches Meer", *RE* 20. Hbbd., 2275-2290.

Huebeck A. 1963: Κιμμέριοι, *Hermes* 91, 490-492.

Huebeck A./Hoekstra A. 1989: *A Commentary on Homer's Odyssey*, Vol. II, Books IX-XVI, Oxford.

Ivančik A.I. 1996: *Kimmeriycy. Drevnevostočnye civilizacii i stepnye kočevniki v VIII-VII vekach do n.e.*, Moskva.

Ivančik A. 1996a: "Die hellenistischen Kommentare zu Homer Il. 13.3-6. Zur Idealisierung des Barbarenbildes – Ephoros und die Philologen der alexandrinischen Schule" in: Funck B. (ed.), *Hellenismus. Beiträge zur Erforschung von Akkulturation und politischer Ordnung in den Staaten des hellenistischen Zeitalters. Akten des Internationalen Hellenismus-Kolloquiums 9. - 14. März in Berlin*, Tübingen 1996, 671-692.

Ivantchik A.I. 1993: *Les Cimmériens au Proche-Orient* (Orbis Biblicus et Orientalis 127), Fribourg.

Jacoby F. 1912: "Hekataios", *RE* VII 2, 2667-2769.

Jacoby F. 1913: "Herodot", *RE* Suppl. 2, 205-520.

Junge J. 1939: *Saka-Studien. Der ferne Nordosten im Weltbild der Antike* (Klio, Beiheft XLI, N.F., Heft 28), Leipzig.

Kačalova N. K./Alekseev A. Yu. 1993: "Arkheologičeskie aspekty kimmeriyskoi problemy" in: Alekseev A. Yu./Kačalova N. K./Tokhtas'ev S. R. 1993, 51-89.

Karyškovskii P. O./Kleyman I. B. 1985: *Drevnii gorod Tira*, Kiev.

Keil J. 1937: "Treres", *RE* 2. Reihe, VIA 2291.

Kristensen A. K. G. 1988: *Who were the Cimmerians and where did they come from?*, Copenhagen.

Kuklina I. V. 1985: *Etnogeografyja Skifii po antičnym istočnikam*, Leningrad.

Lanfranchi B. I. 1990: *Cimmeri. Emergenza delle élites militari iraniche nel Vicino Oriente (VIII-VII sec. a. C.)*, Padova.

Lehmann-Haupt C. F. 1921: "Kimmerier", *RE,* Hbbd. 21, 397-434.

Lendle O. 1992: *Einführung in die griechische Geschichtsschreibung: von Hekataios bis Zosimos*, Darmstadt.

Leskov A. M. 1981: *Kurgany, nachodki, problemy*, Leningrad.

Lesky A. 1967: "Homeros", *RE*, Suppl. XI, 687-846.

Makhortykh S. V. 1994: *Kimmeriycy na Severnom Kavkaze*, Kiev.

Malitz J. 1983: *Die Historien des Poseidonios* (Zetemata 79), München.

Melyukova A. I. 1989: "Predskifskii period v stepiach Severnogo Pričernomorya" in: A. I. Melyukova (ed.) *Stepi evropeyskoi časti SSSR v skifo-sarmatskoe vremia*, Moskva, 10-16.

Melyukova A. I. 1990: "The Scythians and Sarmatians" in: D. Sinor (ed.) *The Cambridge history of early Inner Asia*, Cambridge 1990, 97-117.

Meuli K. 1921: *Odysse und Argonautika*, Basel.

Olbrycht M. J. 1998: *Parthia et ulteriores gentes. Die politischen Beziehungen zwischen dem arsakidischen Iran und den Nomaden der eurasischen Steppen* (Quellen und Forschungen zur antiken Welt, Bd. 30), Tuduv-Verlag, München.

Parker V. 1995: "Bemerkungen zu den Zügen der Kimmerier und der Skythen durch Vorderasien", *Klio* 77, 7-34.

P'yankov I. V. 1975: "Massagety Gerodota", *Vestnik Drevnei Istorii* 1975, No. 2, 46-70.

Plezia M. 1959/1960: "Hekataios über Völker am Nordrand des skythischen Schwarzmeergebietes", *Eos* 50, 27-42.

Pogrebova M. N./Raevskii D. S. 1992: *Rannie skify i Drevnii Vostok. K istorii stanovleniya skifskoi kul'tury*, Moskva.

Pstrusińska J. 1996: "Why the Celto-Asiatic Seminar? I. Celtic versus Indo-Iranian" in: A. Krasnowolska (ed.), *Cracow Iranian Studies in Memory of Władysław Dulęba*, Cornelius Publishing House, Cracow, 195-215.

Rohde E. 1901: *Kleine Schriften*, Bd. I, Tübingen-Leipzig.

Samokvasov D. Ja. 1908: *Mogily russkoi zemli*, Moskva.

Sulimirski T. 1959: "The Cimmerian Problem" in: *Bulletin of the Institute of Archaeology of London*, 2, 45-62.

Sulimirski T. 1985: "The Scyths" in: *The Cambridge History of Iran*, 2, 142-199.

Terenožkin A.I. 1976: *Kimmeriycy*, Kiev.

Tokhtas'ev S. R. 1993: "Antičnaya literaturnaya tradiciya o kimmeriycach" in: Alekseev A. Yu./Kačalova N. K./Tokhtas'ev S. R. 1993, 9-50.

Trubačev O. N. 1976: "O sindach i ich iazyke", *Voprosy iazykoznaniya* 1976, No. 4, 39-63.

Vinogradov Ju. A./Marčenko K. K. 1989: "Das nördliche Schwarzmeergebiet in der skythischen Epoche", *Klio* 71, 539-549.

Willamowitz-Moelendorf U. von 1920: *Die Ilias und Homer*, Berlin.

Winckler H. 1897: *Kimmerier, Skythen, Ašguzäer* (Altorientalische Forschungen, Heft VI), Leipzig.

Marek J. Olbrycht
(Cracow)

Notes on the presence of Iranian peoples in Europe and their Asiatic relations

The scope of the problems involving the history of steppe Iranian-speaking peoples in Europe is large and continues to grow as new information becomes available. For this reason this paper is limited to the most important aspects. The very significant role that the Scythians, Sauromatians, and various so-called "Sarmatian" tribes (including the Royal Sarmatians, Iazygs, Aorsi, and Alans) played in the history of Southeastern Europe has commonly been recognized. This is, however, not the case with their role in the history of Central and Western Europe.

In the 1st millenium B.C. and in the first centuries A.D., the native populations of Southeastern and Central Europe were faced with the expansion and movement of the Central Asian peoples pressing westwards. Some indigenous tribes retreated, setting in motion other peoples, others mingled with the newcomers, giving rise to new hybrid cultures. The contribution of Iranian peoples to the cultures of ancient Europe is discernible in many aspects, including Germanic religion, Celtic folk-poetry, and early Slavic civilization. The influx of Iranian steppe peoples in Europe was linked with tribal movements in Central Asia. This was a consistent pattern, for we have evidence of several great migrations in the 1st millenium B.C. and the 1st millenium A.D. Already Herodotus (4.13), living in the 5th century B.C., had observed such processes: "Except the Hyperboreans, all these nations (and first the Arimaspians) ever make war upon their neighbours; the Issedones were pushed from their lands by the Arimaspians, and the Scythians by the Issedones, and the Cimmerians, dwelling by the southern sea, were hard pressed by the Scythians and left their country"[1].

[1] In this paper, unless otherwise stated, translations are drawn from Loeb editions with my own improvements.

It was M. Rostovtzeff who stressed the necessity to connect the effects of the unrest in Inner Asia with the nomad incursions into Europe: "Wenn die ersten sarmatischen Verschiebungen in Südrußland den Ereignissen aus der Zeit Alexanders entsprechen, so können die weiteren – das Erscheinen der Jazygen, Roxolanen, Aorsen, Siraken usw. sehr gut mit der sako-parthischen Bewegung verbunden sein. Das Erscheinen der Alanen würde dann dem Vordringen der Ye-tschi entsprechen. (...) Ich muß nur betonen, daß alle die Sarmatenwellen nach Südrußland aus Gegenden kommen, welche für eine lange Zeit mit der Kulturwelt der persischen und frühhellenistischen Reiche in Zentralasien verbunden waren, und daß die letzte auch mit China in Verbindung stand" (Rostovtzeff 1931, 609).

The first nomadic waves of the 1st millenium B.C. in Europe – the archaeological Chernogorovka-Novocherkassk complex

The Cimmerians were one of the steppe peoples who had to abandon their homeland on the northern shore of the Caspian Sea in the 8th century B.C. The Cimmerians' activities affected only the southeastern periphery of Europe as that people retreated through the Caucasus into Western Asia. For Cimmerian history, Diakonoff (1985, 93) is fully correct to emphasize that: "We possess no factual data to show that the Cimmerians at any time represented the basic mass of the population of the steppes north of the Black Sea". However, archaeologists use the designation "Cimmerian" for archaeological finds of nomadic origin widely attested in the area from the Caucasus to the Hungarian plain and Central Europe (Makhortych/Ievlev 1992, 114f.; Chochorowski 1993, 262f.). It seems that a more suitable designation for the archaeological remains of that period would be the Chernogorovka-Novocherkassk complex, a term already used to label two chronological stages or two regional variations of the archaeological "Cimmerian" culture. Amongst the archaeological finds of the Chernogorovka-Novocherkassk complex in the North Pontic steppes a strong Eastern impact originating in Central Asia and Sibiria (elements of the Karasuk, Arzhan, and Altai type) is discernible (Murzin 1990, 25ff.; Chochorowski 1993, 263). Apparently, nomadic groupings from Central Asia moved westwards and created new tribal confederations in the Ponto-Caspian steppe expanses (Chochorowski 1993, 268f.). An important part in the development of the Chernogorovka-Novocherkassk civilization was played by the Kuban culture of the North Caucasus. The appearance of North Caucasian weapons and horse etrated by the steppe tribes (Chochorowski 1993, 266; Dudarev 1991; Dudarev 1995). As a whole, the steppe groupings exerted a strong influence on the local cultures of Central Europe, including the Hallstatt civilization (Chochorowski 1993, 268ff.).

There were many components which contributed to the successful expansion of Central Asian peoples into Eastern Europe. Of crucial significance for that period was the development of a mobile, mounted nomad pastoralism. The nomadic way of life became extremely warlike and the nomads were provided with highly effective weapons. Their tactics were based upon the use of horses.

The development of the Chernogorovka-Novocherkassk culture was disturbed again in the 8th-7th centuries B.C., when new waves of Central Asian nomads entered Europe. Their advance was mainly directed towards the Caucasus. These tribes can be to some extent identified in historical sources as the Scythians. According to some archaeologists, it was the so-called second proto-Scythian wave which formed the beginnings of the Scythian culture in Europe (Murzin 1990, 275). At first, the Scythians occupied the areas between the Volga, the Caucasus, and the Sea of Azov and carried out raids into Western Asia. South of the Caucasus, they played an important part alongside Assyria, Urartu and the Medes. The new nomadic groupings must have adopted many elements of the much higher cultures flourishing in their new homeland north of the Caucasus. Moreover, it seems that Scythian pressure affected some steppe as well as forest-steppe areas of Southeastern Europe and ultimately forced a number of peoples of the North Pontic steppes to retreat into more remote areas. One of those threatened neighbours were the Agathyrsi (Chochorowski 1993, 275).

The Agathyrsi – the presumed survivals of the pre-Scythian period

The Agathyrsi are known mainly due to Herodotus who appears to locate them in Moldavia north of the Danube and east of the Carpathians (Hdt. 4.48, 78, 100, 125. cf. Chernenko 1984, 88; Chochorowski 1993, 255ff.). Herodotus (4.104) maintains that Agathyrsian customs were similar to those of the Thracians. However, the names of the known kings of the Agathyrsi – Agathyrsus and Spargapeites – are Iranian (for details see R. Schmitt in: *Compendium Linguarum Iranicarum*, Wiesbaden 1989, 93 and Chochorowski 1993,

254f. with further literature). An interesting sidelight is provided on the origins of the Agathyrsi by Herodotus in his Scythian account (Hdt. 4.8-10). This passage states that Heracles and a serpent-woman had three sons named Agathyrsus, Gelonus, and Scythes. Herodotus' account reflects real historical events relating to the emergence of Scythian power in the North Pontic steppes (Murzin 1990, 30). Clearly Agathyrsus represents the oldest tribe of the Scythian world which was pushed westwards from the steppes and lived thereafter close to Scythia. Similarly Gelonus bears the name of a people outside the confines of Scythia proper (cf. Chochorowski 1987, 147). To sum up, the Agathyrsi are to be treated as one of the pre-Scythian populations of the North Pontic area which were supplanted by their kindred folk, the Scythians. According to the 1st century Roman geographer Pomponius Mela (2.2) the Agathyrsi were located next to Lake Maiotis (the Sea of Azov) and the Sauromatians. Mela's statement is based upon an ancient Greek source. Another writer, Ammianus Marcellinus (4th century A.D.), also locates the Agathyrsi in the vicinity of Lake Maiotis (22.8.30). Thus it is probable that the Agathyrsi had inhabited the Azov Sea region before they retreated westwards. It should also be noted that the relations between the Agathyrsi and the Scythians were hostile as reflected in several episodes of their history (Hdt 4.78; 4.119).

As stated above, the Agathyrsi had to retreat westwards before the Scythian menace. Most of them settled in Moldavia and gradually mingled with the local population of Thracian stock. In archaeological terms, attributable to the Agathyrsi is the cemetery at Stoicani dated to the 8th-7th centuries B.C. (Chochorowski 1987, 155ff.). Furthermore, archaeological materials suggest that the Agathyrsi belonged to the tribes of the culture with fortified settlements of the Stincesti-Cotnari type, whose beginnings date to the 6th century B.C. These settlements are to be regarded as the centres of the Getic groups who would be partially transformed into the Dacian culture (Chochorowski 1987). Apparently, the Agathyrsi were assimilated in the Geto-Thracian environment. A poorly-known passage in Stephanus of Byzantium (s.v. Αγάθυρσοι) seems to provide a more certain attestation for the location of the Agathyrsi in Thracia; it situates them in the Thracian "mons Haemus". Epigraphic evidence from Italy of the 1st-2nd centuries A.D. suggests that an important part of the Dacians was formed by the population of Agathyrsian origin (for a convincing discussion of this problem see Kolosovskaya 1984. cf. also Chochorowski 1987, 148). After Herodotus, there are only few mentions of the Agathyrsi in classical sources (Mela

2.2, 10; Dionysius *Per.* 310ff (= *GGM* II 120); Ptolemy *Geogr.* 3.5.10, 22; Marcian of Heraclea Pontica *Per. Mar. Ext.* 2.39 (= *GGM* I 559).

The Siginni in Central Europe

Herodotus' knowledge of the lands beyond the Danube is extremely scanty. He is, nevertheless, well informed about the Siginni living north of that river (Hdt. 5.9). For a discussion of this problem, see Chochorowski 1987, 182-207 and Chochorowski 1993, 244ff. cf. also Markwart 1932). According to Herodotus, the Siginni wore Median clothes and used small ponies unable to carry their horsemen. They claimed to be Median colonists. Apollonius Rhodius (3rd century B.C.) in his poem *Argonautika* locates the Siginni in the "Laurion" plain (*Argon.* IV 320, ed. Vian, Paris 1981). Based upon the above mentioned sources, the hypothesis can be brought forward that the Siginni inhabited the Hungarian plain, probably its eastern part (Chochorowski 1993, 245f.).

In archaeological terms, the Siginni are identified as a people connected with the Mezöcsat group and the southern group of the Vekerzug culture (Sulimirski 1961, 795; Chochorowski 1987, 185-197; Chochorowski 1993, 251). Archaeological evidence suggests that the Siginni occupied the Hungarian plain in the Novocherkassk phase, probably in the 8th century B.C., and contributed to the emergence of the culture known as the Mezöcsat group (Chochorowski 1998, 486). Afterwards, their culture seems to have been affected by Scythian influences, and, under such circumstances, the Vekerzug culture was formed (Chochorowski 1993, 181f.; Chochorowski 1998, 475f.).

According to the Roman geographer Strabo, it was the Medes who were the originators of customs and clothing for the Persians. The most important elements of Median and Persian dress were tunics with sleeves and trousers (Strabo. 11.13.9. Herodotus, 7.61, makes similar comments on Persian dress). It should be kept in mind that trousers were not used by the autochthonous tribes of Central Europe before the coming of the steppe groupings.

Some light has been thrown by the archaeological finds on the Asiatic relations of the Siginni. Therefore, the historian must bear the results of the excavations conducted in Hungary in mind. It seems that the population of the Mezöcsat group and of the Vekerzug culture (its southern group) used dress of the Median or Persian type. Such an assumption is supported by archaeological finds from the area embracing these cultures and datable mainly to the 6th-5th centuries B.C.; they do not contain fibulae and pins which are indispensable for the wearing of traditional local clothes attested in the most parts of the Danubian region (Chochorowski 1993, 247f.). In addition, in the barrow graves investigated at Szentes-Vekerzug 16 skeletons of small horses (tarpans) have been found (Harmatta 1968, 153-157; Sulimirski 1961, 795; Chochorowski 1993, 248). Such horses are described in Herodotus as used by Siginni. Furthermore, the population of the Vekerzug culture used so-called pintaders – clay stamps intended to mark tattooed pictures on someone's skin (Chochorowski 1998, 484ff.). Such objects are attested beyond the Vekerzug culture in the North Caucasus (especially the Kuban culture) and in Transcaucasia. Thus, the pintaders are more definite evidence of Asiatic connections of the Vekerzug culture. Moreover, at several sites associated with this culture, some objects of Near Eastern origin have been found (Chochorowski 1998, 486).

The Siginni are regarded in Herodotus as Median colonists. If Herodotus is right, it would seem that Siginni came from Iran. An interesting passage relating to this question is provided by Strabo (68 B.C.-A.D. 20). According to his account, the Siginni imitated the Persians in all their customs, except that they used ponies which were small and shaggy and, though unable to carry a horseman, were yoked together in a four-horse team (Strabo 11.11.8). However, Strabo's description lists the Siginni alongside the Derbices, Hyrcanians, and Tapyri; all peoples of northern Iran inhabiting the areas south of the Caspian Sea. On the other hand, the Orphic poem about the Argonauts (*Orpheus Argonautika* 756) locates the Siginni between Phasis and Sinope in northern Asia Minor (Chochorowski 1993, 252). Stephanus of Byzantium (s.v. Σίγυννος) seems to locate the Siginni/Sigynni southeast of the Black Sea (Markwart 1932, 14f.). The above-mentioned sources clearly document that, as far as can be judged at the present state of research, the Siginni came from Iran and were known in the north Danubian lands for their "Persian" or "Median" customs. During their migration, the Siginni moved through the Caucasus into the North Pontic steppes and established themselves in the Hungarian plain.

According to a widely accepted, but unproven, theory, the Siginni are thought to be an Iranian people affected by the Scythian invasions (Chochorowski 1993, 275f.). However, we are not able to determine their language or ethnic affiliation. They may be considered as an Iranian or pre-Iranian tribe. The Siginnian presence, whatever may have been the ethnic affiliations of this people, brought about the ethnic and cultural transformation of the Hungarian plain.

In some Classical texts there are a number of mentions of the Sindi. This tribe is located in the most sources in the Taman Peninsula or in the adjacent areas (e.g. Herodotus 4.28, 4.86; Strabo 11.2.11. For more details and further references, see Machinskiy 1971, 33 and Chochorowski 1993, 252f.). Apollonius Rhodius locates the Sindi in the Laurion plain (*Argon.* IV 322, ed. Vian, Paris 1981, cf. Chochorowski 1993, 246). This statement suggests that the Sindi moved from the Azov Sea area to Central Europe. This migration probably took place in the 7th-6th centuries B.C. in connection with the Scythian expansion in Central Europe; some groups of the Sindi settled in the Hungarian plain. Nevertheless, it seems that the bulk of the Sindi remained in the North Caucasus as they are attested there in many sources, including Bosporan inscriptions of the Roman period (Gardiner-Garden 1986, 207ff.).

Persian activities in the Iberian Peninsula seem to be mentioned in Pliny's *Natural History* (3.1.8) who writes, following Marcus Varro, that Spain was penetrated by invasions of Iberians, Persians, Phoenicians, Celts, and Carthaginians. There is, however, no evidence supporting Pliny's statement of a Persian invasion in Spain. Some scholars suppose that Pliny had knowledge of some tribes using dress similar to that of the Persians, a phenomenon originated in connection with nomad invasions of the pre-Scythian and Scythian periods (Schüle 1969, 55-57).

The Scythians in Europe – some considerations

The earliest written testimonies of Scythian activities in Western Asia – the Assyrian texts – date to the seventies of the 7th century B.C. (Diakonoff 1985, 96f.). Some fragments in the *Histories* of Herodotus also relate to the Scythian presence in the Near East. For some decades, the Scythians were one of the main political and military factors in Western Asia and Herodotus speaks of a period of Scythian hegemony there (Diakonoff 1994). According to Herodotus (1.106), the Medes under their king Kyaxares eventually forced the Scythians to return to their homeland (about 625 B.C.). This may be true of the bulk of the invading tribes, but some Scythian groups settled in Transcaucasia and Azarbaijan (Diakonoff 1985, 100; 118ff.). Some excavated archaeological remains in the Near East can be linked with the Scythian presence (cf. Sulimirski 1954; Diakonoff 1994; Raevskiy 1995, 93). The Oriental civilization of Western Asia played an important role in the formation of the Scythian culture.

The question of the origin of the Scythians greatly intrigued contemporary writers. Valuable information on this issue is provided by Diodorus Siculus (2.43.1-2):

"This people (i.e. the Scythians, M.J.O.) originally possessed little territory, but later, as they gradually increased in power, they seized much territory by reason of their deeds of might and their bravery and advanced their nation to great leadership and renown. At first, then, they dwelt on the Araxes river, altogether few in number and despised because of their lack of renown; but since one of their early kings was warlike and of unusual skills as a general they acquired territory, in the mountains as far as the Caucasus, and in the steppes along the ocean and Lake Maeotis and the rest of that country as far as the Tanais river".

Diodorus, living in the 1st century B.C., composed a huge work of world history in 40 books. As regards the peoples of the Ponto-Caspian steppes, Diodorus' sources are often very reliable and offer much information not attested in other writers (see Schneider 1880). O. Lendle (1992, 242f.) has pointed out that "Die Bibliothek stellt eine große Kompilation dar, deren Wert sich aus der Tatsache ergibt, daß Diodor die zahlreichen von ihm ausgeschriebenen Quellen der Sache nach relativ treu bewahrte". At present, Diodorus' reliability is more highly regarded than it has been in the past (cf. Meister 1997).

In his Scythian account, Diodorus apparently used some valuable sources independent of those drawn on by Herodotus. It is worth noting that Diodorus' account describes the Scythian kingdom as situated north of the Caucasus. Thus, his source must have been earlier than the sources for the Herodotus' account which focus on the period of Scythian hegemony in the North Pontic steppes. As regards the origins of the Scythians, Herodotus reports that they were nomads living in Asia and, when the Massagetae harassed them in war, the Scythians went in search of home across the river Araxes (i.e. the Volga) to the lands of the Cimmerians (Hdt. 4.11). Using the testimonies of Diodorus and Herodotus we can state that the Scythians came from Central Asia. From Greek and Persian records we know that in the 6th-3rd centuries B.C.

large areas of western Central Asia were dominated by a people called Massagetae (Sakā Tigraxaudā of Achaemenid inscriptions, cf. Olbrycht 1998, 28ff.). In the 6th century B.C., the Massagetae caused the Achaemenids much trouble. Thus, Cyrus the Great met his death while fighting against this powerful tribe (530 B.C.). It is certain that the power of the Massagetae, so striking in the 6th century, lasted for a long time and may have been established in the 8th-7th centuries BC, when this expanding people supplanted the Scythians into the Caspian and North Caucasian steppes.

Archaeological evidence fully vindicates Diodorus' account of the Scythian realm existing north of the Caucasus (Pogrebova/Raevskiy 1992). As a whole, archaeological finds, including the famous kurgans at Kelermes, Krasnoe Znamya in Stavropol, Ulskiy Aul, and Kostromskaya Stanitsa show that during the 7th century B.C. the Scythian rulers held their headquarters in the steppe expanses north of the Caucasus (Makhortykh 1991; cf. also Murzin 1990, 26 and Raevskii 1995, 91). The huge impact of Oriental civilization on the Scythians is reflected in their rich barrow-graves. The style and technique of finds as well as the dress and armour were heavy influenced by Western Asiatic elements.

Not content with their dominions in the North Caucasian steppes, the Scythians subjugated the North Pontic area. It seems that in the second half of the 7th century and in the course of the 6th century B.C., the bulk of the Scythians moved from the North Caucasus into the North Pontic steppes. Most Scythian kurgans in the North Pontic area date to the 4th century B.C. (e.g. Nikopol, Solokha, Chertomlyk, Alexadropol), only few are attributable to the 5th century B.C.

From their North Pontic areas the Scythians made frequent raids on other regions, especially Central Europe. At the turn of the of the 8th and 7th centuries B.C., a number of new objects of steppe origin appeared in Central Europe. On the basis of their distinctive weapons and horse-equipment, these finds, coming mostly from burial assemblages, have been suggested as reminants of the Scythian culture spreading through Europe (Sulimirski 1945; idem 1961). Scythian forays reached Transylvania (Chochorowski 1998, 480), Podolia (Chochorowski 1998, 479f.), and the Hungarian plain (Chochorowski 1998, 481). At the same time, the Scythians destroyed a number of fortified settlements of the Lausatian culture (Chochorowski 1998, 481). Finds of Scythian origin have been found on several Polish and Slovak sites including Witaszkowo

(Vettersfelde), Wicina, Strzegom, Polanowice, and Smolenice-Molpir (Chochorowski 1994, 49ff.). There is an alternative interpretation, although weaker in my opinion, of the nature of Scythian activities in Central Europe. H. Parzinger (1998) maintains that the settlements such as Smolenice-Molpir and Wicina, connected with the local populations, were not destroyed by the Scythians. In his opinion, the East Hallstatt culture and the Lausitian culture underwent a strong Scythian impact and borrowed from the nomads types of weapons and horse harness.

Regrettably, we have no written evidence concerning the Scythian advances in Central Europe. Towards the end of the 4th century B.C., the Scythian power in the North Pontic area was crushed by the Sarmatians. In the course of the 3rd century B.C., the Celts and Bastarnae extended their dominions at the expanse of the Scythians. Scythian remnants retreated to the Crimea, present-day Dobruja and the adjacent areas.

The Sauromatians and their "gynaecocracy"

One of the important groupings among the Iranian-speaking peoples were the Sauromatians who roamed east of the Tanais/Don. Diodorus Siculus (2.43) offers a short description of this people in connection with Scythian history. First, he describes the Scythian invasions reaching Egypt and Thracia and then writes about some outstanding rulers of the Scythians:

"It was by these kings that many of the conquered peoples were removed to other homes, and two of these became very great colonies: the one was composed of Assyrians and was removed to the land between Paphlagonia and Pontus, and the other was drawn from Media and planted along Tanais, its people receiving the name Sauromatae" (Diod. 2.43.6).

Pliny, a Roman writer of the 1st century A.D., provides a similar passage:

"Next come the two mouths of the river Don (Tanais), where the inhabitants are the Sarmatae, said to be descended from the Medes, and themselves divided into a number of sections. The first of these are the Matriarchal Sauromatae (Sauromatae Gynaecocratumeni), the husbands of the Amazons" (Pliny *Nat.Hist.* 6.19).

Judging from what Diodorus and Pliny say, the Sauromatians came into the steppes east of the Tanais from Iran. Pliny's passage suggests that women occupied a high position in Sauromatian society. A similar motif connecting the Amazons and the Sauromatians' forefathers is found in Herodotus (4.110ff.). In his account, the Sauromatians were the descendants of Amazons and young Scythians who inhabited the area beyond the Tanais and Lake Maiotis. Moreover, according to Herodotus, the Sauromatians used a corrupted version of the Scythian language. He also states (4.21) that the Sauromatians' land stretched "fifteen days journey northward from the northern tip of Lake Maiotis" (for the location of the Sauromatians see Machinskiy 1971, 40f.). Of particular interest is the position of women among the Sauromatians reported in a number of classical sources (Mela 1.116; Pliny *Nat.Hist.* 6.19; Dionys. *Per.* 652ff. (= *GGM* II 144); Avien. *Descr. Orb.* 854ff. (= *GGM* II 184); Prisc. *Per.* 645 (= *GGM* II 195); Ps.-Scyl. 70 (= *GGM* I 59). The wives of the Sauromatian men kept to the ancient "Amazon" mode of living, going out on horseback to hunt, joining their husbands in war, and wearing the same dress as men. This is why the Greeks associated the Sauromatians with the Amazons of their mythological tradition. During the invasion of Darius (about 514-512 B.C.), the Sauromatians supported the Scythians (Hdt. 4.119ff.). Herodotus' account of the Sauromatians' origins probably derives from folk tales from Olbia which contained some legendary motifs typical of Greek tradition, including the Amazon story. Herodotus' version does not provide statements linking the Sauromatians with the Near East.

Diodorus Siculus and Pliny in their accounts relating to the origins of the Sauromatians differ in some details from that given by Herodotus. All these authors, however, locate the Sauromatians as living to the east of the Tanais/Don or on the Tanais/Don, regarding them as the neighbours of the Scythians. As to the Sauromatians' original homeland, Herodotus writes about the establishment of a new, Sauromatian tribe in the steppes, whereas according to Diodorus and Pliny the Sauromatians came from Iran. Despite these differences, all three writers believe that the Sauromatians were a new tribe in the steppe area. If we believe the chronology given in Herodotus, they were formed after the Scythians had dominated the North Pontic steppes, i.e. not earlier than in the 7th century B.C.

Besides the fragments mentioned above, classical sources offer only few fragments relating to the early Sauromatians. Most records situate the

Sauromatians next to the Tanais/Don (Mela 1.116; Ps.-Scyl. 70 (= *GGM* I 59); Diod. 2.43; Pliny *Nat.Hist.* 6.19). Pseudo-Hippocrates (*De Aere, Locis et Aquis* 17) describes the Sauromatians as living in Europe by Lake Maiotis and observes matriarchal elements in their society (Machinskiy 1971, 39). Some accounts suggest that there were close ties between Sauromatians and Maiotians, a people living next to the Sea of Azov (Lake Maiotis) north of the Caucasus (Machinskiy 1971, 41). According to Ephorus (4th century B.C.), the tribe of the Maiotae was composed of Sauromatians. Another writer, Demetrius of Kallatis (end of the 3rd century B.C.) maintains that the Maiotians were called Iazamatae, a name which seems to be of Iranian origin. Both authors are cited by pseudo-Scymnus in his *Periegesis (*860-880, = *GGM* I 232-233. cf. Machinskiy 1971, 44f.; Dilke 1985, 144; Gardiner-Garden 1987, 7ff.).

The Sauromatians were probably an Iranian grouping who came from Media during the course of the migrations of the 7th century B.C. At first, they occupied the area on the Tanais/Don not far from Lake Maiotis north of the Caucasus. It is highly probable that they merged with some indigenous tribes, especially the Maiotians. An echo of such a merging may be detected in Herodotus' and Pliny's accounts of the Amazons uniting with the Sauromatians' ancestors. The important part played by women in Sauromatian society is also attested in the history of the Maiotians (Ps.-Scymn., *loc. cit.*; Anon. *Per. Pont. Eux.* 45 (= *GGM* I 412). A semi-legendary Maiotian queen called Tirgatao is described by Polyaenus (*Strateg.* 8.55). In all likelihood, the Sauromatians were formed on the basis of Maiotian groupings whose customs were to some extent matriarchal. Such customs were probably widespread amongst the peoples of the Caucasus region and are reflected in the Greek stories of the Amazons.

In the 4th century B.C., the name *Sarmatae* or *Syrmatae* makes its first appearance in classical sources in Pseudo-Scylax (*Peripl.* 68-70) and Eudoxus of Cnidus (circa 390-340 B.C.), both preserved by Stephanus of Byzantium, s.v. Συρμάται (cf. Gardiner-Garden 1988, passim). Pseudo-Scylax wrote a compilation, dating no earlier than in the 4th century B.C. (Dilke 1985, 133f), based on earlier *periploi* and contemporary sources. According to M. I. Rostovtzeff, the designations Sarmatian and Syrmatians are to be equated (cf. Machinskiy 1971, 48). Later classical writers, especially those of the Roman period, regard the Sarmatians as a group name for the tribes of the Ponto-Caspian steppes. Most classical writers of the late Hellenistic and Roman periods used the names

Sauromatians and Sarmatians interchangeably and "applied freely to the Sarmatae of their own times what Hecataeus, Herodotus, and other early authors had to say of the Sauromatae" (Rostovtzeff 1936, 91). However, it is necessary to emphasize that several classical writers clearly distinguished between the Sauromatians and Sarmatians/Syrmatians (Ps.-Scyl. *Peripl.* 68-70; Ps.-Scym. *Per.* 876-881; Pliny *Nat.Hist.* 6.16. On this issue see Machinskiy 1971, 48f.). Although the Latin writers of the Roman period preferred the term Sarmatians (*Sarmatae*), in some literary sources and inscriptions of the Imperial period the personal name Sauromates occurs (cf. Vinogradov 1994, 11).

M. I. Rostovtzeff denied the possibility of any genetic relation between the Sauromatians known from Herodotus, as well as some other writers, including Ephorus and Hippocrates, and the Sarmatians. For Rostovtzeff (1931, 103), the particular position of women among the Sauromatians was "ein schlagender Beweis dafür, daß die Sauromaten mit den Sarmaten nicht identisch waren". At present, however, most scholars equate the Sauromatians and the Sarmatians (e.g. Smirnov 1980).

Contemporary archaeologists associate the historical Sauromatians with the archaeological finds which form the so-called Volga- and Samara-Ural groups. These groups belong to the so-called Sauromatian culture. Most archaeologists derive this culture from the people of the Srubnaya culture of the Bronze Age (Melyukowa 1990, 111). In historical terms, it is hardly possible to attribute the whole Volga-group and the Samara-Ural group to the Sauromatians. In particular, the Samara-Ural group of the so called "Sauromatian" culture cannot be identified with the historical Sauromatians who are attested only for the area on the Tanais/Don and not beyond the Volga in the east.

The peoples who dominated the steppes between the Don and the Volga during the 4th century B.C. and at the beginning of the 3rd century B.C. were organized into several tribes. Initially, these tribes had no common designation known to western writers. In all likelihood the most important components of this wave of peoples can be identified as the later Iazygs and Royal Sarmatians. The surviving Sauromatians joined the conquerors and were able to preserve for a long time their separate position, as reported in some sources which distinguish the Sauromatians from the Sarmatians. The name of the Sauromatians, although in the slightly modified form "Sarmatians", was transferred into the designation of all tribes who subjugated the steppes east of Scythia proper. According to Rostovtzeff (1936, 91), it is possible that the names Sarmatians and Sauromatians were only different spellings of the same Iranian name. Both forms can be derived from the old Iranian dialects (Abaev 1979, 305 and 349). Like the Sauromatians, some Maiotian tribes were incorporated into the new victorious peoples. The Maiotians must have been numerous enough to maintain a historical tradition of their own, since the name of the "Sarmatian" Iazygs can be derived from the appellation *Iazamatai*, one of the Maiotian groupings.

The paucity of available information does not allow the creation of a detailed account of the struggles between Sauromatians and newcomers from the east, but it is clear that the latter were victorious and that the surviving Sauromatians joined the victors in their further expansion. The indigenous Sauromatians were to some extent absorbed by the new waves of eastern nomads, being identified under the appellation "Sarmatians". These new tribes in all likelihood came from Central Asia. It is interesting that Pliny in his *Natural History* (6. 48) mentions a people called Syrmatae next to the Drebices, i.e. in living in the Transcaspian plains in Central Asia.

We can assume that some of the new steppe tribes, having dominated the Ponto-Caspian area, preserved also Sauromatian cultural elements. The occurrence of the term *farn* in a few "Sarmatian" names is probably one such element. This term seems to be of Median origin as it is attested in sources relating to the Medes (cf. the names *Čiθra-farnah* and *E-farnah* (Diakonoff 1985, 103 and 140).

Evidence for the pre-Achaemenid links between the steppe nomads and Iran – the Zariadres story

In the 8th century B.C., a new political factor emerged in Western Asia: the nomads from beyond the Caucasus who penetrated into the Near East during the second half of the 8th century B.C. and in the 7th century B.C. (cf. Diakonoff 1985, 89ff.; idem 1994). The earliest nomads of that time were the Cimmerians who advanced into Transcaucasia, Iran, and Asia Minor. Soon after the Cimmerians, the Scythians invaded Western Asia. According to Herodotus (1.106) the Scythians ruled the Near East for almost 30 years until the Median king Kyaxares killed their chiefs. On the other hand, Scythian arms and tactics were used by the victorious Medes. According to Herodotus (1.73), Medes took instruction from Scythians in archery. Herodotus relates that the Scythians returned to their homeland which is to be located north of the Caucasus. As stated above, in the culture and art known from the Scythian North Caucasian burials, there are many elements which originate in Western Asiatic civilization, including Iranian artefacts and motifs.

A Greek writer living in the second half of the 4th century B.C., Chares of Mytilene, has transmitted the charming Iranian tale of Zariadres. According to this story, Hystaspes and Zariadres, who were the sons of Aphrodite and Adonis, reigned in powerful countries. Hystaspes ruled Media, and Zariadres the areas above the Caspian Gates up to the Tanais. Beyond the river Tanais lived the Marathoi under their king Omartes. After many adventures and miracle events, Zariadres married Omartes' daughter, Odatis. Chares stresses that the barbarians of Asia placed great value on this tale, and many scenes from it were painted in the houses and palaces of Asia. The story is preserved in Athenaeus (*Deipnosophistae* 13.35, p. 575 = F. Jacoby, *FrGrHist* 125, fr. 5). The tale has been studied in depth by several scholars (Boyce 1955, 463ff.; Yarshater 1983, 467ff. cf. also Nöldeke 1896, 4f. and Markwart 1938, 126ff.). M. Boyce (1955, 470) came to the conclusion that "the story of Zariadres and Odatis was in fact a Median legend, already ancient when Chares heard it". Some scholars pointed out striking similarities of Chares' story to a tale told by Firdausi and Thāᶜālibī about Gushtasp (Markwart 1938, 130; Boyce 1955, 463).

The geographical setting of the Zariadres' realm and the Marathoi remains fairly unclear. J. Markwart (1938, 126) believes that Chares must have identified the Tanais with the Iaxartes/Syr Darya. Consequently, we should locate the Marathoi in Central Asia. However, it must be kept in mind that in the ancient period there was a confusion between the Central Asian Tanais/Syr Darya and the European Tanais/Don. The second question which might be addressed to Chares' story is a textual one. The manuscripts offer the form Marathoi, Gen. Μαραθῶν, which seems to be not reliable.

The Persian national epic, the *Šahnāme,* differs in some respects from the Zariadres story transmitted by Chares. In the *Šahnāme*, the main hero is Gushtasp, brother of Zarer. A daughter of a Roman emperor called Katāyūn is to choose a husband. The emperor's residence in the Sasanid period was built by Salm who was considered the ancestor of the Romans, but in earlier times had been regarded as ancestor of the Sarmatians (Markwart 1938, 130). "Dies führt aber auf die Vermutung, dass Marathoi eine persische oder griechische Verdrehung von *Þarama = aw. Sairima ist" (Markwart 1938, 131). Under these circumstances, some scholars restored the text of Chares with the term Σαρματῶν instead of Μαρατῶν (cf. Markwart 1938, 131, note 2). This textual conjecture may be strengthened by two further factors. First, the name Zariadres, known from Chares, is historically attested in Armenia (Justi 1895, 382f.; Boyce 1955, 466). Thus, in the 2nd century B.C., a Zariadres (Zareh) ruled the Armenian principality of Sophene (Strabo 11.14.15). Second, the Medes in the 7th century B.C. were involved in the developments in the Caucasus region as partners and enemies of the Scythians which also makes the location of the Zariadres story in the west more probable.

On the whole, it seems that Chares' story is related to the region of the Caucasus and the Caspian and North Pontic steppes. This tale may be considered weighty evidence in favour of the existence of close connections between Media and peoples from beyond the Caucasus.

Changing events in Scythia – the Sarmatian invasion

The central Eurasian steppes were inhabited by different nomadic tribes which can be called, with some caution, "Sarmatian". The Sarmatians belonged to the northern branch of the Iranian-speaking peoples (Bielmeier 1989). They were never a homogenous ethnic entity and T. Sulimirski (1970a, 23f.) stresses that "It is a mistake to treat all the Sarmatians alike with the result that some special practices and features characteristic of one branch only, e.g. cranial deformation, have been presented as typical of all the Sarmatian peoples". The designation "Sarmatian" has been differently used by our sources and modern scholars. The first Sarmatian tribes to be known by this name are attested in Classical sources as Sarmatae (Σαρμάται). In later ancient sources, espectially from the 1st century B.C. onwards, the terms Sarmatae (Σαρμάται) and Sauromatae (Σαυρομάται) were often used as synonyms. The name Sarmatian was applied by ancient authors to the most steppe tribes which were moving into the Ponto-Caspian steppes from Central Asia after the collapse of Greater Scythia until the coming of the Huns (on the Sarmatians see Kretschmer 1920; Kretschmer 1921; Rostovtzeff 1922, 113ff:; Rostovtzeff 1931, 100ff.; Rostovtzeff 1936, 91ff.; Junge

1939, 72ff.; Harmatta 1970, 8ff.; Sulimirski 1970; Sulimirski 1970a; Machinskiy 1971; Machinskiy 1974; Smirnov 1980; Moshkova 1989, 153-154; Olbrycht 1998, *passim*). It is clear that there were striking differences amongst the steppe Iranian peoples of the post-Scythian period, including in their culture and religion. As the earliest reference to the Sarmatians is often considered to be the term *Sairima-* found in the *Avesta*, and later found as *Slm* **Sarm* and *Salm* (Bailey 1985). This nomenclature is found in the *Farvardīn Yašt* (13.143) alongside some other ethnonyms, including the Aryan, Tūira, Sāinu, and Dānu lands. It is, however, not certain whether this passage is not a later interpolation. On the other hand, V. A. Livshits tends to date this Yašt to the 5th century B.C. (in a letter of November 10, 1997). If this date is reliable, the Avestan Sairima could not be an earlier designation than the Sauromatians of Herodotus who wrote in the 5th century B.C., but his sources relating to the Sauromatians may be dated to the 6th century B.C.

The early history of the Sarmatians in the 4th-2nd centuries B.C. is poorly documented (Rostovtzeff 1925, 23ff.; Machinskiy 1971, 45; Gardiner-Garden 1988). The accounts which have been preserved provide evidence that Sarmatian groups moved westwards and carried out devastating raids (cf. Rostovtzeff 1931, 101ff.; Moshkova 1989, 154.; Rostovtzeff 1993, 37f.). Sarmatian attacks against the Scythians are reported by Lucian (Tox. 39) and, more accurately, by Diodorus Siculus (2.46.1-2). Diodorus says: "Many years later this people (i.e. the Sauromatae) became powerful and ravaged a large part of Scythia, and destroying utterly all whom they subdued they turned most of the land into a desert. (Diod. 2.43.7). In Diodorus, the term Sauromatian is equated with the designation Sarmatian.

The chronology of the Sarmatian advances into Scythian territory is disputed, suggestions ranging between the second half of the 4th century B.C. and the 2nd century B.C. Machinskiy (1971, 52) believes that the Sarmatians deprived the Scythians of their leading position in the North Pontic steppes shortly before 310 B.C. His hypothesis is based upon Heracleides' of Pontus and Theophrastus' statements concerning the alleged Sarmatian activity to the west of Tanais/Don and the posited date 310 for the year of Heracleides' death. The most recent viewpoints concerning the chronology of the Sarmatian advances in the North Pontic area are given by Vinogradov/Marchenko/Rogov (1997) and Vinogradov (1997). They are inclined to date the Sarmatian invasion towards the end of the 4th and beginning of the 3rd century B.C.

Historical sources document that in the second half of the 4th century B.C. Scythian dominance over the North Pontic steppes was heavily affected by some defeats. Thus in 339 B.C. the powerful Scythian king Atheas was defeated and killed in battle with Philip of Macedon. In 313 B.C., the Scythians invaded the area south of the Danube, but were beaten off (Diod. 19.73). Furthermore, the Scythians took an active part in the struggles in the Bosporan kingdom in 309 B.C. (Diod. 20.24). The decline of the Scythians was mainly due to invasions by Sarmatian peoples. After conquering Scythia, the Sarmatian tribes became the main political factor in the North Pontic steppes. In the second half of the 3rd and in the 2nd centuries B.C., two Little Scythias arose in the Crimea and in Dobruja (cf. Strabo 7.4.5. See also Machinskiy 1971, 53 and Marchenko 1996, 76f.). In this period, the Scythians were under pressure not only from the Sarmatians, but also from the Getae and the Bastarnae in the west (Marchenko 1996, 77).

The expansion of the Sarmatian tribes from the steppe expanses east of the Don to the North Pontic steppes took place in the late 4th and early 3rd century A.D. in connection with the disturbances set off by the wars of Hellenistic states against the nomads of Central Asia. Under the Achaemenids, different forms of co-existence between nomads and sedentary population were developed in Central Asia and northeastern Iran. The Iranian tribes of the Massagetae, Sakas, and Dahae settled in the steppes on the borders of the Persian empire. Alexander's campaigns in Central Asia dealt a shattering blow to the relation of nomads with sedentary areas. The pastoral steppe tribes were driven back and cut off from the settled population. In all areas adjoining to the steppe expanses (Parthia, Areia, Margiana, and Transoxiana) resistance to the conqueror was stronger than elsewhere in the Achaemenid empire. Moreover, the sedentary population of these provinces gained the support of nomads: the Sakas beyond the Iaxartes/Syr Darya, and the Dahae, as well as the Massagetae. Under Greek rule, Central Asia and Iran experienced great urban growth. The cities were instruments of colonization and served as military as well as economic centres. Nomadic tribes roaming beyond the frontiers of the Hellenistic world tried to gain more influence on the borderland and challenge the restrictive Hellenistic system. As regards this development, there are striking analogies to be found in nomadic-Chinese interactions, as shown in the studies of Barfield (1989) and Jagchid/Symons (1990). The greatest early Hellenistic undertaking in the steppes was the expedition led by Demodamas prior to 305 B.C. in which he crossed the

Syr Darya and then marched into the steppe (Olbrycht 1998, 44). The nomadic response to the Seleucid attack came in invasions carried out against Seleucid possessions. The turmoil in the steppes and the movements of the Dahae resulted in the westward migration of the Sarmatian tribes. At the end of the 4th century B.C., nomads, including the Dahae, penetrated Seleucid territory and appear to have succeeded in destroying some cities, as well as devastating areas of northern Iran. The Dahae had lived in the lands along the Syrdaria at the borders of Sogdiana and Khorasmia at the time of Alexander. By the middle of the 3rd century B.C., they had advanced to the frontiers of the Seleucid kingdom in the vicinity of northern Parthia (present-day Turkmenistan). Seleucid policy towards the nomads recalls Sāmānid activity in the steppes under Ismāᶜīl at the end of the 9th century A.D. (Bosworth 1978). This resulted in the westward migration of the Hungarians from the North Pontic steppes to Pannonia. Within one decade after the Sāmānid attacks against the Oghuz in Central Asia (A.D. 893), the Hungarians managed to subjugate the whole Carpathian basin (Györffy 1985, 234ff.).

Early Sarmatian expansion in the North Pontic steppes is hardly discernible in archaeological finds. Most Greek and native settlemens in the Pontic area were destroyed in the 70-60s of the 3rd century B.C. through Sarmatian pressure (Vinogradov/Marchenko 1989, 548f.; Marchenko 1996, 74). It seems that the centre of gravity of Sarmatian power in the 4th-3rd centuries B.C. should be located in the areas to the north of the Caucasus. Here, new types of graves, apparently of Sarmatian origin, are attested in the second half of the 4th century B.C. (see Abramova 1991 and eadem 1992). In the 3rd century B.C., the most significant Sarmatian centres were located in the lower Don area, Kalmykia, the Kuban region, and the Central Caucasus. At this time, there were practically no Sarmatian burials in the North Pontic area. According to the present state of research, the appearance of Sarmatian graves in the southern Ukrainian steppes next to the Black Sea followed in the 2nd century B.C. (Simonenko 1993).

The hegemony of the Royal Sarmatians in the North Pontic Steppes and the infiltration of steppe tribes in the Carpathian Basin

The major Sarmatian migration to the areas encompassing the lands between the Don and Dnieper and the territories further to the west took place about 175-150 B.C. The Sarmatians now lived in close proximity to many Greek and indigenous settlements on the Black Sea (Marchenko 1996, 72). These developments were responsible for the appearance of a number of Sarmatian graves, which are particularly attested from the 2nd century B.C. onwards (cf. Simonenko 1993).

There are very few classical sources dealing with the peoples of the Ponto-Caspian steppes during the period extending from the 3rd century B.C. to the time when Rome established close contacts with these tribes. The scarcity of the sources is stressed by the Greek historian of the 2nd century B.C. Polybius (38.2-3). For a convincing discussion of this problem, see Machinskiy (1971, 122ff.). It is significant that Pseudo-Scymnus (writing at the end of the 2nd/beginning of the 1st century B.C.) relies on much older authors, including Ephorus. Polyaenus in his *Strategemata* (8.56) offers an interesting account of a Sarmatian queen called Amage. She intervened against her vassals, the Crimean Scythians, and put a rebellious Scythian ruler to death. Amage was allied with the people of the Crimean Chersonesus. This account should be dated to the 3rd century B.C. (Rostovtzeff 1931, 16).

One of the most important sources relating to Sarmatian and Scythian history of the 3rd century B.C. is the decree in honour of Protogenes discovered at Olbia (*IOSPE* I², 32). This document dates to the 220s-210s B.C. (Vinogradov 1989, 182, n.16. For a detailed discussion see Vinogradov 1989, 179ff). The decree shows that the Olbians were repeatedly forced to pay tribute to the Saii, apparently a Sarmatian tribe, and their king Saitapharnes (*IOSPE* I², 32A: 11, 34,44,84-92). The Scythians are also recorded in the decree, but as an insignificant tribe. Mention is also made of some other groups, including the Thyssamatae and Saudaratae, whose names should be regarded as Iranian (Harmatta 1970, 12; Abaev 1979, 304; Vinogradov 1989, 183). The Saii can be identified as the Royal Sarmatians (Machinskiy 1971, 47; Vinogradov 1989, 181). The Royal Sarmatians are attested in Strabo (7.3.17) and Appian (*Mithr*. 69). A hint about the origins of the Saii is found in their name. J. Harmatta (1970, 11f. and 98) has explained this as an Iranian derivative from **xšaya* "Herrscher". The name Saitapharnes is, without a doubt, an Iranian proper name (Harmatta 1970, 11 and 94; Abaev 350). The element *farn* is also attested in other Sarmatian names (cf. the names Arifarnes in Diod. 20.22-23 and Uatafarnes is found in epigraphic fragments cited by Machinskiy 1971, 47).

The dominant position of the Sarmatians in the steppes next to the Black Sea in the 2nd century B.C. is shown by another source. The 2nd century historian Polybius mentions the "Sarmatian" king Gatalus, whose power is illustrated by the fact that he is named in the peace treaty concluded about 179 B.C. by Pharnaces, king of Pontus with his adversaries (Polyb. 25.2.13. cf. Machinskiy 1971, 46f.).

The principal source for the history of the Ponto-Caspian steppes in the 2nd-1st centuries B.C. constitutes the *Geography* by Strabo of Amaseia. He used relations connected with the activities of Mithridates VI Eupator in the North Pontic region (cf. Strabo 1.2.1). Thus, his description dates, for the most part, to the last decades of the 2nd and to the 1st century B.C., but to some extent mirrors the state of affairs during the whole of the 2nd century. Strabo enumerates the following peoples in the North Pontic steppes:

"Then the country of the Tyregetae; and after it the country of the Iazygian Sarmatians and that of the people called the Basileians (Royal) and that of the Urgi, who in general are nomads, though a few are interested also in farming (...). In the interior dwell, first, those Bastarnians whose country borders on that of the Tyregetans and Germans (...). The Roxolani (...) roam the plains between the Tanais and the Borysthenes" (Strabo. 7.3.17).

Judging from what Strabo says, it was the Royal Sarmatians and the Iazygs who made up the first wave of Iranian nomads of the post-Scythian period. It is possible that the Royal Sarmatians are to be identified with the Saii known from the Protogenes decree. The Iazygs may be identified with the earlier tribe of Iaxamatae/Iazamatae (Rostovtzeff 1936, 93; Sulimirski 1970a, 102). The Iaxamatae are mentioned in a number of sources (Ixomatai in Polyaenus *Strat*. 8.55; Iaxamatae in Mela 1.114; Ixibatai in Hecataeus. *ap*. Steph. Byz. *s.v.* (= *FGrHist* 1 F 216); Iaxamatai in Ptol. *Geogr.* 5.8.10, 12; Iazabatai in Steph. Byz. *s.v.*; Iazamatai in Ps.-Scymn. 879 (= *GGM* I 223), and in Anon. *Per. Pont. Eux*. 45 (= *GGM* I 412); Exomatae in Val. Fl. 6.144, 146, 569).

After the Iazygs, Strabo names the Roxolani whose movements followed the migrations of the former. According to Strabo, this tribe lived between the Dnieper and Don. The Roxolani carried on war with Diophantus, the general of the Pontic King Mithridates Eupator. The Scythians appealed to them for help against Diophantus, but they were finally defeated as reported by Strabo (7.3.17). It is strange that the Roxolani, treated by most scholars as a Sarmatian tribe, acted as allies of the Scythians in their campaigns against the Chersonesus and Pontus. Previously, the Sarmatians had been the principal enemies of the Scythians. Diophantus' activities on the northern Black Sea shore are recorded in the decree dedicated by the Chersonesians in his honour. Judging from this inscription, Diophantus fought against the Reuxinali who are probably identical with the Roxolani known from Strabo. However, Ptolemy (*Geogr.* 3.5.7; 3.5.10) knows both appellations.

According to Strabo (2.5.7), the Roxolani were the most remote of the Scythians. The same writer defines the Roxolani as a tribe of the Bastarnae living between the Borysthenes and the Tanais (7.3.17). The Bastarnae were probably of Germanic stock (Pliny *Nat.Hist.* 4.81). They are attested from about 233 B.C. onwards on the area extending from Olbia to the Danube (Batty 1994). In all events, the ethnic identity of the Roxolani is not clear, perhaps they were a mixed Scytho-Sarmatian group. The presence of the Roxolani close to the Roman frontier in Walachia is recorded in the 60s of the 1st century A.D., when the governor of Moesia, Plautius Silvanus Aelianus, had to defend the Roman frontier on the Danube (Anderson 1934, 775ff.). The nomadic pressure is attested in his epitaph (*ILS* 986. cf. Bosworth 1977, 222; Olbrycht 1998, 194).

Strabo (7.3.17) mentions another tribe in the North Pontic steppes, the Urgoi, who are otherwise unknown. Their name is Iranian (Abaev 1979, 308 interprets it as meaning "wolves").

In the 1st century B.C., the hegemony of the Sarmatian tribes in the steppes continued. The Sarmatians were amongst the allies of Mithridates Eupator in his wars against Rome (App. *Mithr.* 15, 57, 69). During the 1st century B.C., different Sarmatian groupings moved westwards towards the Danube, reaching the Hungarian plain. On the lower Danube, the steppe tribes pressed against the Roman frontier (Anderson 1934; Harmatta 1970, 26ff.; Bachrach 1973; Fitz 1979; Batty 1994). One of the first Sarmatian attacks on Roman Thracia is recorded by Cassius Dio in 16-15 B.C. (Dio 54.20.1-3). In the Augustan period, some Sarmatian tribes (perhaps the Aorsi) sent embassies to Rome (*Res Gestae* 31.2). Ovid speaks of Sarmatian and Iazygian herdsmen (Batty

1994, passim). Prior to A.D. 50, the Iazygs established themselves in Pannonia (Tac. *Ann.* 12.29-30. cf. Machinskiy 1974, 129). Sarmatian tribes, especially the Iazygs and the Roxolani, played an important part in the history of the Carpathian basin of the 1st-4th centuries A.D.

The Aorsi, Upper Aorsi and Siraces

In his description of the steppes beyond the Tanais Strabo (7.3.17; 11.2.1; 11.5.8) enumerates the Aorsi, Upper Aorsi, and Siraces (cf. Nicolai 1984). In the most important passage he gives the following account of those peoples:

"The next peoples to which one comes between Lake Maeotis and the Caspian Sea are nomads, the Nabiani and the Panxani, and then next the tribes of the Siraces and the Aorsi. The Aorsi and the Siraces are thought to be fugitives from the upper tribes of those names and the Aorsi are more to the north than the Siraces. Now Abeacus, king of the Siraces, sent forth twenty thousand horsemen at the time when Pharnaces held the Bosporus; and Spadines, king of the Aorsi, two hundred thousand; but the Upper Aorsi sent a still larger number, for they held dominion over more land, and, one may almost say, ruled over most of the Caspian coast. And consequently they could import on camels the Indian and Babylonian merchandise, receiving it in their turn from the Armenians and the Medes, and, also, owing to their wealth, could wear golden ornaments. Now the Aorsi live along the Tanais, but the Siraces live along the Achardeus, which flows from the Caucasus and empties into Lake Maiotis".

This description derives basically from Hypsicrates (for a detailed disscussion of Strabo's sources, see Lasserre 1975, 22-24 and Olbrycht 1998, 133ff. cf. Rostovtzeff 1931, 126ff. and Harmatta 1970, 14). He was one of the historians of the wars fought by Mithridates VI Eupator (120-63 B.C.) against the tribes of the Black Sea region. Moreover, in 48-47 B.C., the Aorsi and Siraces gave support the Bosporan kingdom and their presence became more apparent to classical writers. The steppe tribes called "Sauromatai" are mentioned in Appian (*Mithr.* 120) as allies of Pharnaces, the king of Bosporus, in his attacks against Theodosia and Pantikapaion (around 47 B.C., cf. Gajdukevich 1971, 323f.).

The royal names given in Strabo's account, Spadines and Abeacus, are Iranian (Humbach 1969, 42). It is striking that Strabo describes the Aorsi and Siraces as refugees from other tribes. Similarly, the Huns, Avars, and Hungarians appeared in Europe "as small bands of gifted adventurers and/or refugees, who were able to forge on newly entered territories a confederation including alien associates" (Pritsak 1988, 749). Apparently both Aorsi and Siraces were fugitives from tribes east of the Volga.

The Siraces are attested in many sources (Mela 1.114; Pliny *Nat.Hist.* 4.83. cf. Olbrycht 1998, 135f.). Their homeland should be located in the Transcaspian plains. This assumption is vindicated by the following data. A country named Sirakene, located on the borders of Hyrcania, appears in Ptolemy's *Geography* (6.9.5). A further important clue is the personal name Sirakes, mentioned in Polyaenus' *Strategemata* (7.12) in connection with Persian attacks against the steppe peoples of Turkestan. This name should be treated as designation derived from an ethnonym. The appellation "Sirakoi" in Polyaenus (*Strat.* 8.26) is, in fact, a conjecture. The sources cited support the theory that the Siraces came from Central Asia. Harmatta (1970, 33-34) has already postulated that the Siraces migrated from Turkestan.

In some modern studies (Sulimirski 1970a, 103; Gardiner-Garden 1986, 215ff.), the Siraces are believed to have taken part in the Bosphoran civil war of 310/309 BC which is described by Diodorus Siculus (20.22-26). However, Diodorus' passage gives the form Θρᾳκῶν which was arbitrarily rejected, with some scholars (e.g. Rostovtzeff 1922, 163 and Gardiner-Garden 1986, 232f.) emending the text to Σιρακῶν. Such a conjecture cannot be vindicated either by philological data or historical circumstances. Thus, the alleged presence of the Siraces in the North Caucasus already in the 4th century B.C. cannot be confirmed by historical records.

The Upper Aorsi controlled the vast area extending from the Caucasus, through Kalmykia and the Nogai steppe in the west, up to the Aral region in the east. Of particular interest is their participation in international trade. In Aorsian territory on the lower Volga, Parthian coins have been found. This evidence clearly documents the existence of trade relations between Iran and the peoples of the Ponto-Caspian steppe and supports Strabo's description of trade routes (Olbrycht 1998, 134). This trade could have flourished only under the protection of the nomadic rulers. Objects of Parthian origin have been found in the forest belt of contemporary Russia and in the North Pontic area (Olbrycht 1998a, passim).

Our sources concerning the Aorsi are rather poor and their historical interpretation is not beyond dispute. The name of the Aorsi is of Iranian origin (Harmatta 1970, 82-85). Besides Strabo, the Aorsi are mentioned in Ptolemy's *Geography* (6.14.10; 3.5.10; 3.5.22), in Pliny's *Natural History* (4.80), and in the *Tabula Peutingeriana* (10.1). An interesting story concerning the Aorsi and Siraces is provided by Tacitus (*Ann.* 12.15ff.) who describes dynastic feuds in the Bosphoran kingdom during the years A.D. 48-49 (Treidler 1961). Mithridates VIII, supported by the Siraces and their king Zorsines, fought against his half-brother, Cotys, who was in alliance with Rome and Eunones, king of the Aorsi. There is, however, a textual problem connected with this text. In our manuscripts the forms *adorsorum, adorsi,* and *aduorsorum* are attested (H. Fuchs in Altheim 1969, 74-75). Lipsius emended the text to *Aorsorum* and he is followed in this conjecture by most scholars (e.g. Harmatta 1970, 83. cf., however, Humbach's objections – 1969, 42, n.2). On the whole, Lipsius' conjecture seems to be well vindicated by historical circumstances. There are also new records concerning the Aorsi. In 1984, a new inscription, dating to the 1st century B.C., was found at Olbia in the Crimea. This mentions an embassy to the "greatest kings of Aorsia" (τοὺς μεγίστους τῆς 'Αορσίας βασιέ[ας, cf. Vinogradov 1994, 10-11). In Chinese records, the Upper Aorsi are known as An-ts'ai/Yen-ts'ai (Olbrycht 1998, 135).

In some classical sources the term "Hamaxobioi" is attested (Mela 2.3: Sauromatae ... Hamaxobiae; Pliny *Nat.Hist.* 4.80: Hamaxobii; Ptol. *Geogr.* 3.5.10: Hamaxobioi; *Tabula Peutingeriana* 7.2-3: Amaxobii Sarmatae). This appellation is derived from the Greek word *hamaxa* which designated in particular the wagons of the Pontic nomadic tribes (cf. Hdt. 1.216; 4.114, 121; Lucian. *Anach.* 18). According to several authors, the nomads of the Ponto-Caspian steppe expanses used wagons in their movements (Tac. *Germ*. 46. cf. Strabo 7.3.17 (Hamaxoikoi), Ovid, *Trist*. 3.10.33 and Horace, *Odes* 3.24.9-16). Pliny (*Nat. Hist.*4.80) says "Hamaxobii aut Aorsi", and this equation seems to be reliable (Machinskiy 1971, 131f.). The Aorsi are probably referred to under the name Hamaxobii in late Roman sources. Some scholars (e.g. Sulimirski 1970a), however, identify the Hamaxobii with the Roxolani.

From the middle of the 1st century A.D. (around 48/49 A.D.) up to the 60s of that century, two steppe rulers, Pharzoios and Inismeus, minted their coins in Olbia. These emissions are known from finds in the Balkans and in the North Pontic area (Gajdukevich 1971, 344; Karyshkovskiy 1982; *idem* 1982a). There is controversy about the ethnic identity of these rulers. According to Yu. G. Vinogradov (in Rostovtzeff 1993, 144) they were kings of the Aorsi, whereas Skripkin (1996) believes they were rulers of Alanic tribes.

The Alans and their eastern relations

In the 60s of the 1st century A.D., a people appeared on the Roman horizon (Lucan. *Phars.* 8.223; 10.454; Sen. *Thyest.* 630. cf. also Val. Flacc. 6.42, 656; Martial 7.30) who changed the balance of power in the Caspian and Pontic steppes (Bachrach 1973; Bosworth 1977, 222ff.; Yatsenko 1993). It bore the name Alans and introduced into the scene of European history an ethnic and linguistic entity of crucial significance for further developments. The origins of the Alans are connected with Central Asia. According to Ammianus Marcellinus (31.2.16), a Roman writer of the 4th century A.D., the Alans even reached India and the Ganges in their expansion. This statement vindicates the view that the Asioi, a powerful tribe which took part in the nomadic invasions of Bactria in the 2nd century B.C., are to be identified as a people closely affiliated to the Alans (Olbrycht 1998, 95f.). The appellations Alans and As are mentioned in many sources of the Islamic period as synonyms (Barthold/Minorsky 1960, 354; Altheim 1969, 54ff.). A clue as to the origins of the As/Alans is the personal name Carthasis born by a Saka king about 330 B.C. The name is interpreted as *kart-as* “sword of the As” and contains the ethnic designation *As* (Abaev 1979, 293).

The location of the Alan homeland in Central Asia can be detected from information given by some classical writers (Jos. *Bell.Jud.* 7.244; Ptol. *Geogr.* 6.14.9. On this issue see Olbrycht 1998, 190ff.). Moreover, the Alans' ancestors originated in the Transcaspian areas according to some writers of the Islamic period whose sources are obviously much earlier. Such references concerning the Alan homeland are given by Al-Bīrūnī, Thāᶜlibī (Marquart 1914, 106f.; Barthold/Minorsky 1960; Harmatta 1970, 64), and the *Shāhnāme* (III 6270, 8101, 8323, 17094, transl. by C. B. Banu-Lakhuti et al., Moskva 1984ff.). This problem has already been studied in depth by Marquart (1914, 106f.) and Monchi-Zadeh (1975, 204ff.).

The designation *Alan* is very archaic and F. C. Andreas has linked it with *arya-*, Arians (Humbach 1969, 34). The Chinese sources reflect the appearance of the name of the Alans (in the *Hou Han-shu* 118, cf. Chavannese 1907, 195f.), and maintain that the Yen-ts'ai changed their name into A-lan (-liao). According to Pulleyblank (1968, 252, note 1), this statement dates to about A.D. 125. Based upon the above mentioned Chinese sources, it can be seen that they report changes in the steppe world reflecting a new state of affairs which apparently occurred due to the emergence of a people which was able to win dominance over other tribes of western Central Asia prior to A.D. 125. The cause of the Alan migration to the west was unknown to classical sources. It seems likely that the immediate catalyst for their movement was the Kang-chü, a powerful nomadic people found in the Syr Darya basin, extending from Farghana to the Aral Sea (Olbrycht 1998, 221). The Kang-chü, well known to Chinese records, can be identified with the Iaxartoi of Ptolemy (*Geogr.* 6.14.10, cf. Olbrycht 1998, 135).

The Classical writers Cassius Dio (69.15.1) and Ammianus Marcellinus (31.2.12; cf. 23.5.16) identify the Alans with the powerful people of the Massagetae, known in the Transcaspian steppes in the Achaemenid and Hellenistic periods. Based upon those statements and the tradition which connects the Alans with Central Asia, one can assume that the Alans were formed when some older tribal groupings embraced the Massagetae. The beginnings of the Alans are reflected in Ammianus Marcellinus in two particularly instructive passages:

"Thus the Halani (whose various peoples it is unnecessary now to enumerate) are divided between the two parts of the earth, but although widely separated from each other and roaming over vast tracts, as Nomads do, yet in the course of time they have united under one name, and are, for short, all called Halani because of the similarity in their customs, their savage mode of life, and their weapons" (31.2.17).

"(...) By repeated victories the Halani wore down the peoples whom they met and like the Persians incorporated them under their own national name" (31.2.13).

Such formations of nomadic confederacies, embracing peoples of different stock, repeatedly took place in the history of the steppe peoples (Khazanov

1975; Olbrycht 1998, 192). The Alans themselves played an important part in such a role in the empire of the Huns (Maenchen-Helfen 1978, 15ff.).

The Alans became repeatedly dangerous to Parthia as they conducted raids into Iran in A.D. 73 and 135. But the first incursion of the Alans into the Caucasus area and Transcaucasia is reported in A.D. 35. In that year Josephus names them as allies of the Caucasian Iberians (Jos. *Ant.* 18.97. cf. Olbrycht 1998, 146-148). Josephus' sources were obviously Parthian. Tacitus, who also offers an account of these events (Tac. *Ann.* 6.33.2), speaks vaguely of Sarmatians. Apparently the Alans remained unknown to our Latin-speaking sources until the 60s of the 1st century A.D. Consequently, most scholars date the appearance of the Alans in the Ponto-Caspian steppes to the 50-60s of the 1st century (see, for example, Machinskiy 1974, 132). The Alans are not mentioned in connection with the civil war in the Bosphoran kingdom of A.D. 48-9. In this episode, only two nomadic peoples, the Aorsi and the Siraces, are named as living in the region north of the Caucasus (Tac. *Ann.* 12.15ff., cf. Olbrycht 1998, 193f.). In the course of time, the Alans expanded westwards across the Volga. As stated above, the Alans firmly appear on the Roman horizon in the 60s of the 1st century A.D. Their advance from Central Asia drove forward various Sarmatian tribes. It was due to their pressure that the Roxolani and the Iazygs remained active in the struggle on the Danube frontier of the Roman Empire. Some of the Aorsi had to move west, other were subjugated by the new power.

The nomadic movements of the 1st century A.D. and the coming of the Alans into the North Pontic steppes brought significant changes in the culture of that area. A powerful impact of eastern elements is reflected in archaeological remains of the 1st-2nd century A.D. In the last decades, several rich burials of that period (mostly of the 1st century A.D.) have been excavated, including kurgan 1 at Kosika, kurgan 10 at Kobyakova by Rostov, and the burial Sokolova Mogila on the Boh (Dvornichenko/Fedorov-Davidov 1989 and 1993; Guguev 1990 and 1992). Oriental components of Central Asian origin are discernible, including polichromy and a new animal style (Treyster 1994; Olbrycht 1998, 195) in the art of this period. Furthermore, this evidence of extensive eastern influence is supported by the finds of Chinese objects discovered in the Ponto-Caspian steppe expanses, mainly dating from the 1st century B.C. onwards (Guguev/Treyster 1995).

In all likelihood, a general northern exchange route existed linking Western Turkestan with the region of the southern Urals and the North Pontic area. Trade between those countries is clearly documented from archeological research. Some coins of the Bosphoran kingdom have been found in Chorasmia. It seems that some finds recovered at Chorasmian centres, including a number of beads, also have their origins in the Sarmatian and North Pontic areas. This evidence can be linked with Ptolemy's account of a northern route in the Pontic and Caspian steppes. Ptolemy apparently received a number of reports from merchants involved in the trade with Central Asia, he is the first classical author to mention the rivers Rha/Volga, Daix/Ural, and Iastos/Emba in the Caspian region (Ptol. *Geogr.* 6.14.1ff. cf. Olbrycht 1998, 211f.; Olbrycht 1998a).

Probably during the 2nd and 3rd century A.D., the old "Sarmatian" territories in the Caspian steppes and in the south Ural region were seized by the Huns. In the North Pontic steppes, Iranian supremacy was ended by the Gothic invasion of around A.D. 200. In the 4th century A.D., most Alans acknowledged Hunnic supremacy and merged with their conquerors (Yatsenko 1993). After this they retreated westwards, inflicting a defeat on the Ostrogothic Kingdom. The Alans played an active role in the political life of Roman Empire in the 4th-5th centuries A.D. (Bachrach 1973). Alan groupings moved into Central and West Europe reaching even Spain and Britain during the upheavals of the Great Migration Period. Alan detachments crossed over into Africa and finally took part in the creation of the Vandal kingdom there. A number of archaeological remains in Western Europe have been associated with the Alans (Sulimirski 1970a, 185ff.; Kuznetsov 1996). It is believed that the Alans influenced Celtic poetry, including the cycle of legends concerning King Arthur and his knights of the Round Table (Abaev 1985, 802 with further references). According to T. Sulimirski (1970a, 166f.), the Western Alans, possibly the Antae, entered even the territory of Poland, and ancient Sarmatian traditions survived in Central Europe for a long time. Sizable Alan elements were also present in Hungary until the 15th century A.D. Some of the Alans remained in the Crimea area and in the Caucasus. The Alans living in the North Caucasus are treated as the ancestors of the present-day Ossets. Alan settlers and soldiers are mentioned even in China in the Mongol period (Barthold/Minorsky 1960; Abaev 1985, 802).

Conclusions

Having surveyed the main historical developments in the Ponto-Caspian steppes and the adjacent areas, we may discern the broad contours of several principal movements. Thus, a preliminary structure of these chronological stages, embracing the influx of respectively new Iranian groupings, can be proposed.

I. The Chernogorovka-Novocherassk phase (10th-7th centuries B.C.)

This phase begins with the gradual infiltration of cultural elements coming from the Caspian and Pontic steppes into Southeastern and Central Europe. This process was a lengthy one and all its stages are poorly documented. It seems, however, that the nomads who penetrated vast areas of Europe in the 10th-8th centuries B.C. were of Iranian stock and their main body came from Central Asia. The remainders of these groupings may have been the Agathyrsi, known as enemies of the Scythians.

II. The period of Scythian hegemony in the North Caucasus and North Pontic steppes (7th-4th centuries B.C.)

At the end of the 8th century B.C., we have some indications that Scythian groups were beginning to raid Southeastern and Central Europe. The Scythians supplanted the Cimmerians from the north Caspian steppes. In the 7th century B.C., the Scythians were closely linked with the state of affairs in Asia south of the Caucasus and subdued Media as well as some other countries of Western Asia. "The North Caucasian Scythians", as we may term the major unit, would prove to be o formidable force in the Near East. Eventually, however, the Scythians were overthrown by the Medes and expelled from Asia (prior to 600 B.C.). In the 7th-6th centuries B.C., the centre of Scythian power shifted westwards and the Scythians firmly seized the North Pontic steppes. At this time, Scythian detachments undertook a number of raids in Central Europe. It seems that the emergence of the Sauromatians on the Don was connected with Scythian activities in Western Asia and the movement of Iranian-speaking groupings coming from Iran. Added to these groupings, were elements from the tribes which inhabited the North Caucasian-Kuban steppes, including some Scythians and Maiotians. In the same way the Siginni advanced from beyond the Caucasus and occupied parts of the Hungarian plain. The memory of earlier relations between Media and the steppe tribes was probably preserved in the Iranian national epic and the Zariadres story can perhaps be connected with the period of close contacts between the Medes and the kindred groupings north of the Caucasus.

III. The Sarmatian period – the Royal Sarmatians and the Iazygs (4th-2nd centuries B.C.)

Probably during the 4th century B.C., various steppe tribes, driven out of their abode by the turmoil in Central Asia, subjugated the Sauromatians and then (at the end of the 4th century B.C. and beginning of the 3rd century B.C.) defeated the Scythians. These new peoples, coming from beyond the Volga, were called the Sarmatians by our later sources. Their core was formed by the Royal Sarmatians and the Iazygs. The newcomers presumably absorbed the Sauromatian tribal groups. It seems that the Sauromatians were, in fact, originally distinct from the Sarmatians, although both tribes were obviously of Iranian stock and certainly spoke similar tongues. In the 3rd century B.C., the Celts and the Bastarnae appeared in the North Pontic area playing an important part in the region.

IV. The hegemony of the Aorsi and Upper Aorsi (2nd century B.C.-1st century A.D.)

Around 175-130 B.C., new steppe tribes appeared in the areas west of the Volga. These groupings, called the Aorsi, Upper Aorsi, and Siraces, crushed the power of the Royal Sarmatians and Iazygs, setting into motion a chain of events that resulted in the arrival of Sarmatian tribes in the Danube area. Strabo expresses the view that the Aorsi and Siraces who came to the Ponto-Caspian steppes were the fugitive remnants of the more eastern tribes.

V. The Alan domination in the steppes (1st-4th century A.D.)

In the period around A.D. 35-60, the Alans quickly made their presence felt in the Caspian and Pontic steppes. The Alans should be identified as the successors of the ancient Massagetae, but their huge confederation contained different ethnic groupings, including parts of the Aorsi and the Upper Aorsi. Around A.D. 200, the North Pontic steppes were subjugated by the Goths.

The Alans living east of the Don were defeated by the Huns about A.D. 370 and joined the victors in their expansion. The era of Iranian predominance in the Ponto-Caspian steppes came to an end.

Most Iranian tribes entering Europe took possession of the last outpost of the Eurasian steppe in Central Europe: the Hungarian plain. Here, they underwent a number of changes and were transformed, both ethnically (as they mingled with the indigenous substratum) and economically (denomadicization). The interaction of these Iranian groups with the local populations of Europe was largely ignored by our written sources. However, archaeology points to considerable cultural interchange. The movements of many steppe tribes toward Europe introduced new ethnic elements of Asiatic origin into this large area. Iranian groupings of the pre-Scythian period, the Scythians, the Sauromatians, various Sarmatian tribes, the Roxolani, the Aorsi, and the Alans contributed to the development of culture not only in the Ponto-Caspian steppes, but also in other areas as they were driven into many countries at different points in time. The history of Southeastern and Central Europe in the ancient period can be properly understood only within the context of the relations between the sedentary tribes and the Eurasian steppe nomads. Such a relationship is clearly visible in the medieval history of Rus, the Hungarians, the Bulgars, as well as in that of Poland.

The Iranian presence in Europe was also connected with the Old Persian Imperial period. For several decades of the 6th and 5th centuries B.C., the Achaemenid Persians managed to subjugate parts of the Balkan area (Hammond 1980; Pająkowski 1983; Balcer 1988) and carried out campaigns against the Scythians of what today is the Ukraine (Chernenko 1984). Persian culture exerted a powerful impact on the Balkan peoples and even after the retreat of the Achaemenids from Europe, Persian influences remained strong (Bouzek/Ondřejova 1987, 86ff.). A fragment of an Old Persian inscription was found in Gherla in Transylvania (Rumania) in 1937 (Harmatta 1954). According to J. Harmatta, the Gherla inscription goes back to Darius I. From Herodotus (4.87) we know that during his campaign against the Scythians, Darius erected several inscriptions in Thrace.

Acknowledgements
This paper was presented at the Celto-Asiatic Seminar at the Jagiellonian University's Institute of Oriental Philology. My best thanks are due to the organizer, Prof. Jadwiga Pstrusińska for her kind invitation and interest in this work.

Bibliography

Abaev V. I. 1965: *Skifo-evropeyskie izoglossy*, Moskva.

Abaev V. I. 1979: Skifo-sarmatskie narechiya in: *Osnovy iranskogo yazykoznaniya. I. Drevneiranskie yazyki*, Moskva, 272-364.

Abaev V. I. 1985: Alans, *Encyclopaedia Iranica* I, 801-803.

Abramova M. P. 1991: Voprosy izucheniya pamyatnikov Tsentralnogo Predkavkazya sarmatskogo vremeni, *KSIA* 204, 18-24.

Abramova M. P. 1992: Nekotorye osobennosti vzaimootnosheniy iranoyazychnykh kochevnikov i osedlykh plemen Predkavkazya, *RA* 1992/2, 20-31.

Altheim F. 1969: *Geschichte der Hunnen*. I. Bd., Berlin[2].

Anderson J. G. C. 1934: The Eastern Frontier from Tiberius to Nero, *CAH* X, 743-780.

Bachrach B. S. 1973: *A History of the Alans in the West*, Minneapolis.

Bailey H. W. 1985: Alans: additional notes, *EncIran* I, 803.

Balcer J. C. 1988: Persian Occupied Thrace (Skudra), *Historia* 37, 1-21.

Barbarunova Z. A. 1989: Nekotorye problemy istorii rannykh Sarmatov (po pamyatnikam Yuzhnogo Priuralya i Nizhnego Povolzhya), *SA* 1989/3, 48-60.

Barfield T. J. 1989: *The Perilous Frontier: Nomadic Empires and China*, Cambridge (Mass).

Barthold W./Minorsky V. 1960: Alān, *Encyclopaedia of Islam* (new ed.), I, Leiden, 354.

Batty R. M. 1994: On Getic and Sarmatian Shores: Ovid's Account of the Danube Lands, *Historia* 43, 88-111.

Bielmeier R. 1989: Sarmatisch, Alanisch, Jassisch und Altossetisch in R. Schmitt (ed.) *Compendium Linguarum Iranicarum*, Wiesbaden, 236-245.

Bosworth A. B. 1977: Arrian and the Alani, *HSCP* 81, 217-255.

Bosworth C. E. 1978, Ismāᶜīl b. Ahmad, *Encyclopaedia of Islam* (new ed.), IV, Leiden, 188-189.

Bouzek J./Ondřejova I. 1987: Some Notes on the Relations of the Thracian, Macedonian, Iranian and Scythian Arts in the Fourth Century B.C., *Eirene* 24, 67-93.

Boyce M. 1955: Zariadres and Zarēr, *BSOAS* 17, 463-477.

Chernenko E. V. 1984: *Skifo-persidskaya voyna*, Kiev.

Chezhina E. F. 1988: Istoriya i sovremennoe sostoyaniye problemy "savromatskogo" zverinogo stilya, *ASGE* 29, 59-64.

Chavannese E. 1907: Le pays d'occident d'après le Heou Han chou, *T'oung Pao* 8, 149-234.

Chochorowski J. 1986: Rola Sigynnów Herodota w środowisku kulturowym wczesnej epoki żelaza na Nizinie Węgierskiej, *Przegląd Archeologiczny* 34, 161-218.

Chochorowski J. 1987: Zur Bestimmung des Siedlungsraumes und des Ursprungs von Agathyrser, *AAC* 26, 139-173.

Chochorowski J. 1993: *Ekspansja kimmeryjska na tereny Europy Srodkowej*, Kraków.

Chochorowski J. 1994: Skifskie nabegi na territoriyu Srednej Evropy, *RA* 1994/3, 49-63.

Chochorowski J. (ed.) 1996: Koczownicy Ukrainy. *Katalog wystawy: Muzeum Śląskie*, Katowice.

Chochorowski J. 1998: Die Vekerzug-Kultur und ihre östlichen Beziehungen in B. Hänsel/J. Machnik (eds.), *Das Karpathenbecken und die osteuropäische Steppe. Nomadenbewegungen und Kulturaustausch in den vorchristlichen Metallzeiten (4000-500 v. Chr.)*, München-Rahden/West., 473-491.

Dandamaev M. A. 1989: *A Political History of the Achaemenid Empire*, Leiden.

Davis-Kimball J./Bashilov V. A./Yablonsky L. T. (eds.) 1995: *Nomads of the Eurasian Steppes in the Early Iron Age*, Berkeley.

Diakonoff I. M. 1985: Media, *CHI* 2, 36-148.

Diakonoff I. M. 1994: Kimmeriytsy i skify na Drevnem Vostoke, *RA* 1994/1, 108-116.

Dilke O. A. W. 1985: *Greek and Roman Maps*, London.

Dudarev C. I. 1995: *K probleme vzaimodeystviya plemeni Severnogo Kavkaza s rannimi kochevnikami v predskivskuyu epokhu*, Armavir.

Dudarev S. L. 1991: *Iz istorii svyazey naseleniya Kavkaza s kimmeriysko-skifskim mirom*, Groznyi.

Dvornichenko V. V./Fedorov-Davydov G. A. 1989: *Pamyatniki sarmatskoy aristokratii v nizhnem Povolzhe in Sokrovishcha sarmatskikh vozhdey i drevnie goroda Povolzhia*, Moskva, 5-12.

Dvornichenko V. V./Fedorov-Davydov G. A. 1993: Sarmatskoe pogrebenie skeptukha I v. n.e. u s. Kosika Astrakhanskoy oblasti, *VDI* 1993/3, 141-189.

Fitz J. 1979: Sarmatae, *KP* IV, 1557.

Gajdukevich V. F. 1971: *Das bosporanische Reich*, Berlin.

Gardiner-Garden J. R. 1986: Fourth Century Conceptions of Maiotian Ethnography, *Historia* 35, 192-225.

Gardiner-Garden J. 1987: *Greek Conceptions on Inner Asian Geography and Ethnography from Ephoros to Erathostenes*, Bloomington (Indiana).

Gardiner-Garden J. 1988: Eudoxos, Skylax and the Syrmatai, *Eranos* 86, 31-42.

Grantovskiy E. A. 1970: *Rannia istoriya iranskikh plemen Peredeney Azii*, Moskva.

Grantovskiy E. A. 1998: *Iran i irantsy do Akhemenidov*, Moskva.

Guguev V. K. 1990: Ein reiches Sarmatengrab in Rostov am Don, *Altertum* 36, 37-42.

Guguev V. K. 1992: Kobyakovskiy kurgan (K voprosu o vostochnykh vliyaniyakh na kulturu sarmatov I v.n.e. – nachala II v.n.e.), *VDI* 1992/4, 116-129.

Guguev V. K./Treyster M. Yu. 1995: Khanskie zerkala i podrazhaniya im na territorii yuga vostochnoy Evropy, *RA* 1995/3, 143-156.

Gutschmid A. v. 1892: Die Skythen, [in:] *Kleine Schriften*, Bd. III, Leipzig, 421-445.

Györffy G. 1985: Landnahme, Ansiedlung und Streifzüge der Ungarn, *AHASH* 31, 231-270.

Hammond N. G. L. 1980: The Extent of Persian Occupation in Thrace, *Chiron*, 53-61.

Hänsel B./Machnik J. (eds.), *Das Karpathenbecken und die osteuropäische Steppe. Nomadenbewegungen und Kulturaustausch in den vorchristlichen Metallzeiten (4000-500 v. Chr.),* München-Rahden/West.

Harmatta J. 1954, A recently discovered Old Persian Inscription, *AAntASH* 2, 1-16.

Harmatta J. 1968: Früheisenzeitliche Beziehung zwischen dem Karpatenbecken, Oberitalien und Griechenland, *AAntASH* 20, 153-157.

Harmatta J. 1970: *Studies in the History and Language of the Sarmatians*, Szeged.

Harmatta J. (ed.) 1994: *History of Civilization of Central Asia, Vol. II: The Development of Sedentary and Nomadic Civilization: 700 B.C. to A.D. 250.*, Paris.

Humbach H. 1969: Die historische Bedeutsamkeit der alanischen Namen in Studia classica et orientalia *Antonio Pagliaro oblata III*, Roma, 33-52.

Jagchid S. 1977: Patterns of Trade and Conflict between China and the Nomads of Mongolia, *Zentralasiatische Studien* 11, 177-204.

Jagchid S./Symons V. Y. 1990: *Peace, War and Trade along the Great Wall. Nomadic-Chinese Interaction through Two Millenia*, Bloomington.

Junge J. 1939: *Saka-Studien. Der ferne Nordosten im Weltbild dr Antike* (= *Klio,* Beiheft XLI, N.F., Heft 28), Leipzig.

Justi F. 1895: *Iranisches Namenbuch*, Marburg.

Karyshkovskiy P. O. 1982: *Olviya i Rim v I v. n.e. in Pamyatniki rimskogo i srednevekovogo vremeni v Severo-Zapadnom Prichernomorye*, Kiev, 6-28.

Karyshkovskiy P. O. 1982a: O monetakh tsarya Farzoya [in:] *Arkheologicheskie pamyatniki Severo-Zapadnogo Prichernomorya*, Kiev, 66-82.

Khazanov A. M. 1971: *Ocherki voennogo dela sarmatov*, Moskva.

Khazanov A. M. 1975: *Sotsyalnaya istoriya skifov. Osnovnye problemy razvitiya drevnikh kochevnikov evraziyskikh stepej*, Moskva.

Kolosovskaja Yu. K. 1984: K voprosu ob agafirsakh [in:] *Etnogenez narodov Balkan i Severnogo Prichernomorya*, Moskva, 181-193.

Kretschmer K. 1920: Sarmatae, *RE* 2. Reihe, 2. Hbbd., 2542-2550.

Kretschmer K. 1921: Sarmatia, *RE* 2. Reihe, 3. Hbbd., 1-12.

Kretschmer K. 1927: Σίρακες, *RE* 2. Reihe, 5. Hbbd., 283-5.

Kuznetsov V.A. 1996: Alany na Zapade: arkheologicheskaya realnost ili mif?, *RA* 1996/4, 71-79.

Lassere F. 1975: *Strabon, Geographika*, T. VIII (Livre XI), texte établi et traduit par F. Lasserre, Paris.

Latyshev V. V. 1993: *Izvestiya drevnikh pisateley o Skifii i Kavkaze*, vol. 2, Sankt-Peterburg.

Machinskiy D. A. 1971: O vremeni pervogo aktivnogo vystupleniya sarmatov v Podneprove po svidetelstvam antichnykh pismennykh istochnikov, *ASGE* 13, 30-54.

Machinskiy D. A. 1974: Nekotorye problemy etnogeografii vostochnoevropeyskikh stepey vo II v. do n.e. – I v. n.e., *ASGE* 16, 122 - 132.

Maenchen-Helfen O. J. 1978: *Die Welt der Hunnen*, Wien-Köln-Graz.

Makhortykh S. V. 1991: *Skify na Severnom Kavkaze*, Kiev.

Makhortykh S. V./Ievlev M. M. 1992: Über die Anfangsperiode der Geschichte der Kimmerier, *AAC* 31, 107-121.

Maksimenko V. E. 1983: *Savromaty i sarmaty na Nizhnem Donu*, Rostov.

Marchenko K. K. 1996: Tretiy period stabilizatsii v Severnom Prichernomore antichnoy epokhi, *RA* 1996/2, 70-80.

Markwart J. 1932: Die Sigynnen, *Caucasica* X, 1-42.

Markwart J. 1938: *Wehrot und Arang*, Leiden.

Marquart J. 1914: "Über das Volkstum der Komanen" in: W. Bang/J. Marquart, *Osttürkische Dialektstudien*, (Abh. Königl. Ges. Wiss. zu Göttingen, Phil.-hist. Kl. N.F. Bd. 13, N. 1), Berlin, 25-238.

Mc Govern W. 1939: *The Early Empires of Central Asia*, New York.

Meister K. 1997, Diodorus Siculus, *DNP 3*, Stuttgart-Wien, 592-594.

Melyukova A. I. (ed.) 1989: *Stepi evropeyskoy chasti SSSR v skifo-sarmatskoe vremya*, Moskva.

Melyukova A. I. 1990: The Scythians and Sarmatians in Sinor D. (ed.) 1990: *The Cambridge History of Early Inner Asia*, Cambridge-New York-Melbourne, 97-117.

Melyukova A. I./Moshkova M. G./Petrenko V. G. (eds.) 1984: *Drevnosti Evrazii v skifo-sarmatskoe vremya,* Moskva.

Monchi-Zadeh D. 1975: *Topographisch-historische Studien zum iranischen Nationalepos* (*Abhandlungen für die Kunde des Morgenlandes* 41.2), Wiesbaden.

Moshkova M. G. 1963: *Pamyatniki prokhorovskoy kultury* (Svod arkheologicheskikh istochnikov, D1-10), Moskva.

Moshkova M. G. 1989: Kratkiy ocherk istorii savromato-sarmatskikh plemen in Melyukova A. I. (ed.) 1989: *Stepi evropeyskoy chasti SSSR v skifo-sarmatskoe vremya*, Moskva, 153-158.

Moshkova M. G. 1991: Osnovnye problemy sarmatskoy arkheologii, *KSIA* 204, 10-18.

Moshkova M. G. (ed.) 1992: *Stepnaya polosa aziatskoy chasti SSSR v skifo-sarmatskoe vremya,* Moskva.

Murzin V. Yu. 1990: *Proiskhozhdenie skifov: osnovnye etapy formirovaniya skifskogo etnosa*, Kiev.

Nicolai R. 1984: Un sistema di localizzazione geografica relativa. Aorsi e Siraci in Strab. XI 5, 7-8 in: F. Prontera (ed.), *Strabone. Contributi allo studio della personalitŕ e dell'opera*, Perugia, 99-125.

Nöldeke Th. 1896: *Das iranische Nationalepos*, Strassburg.

Olbrycht M. J. 1996: "Die Beziehungen der Steppennomaden Mittelasiens zu den hellenistischen Staaten (bis zum Ende des 3. Jahrhunderts vor Chr.)" [in:] B. Funck (ed.), *Hellenismus. Beiträge zur Erforschung von Akkulturation und politischer Ordnung in den Staaten des hellenistischen Zeitalters. Akten des Internationalen Hellenismus-Kolloquiums 9. – 14. März in Berlin*, Tübingen, 147-169.

Olbrycht M. J. 1998: *Parthia et ulteriores gentes. Die politischen Beziehungen zwischen dem arsakidischen Iran und den Nomaden der eurasischen Steppen* (Quellen und Forschungen zur Antiken Welt, Bd. 30), Tuduv-Verlag, München.

Olbrycht M. J. 1998a: "Die Kultur der Steppengebiete und die Beziehungen zwischen Nomaden und der seßhaften Bevölkerung (Der Arsakidische Iran und die Nomadenvölker)" in: J. Wiesehöfer (ed.) *Das Partherreich und seine Zeugnisse. Beiträge des Internationalen Colloquiums, Eutin (27. – 30. Juni 1996)* (*Historia. Einzelschriften*. Heft 122), Stuttgart, Steiner, 11-43.

Pająkowski W. 1983: Einige Bemerkungen zur Lokalisierung der persischen Provinz (Satrapie) Skudra, *Eos* 71, 243-255.

Parzinger H. 1998: Stepnye kochevniki na Vostoke Tsentralnoy Evropy. Nakhodki i pamyatniki v svete sravnitelnoy arkheologii, *VDI* 1998/2, 104-115.

Pogrebova M. N./Raevskiy D.S. 1992: *Rannie skify i Drevniy Vostok*, Moskva.

Pritsak O. 1988: "The Distinctive Features of the Pax Nomadica" in: *Popoli delle steppe: Unni, Avari, Ungar*, 2 vols., Spoleto, 749-780.

Pulleyblank E. G. 1968: "Chinese Evidence for the Date of Kaniska" in: A. Basham (ed.) *Papers on the Date of Kanishka*, Leiden, 247-258.

Raevskiy D. S. 1995: Rannie skify: sreda obitaniya i khozyaystvenno-kulturnyi tip, *VDI* 1995/4, 87-96.

Rostovtzeff M. 1922: *Iranians and Greeks in South Russia*, New York (reissued 1969).

Rostovtzeff M. 1929: *The Animal Style in South Russia and China*, Princeton (reissued New York 1973).

Rostovtzeff M. 1936: The Sarmatae and Parthians, *CAH* XI, 91-130.

Rostovtzeff (Rostowzew) M. 1931: *Skythien und der Bosporus, Band I. Kritische Übersicht der schriftlichen und archäologischen Quellen*, Berlin.

Rostovtzeff (Rostowzew) M. 1993: *Skythien und der Bosporus, Band II. Wiederentdeckte Kapitel und Verwandtes*, übersetzt und herausgegeben von H. Heinen, Stuttgart (Historia. Einzelschriften 83).

Schneider G. I. 1880: *De Diodori Fontibus (Libr. I-IV)*, Diss., Berolini.

Schüle W. 1969: *Die Meseta-Kulturen der Iberischen Halbinsel. Mediterrane und eurasische Elemente in früheisenzeitlichen Kulturen Südwesteuropas*, Berlin.

Shchukin M. 1982: Tsarstvo Farzoya. Epizod iz istorii Severnogo Prichierno-morya, *ASGE* 47, 35-38.

Simonenko A. V. 1993: *Sarmaty Tavrii*, Kiev.

Sinor D. (ed.) 1990: *The Cambridge History of Early Inner Asia*, Cambridge, New York, Melbourne.

Skripkin A. S. 1982: Aziatskaya Sarmatiya vol. II-IV vv., *SA* 1982/2, 43-56.

Skripkin A. S. 1996: K voprosu etnicheskoi istorii sarmatov pervych vekov nashei ery, *VDI* 1996/1, 160-169.

Smirnov K. F. 1972: Sarmatskie katakombnye pogrebeniya Yuzhnogo Priuralya-Povolzhya i ikh otnoshenie k katakombam Severnogo Kavkaza, *SA* 1972/1, 73 - 81.

Smirnov K. F. 1975: *Sarmaty na Ileke*, Moskva.

Smirov K. F. 1980: Sauromates et Sarmates, *Dialogues d'Histoire Ancienne* 6, 139-153.

Smirnov K. F. 1984: *Sarmaty i utverzhdenie ikh politicheskogo gospodstva v Skifii*, Moskva.

Stolba V. F. 1993: Demograficheskaya situatsiya v Krymu v V-II vv. do n. e. (po dannym pismennych istochnikov), *PAV* 6, 56-61.

Sulimirski T. 1945: Scythian Antiquities in Central Europe, *The Antiquaries Journal* 25, London, 1-11.

Sulimirski T. 1954: Scythian Antiquities in Western Asia, *Artibus Asiae* 17, 282-318.

Sulimirski T. 1961: *Die Skythen in Mittel- und Westeuropa in Bericht über den V. Kongress für Vor- und Frühgeschichte (Hamburg 1958)*, Berlin, 793-799.

Sulimirski T. 1970: *Sarmaci*, Warszawa.

Sulimirski T. 1970a: *The Sarmatians*, London.

Sulimirski T. 1970b: *Prehistoric Russia. An Outline*, London-Dublin.

Sulimirski T. 1985: The Scyths, *CHI* 2, 149-199.

Treidler H. 1961: Uspe, *RE* 2. Reihe, 17. Hbbd., 1092-1093.

Treyster M. Yu. 1994: "Sarmatskaya shkola khudozhestvennoy torevtiki (K otkrytiyu serviza iz Kosiki)", *VDI* 1994/1, 172-203.

Vinogradov Yu. A./Marchenko K. K. 1989: Das nördliche Schwarzmeergebiet in der skythischen Epoche, *Klio* 71, 539-549.

Vinogradov Yu. A./Marchenko K. K./Rogov E. Ya. 1997: Sarmaty i gibel "Velikoy Skifii", *VDI* 1997/3, 93-103.

Vinogradov V. B. 1966: Lokalizatsiya Akhardeya i sirakskogo soyuza plemen, *SA* 1966/4, 38-50.

Vinogradov Yu. G. 1989: *Politicheskaya istoriya olbiyskogo polisa VII-I vv. do n.e.*, Moskva.

Vinogradov Yu. G. 1994: Greek Epigraphy of the North Black Sea Coast, the Caucasus and Central Asia (1985-1990), *Ancient Civilizations from Scythia to Syberia* (Special Sample Issue), 1-12

Vinogradov Yu. G. 1997: Khersonesskiy dekret o "nesenii Dionisa" IOSPE I2 343 i vtorzhenie sarmatov v Skifiu, *VDI* 1997/3, 104-124.

Yarshater E. 1983: "Iranian National History" in: *CHI* 3(1), 359-477.

Yatsenko S. A. 1993: Alany v Vostochnoy Evrope v seredine I – seredine IV vv. n. e (lokalizatsiya i politicheskaya istoriya)", *PAV* 6, 83-88.

Zubar V. M. 1994: "Olbiya, sarmaty i Rim vo vtoroy polovine I v.", *VDI* 1994/3, 218-222.

Abbreviations

AAC	=	*Acta Archaeologica Carpathica.*
AAntASH	=	*Acta Antiqua Academiae Scientiarum Hungaricae.*
AArASH	=	*Acta Archaeologica Academiae Scientiarum Hungaricae.*
AHASC	=	*Acta Historica Academiae Scientiarum Hungaricae.*
ASGE	=	*Arkheologicheskiy Sbornik Gosudarstvennogo Ermitazha.*
DNP	=	*Der Neue Pauly.*
GGM	=	*Geographi Graeci Minores*, ed. C. Müllerus, vol. I-II, Parisiis 1855-61.
HSCP	=	*Harvard Studies in Classical Philology*
IOSPE	=	*Inscriptiones Orae Septentrionalis Ponti Euxini.*
KP	=	*Der Kleine Pauly.*
KSIA	=	*Kratkie Soobshcheniya Instituta Arkheologii.*
KSIIMK	=	*Kratkie Soobshcheniya Instituta Istorii Materialnoy Kultury.*
MIA	=	*Materialy i Issledovaniya po Arkheologii.*
PAV	=	*Peterburskiy Arkheologicheskiy Vestnik.*
RA	=	*Rossiyskaya Arkheologiya.*
SA	=	*Sovetskaya Arkheologiya.*
VDI	=	*Vestnik Drevney Istorii.*

Zygmunt Pucko
(Cracow)

A cult of severed heads in Cracow? *

It is difficult to precisely give the time of Celtic immigration into the area of the Polish lands though several ethnographers date the Celts' arrival in the 4th century B.C.[1] Some Polish researchers maintain that the influence of Celtic culture both spiritually as well as materially on the development of the Proto-Slavs living in the areas of present day Poland was quite large. This is borne out by the preservation up until our times of clear Celtic traces in various forms[2]. These traces are present not only in the areas of Lower and Upper Silesia and the Kujawy area, but first and foremost in Little Poland (Małopolska), and there chiefly in Cracow. In the area of Cracow are preserved the greatest diversity of Celtic sources in Poland[3], starting from the largest Celtic settlement in Poland representing a closed entity surrounded by ramparts. These settlements were in the vicinity of the so-called Krakus and Wanda mounds. In the area of the former Celtic settlements are found skeleton graves and crematories together with a whole inventory of artifacts. Neither type of grave included any articles of local production, while their contents were wholly Celtic[4]. For example the warrior burial found here was according to a Celtic ritual used in the burial of the highest class of warrior[5].

---

* This is a revised version of the paper given in August 1995 at the Centre for Advanced Welsh and Celtic Studies, University of Wales, Aberystwyth.

1 J. Rosen-Przeworska, *Tradycje celtyckie w obrzędowości protosłowian*, Warszawa 1964, p. 1.

2 E. g. T. Makiewicz, "Kulturowe paleniska ornamentowe w Europie" [in:] *Z otchłani wieków*, (1976), no. 2, p. 124-132.

3 J. Rosen-Przeworska, *op. cit.*, p. 14.

4 *Ibidem*, p. 47.

5 *Ibidem*, p. 154.

It is known from many sources that the Celts had the custom of cutting off the heads of their enemies, of collecting them, and that the head had a very significant meaning in their culture, both materially as well as spiritually. Diodorus Siculus writes, for example, that heads were nailed to houses and preserved like treasures. Livy describes on the other hand that captured heads were tied to horses or attached to lances. The head of a valued enemy was placed in local holy places, in lesser temples, and, in later times, in more significant ones. The heads were even decorated with gold and used as drinking vessels. Many Celtic heroes according to some accounts sat down to eat with severed heads arranged in front of them on the table[6]. The motif of the severed head commonly appears in Celtic iconography on many varied articles[7]. Researchers are of the opinion that the symbol of the severed head has many meanings, including sacral ones. A severed head can, as the most important element of the whole, even be a representation of a pagan deity. It also expressed the essence of existence, the centre of intellectual-spiritual activity, as well as the abode of the spirit and the place inhabited by a deity[8]. It is more than likely that the severed head, according to several celtologists, also fulfilled the role of defending the person who carried the effigy of the severed head from sorcery, spells, suffery, and death[9].

In the second half of the nineteenth century, however, there arose a new interpretation of the symbolism of the severed head based on written sources[10]. According to this new concept, the severed head is connected with the belief in life beyond the grave as well as the idea of reincarnation, the repeated, and possibly even manyfold, incarnation of the soul in a new life[11]. Maybe the effigy of the severed head was a reminder of eternal life, and a preparation for a courageous life which guaranteed reward in the land of eternal happiness. It is not out of the question that the effigy also fulfilled the role of guide in the other world, which would explain the widespread presence of the severed head on Celtic swords, belt buckles, harness buckles, bronze utensils, and shields[12].

---

[6] N. Chadwick, *The Celts*, Victoria 1970, p. 49.

[7] J. Rosen-Przeworska, *Ikonografia wschodnioceltycka*, Wrocław 1976, p. 93.

[8] *Ibidem*, p. 113.

[9] *Ibidem*, p. 113.

[10] *Ibidem*, p. 114.

[11] *Ibidem*, p. 116.

[12] *Ibidem*, p. 99.

The exposure of the severed head, as well as its cult which everywhere in time changed in a natural way, for obvious reasons, into the cult of the skull, exists equally in Cracow, through of course only as a relic of the past – and is a relatively little known relic. I would like here to mention the cult of skulls which is continued probably very clearly, though not in a totally conscious way, in the rites still performed in the *Brotherhood of the Good Death* in the Franciscan Order in Cracow. The link of the Brotherhood with the Church dates to the pre-war period. Firstly the Brotherhood received a permanent and independent place to fulfil the cult practices which was the chapel in their church, and secondly the link with the Cracovian Franciscans came through a Franciscan prefect who fulfilled from a certain time the function of chaplain.

The said Brotherhood is not a local creation. The idea for it wandered its way to Cracow several centuries ago from western Europe and more than likely took on a character formulated by an existing local folk rite[13], or the borrowed patterns overlapped similar local ones.

The Brotherhood possesses a lot of autonomy and has a developed organisational structure. All positions were held by people selected by members of the Brotherhood. The Brotherhood was only directly responsible to the bishops. It is still an open association for people from various social sections of an impeccable moral standing. The present Brotherhood takes part in passion services during which it performs in traditional costumes and displaying distinct insignia.

In all the services performed in Cracow from the end of the sixteenth century by members of the *Brotherhood of the Good Death*, skulls have been an extremely important and indispensable requisite. The members of the Brotherhood enter during the liturgy processions to the shrine holding saplings at the end of which are skulls[14]. The skulls carried by the members of the Brotherhood are well maintained and carefully preserved, and some of them are even decorated. It happens that they are even placed on the sapling in a richly decorated gilded frame. The saplings with the skulls are held by the members of the Brotherhood for the whole duration of the sacral rite, right up until the moment of its completion.

---

[13] R. Godula, "Memento mori", *Peregrinus Cracoviensis*, Kraków 1995, p. 101.

[14] *Ibidem*, p. 106.

Equally on the liturgical gowns of the Brotherhood are sewn or painted skulls surrounded by colourful garlands of flowers, most often ivy, or symbols of death like for instance a scythe, spear, sword, hatchet, or a cross. The skulls also appear on banners and on the catafalque encircling a prostrate cross. Two skulls on cross bones are laid equally on the fastened *Book of Life* in which allegedly are written the names and deeds of all people. The *Book* is carried round by members of the Brotherhood during the liturgy as is the case with other requisites[15]. During the ceremony members of the Brotherhood kiss the relics of the cross as well as the skulls placed on the reliquary and pay homage to them. All the relics used in the ritual after the service are stored away in the shrine in a specially segregated chapel exclusively for the use of the Brotherhood. Until recently the ceremonies of the *Brotherhood of the Good Death* had a public character and took place several times a month and also during certain religious holidays, e.g. carnival Sundays, holidays of the Holy Cross and the raising of the Cross, the discovery of Christ in the Temple, and during Lenten Fridays. The present Brotherhood upholds the ceremony once a year on Good Friday.

It is worth remembering in this context that the particular forms of prayer of the Brotherhood do not connect in a strict sense with either the idea of Christ's suffering or penance and redemption[16]. They have the character as well as significative threads which are clearly old and pagan, but their presence in the rituals of the aforementioned ceremonies gives them a sacral role. These threads present themselves at various moments of the action along side the Christian contents, a combination which is seemingly without logic[17].

However if we consider this in the light of more universal ideas, it turns out that maybe it is only perceived chaos, because equally the threads of Christianity, like those of paganism, base themselves on one basic motif: the all pervasive idea of life and death[18]. The ceremonies carried out do not simply have the aim of acquainting man with death, but equally freeing him from fearing it, and informing him of his eternal existence, but in a different dimension. Maybe the symbol of the skulls in the context of the whole ceremony, gestures, requisites and texts should be

[15] R. Godula, *op. cit.*, p. 106.

[16] *Ibidem*, p. 109.

[17] *Ibidem*, p. 109.

[18] *Ibidem*, p. 109.

perceived not only as the borders between life and death, but also as the terrain on which two realities meet, the completed with the uncompleted, which mutually penetrate one another and complement one another[19].

One, could of course interpret it in this way, though is there any need in actual fact for skulls adorning, a sapling skilfully decorated, surrounded by ornaments and clearly surrounded by cult worship which reminds us of the customs of the ancient Celts? Why, it would be sufficient for the skulls to be in an "ordinary" state. In the way an old Breton hymn describes, saying... *You see there the fragments scattered...hear their wisdom, hear it well...*[20]. In other cloisters in Cracow one can find skulls which are normally the result of the burial of monks within the area of the monastery's buildings. The rituals of the *Brotherhood of the Good Death* are however clearly of a different nature.

Of course, severed heads appear in Cracow in the shape of architectural elements, in both secular and religious buildings, though this can be observed in many European cities. Nevertheless one building of this type in Cracow deserves however a special mention. This is one of the chambers in Wawel, the Royal Castle. Here in the past were hung, under the ceiling in geometric frames, the image of the severed heads of, as it is rightly or wrongly suspected, illustrious patricians of Cracow.

These are the so-called Wawel heads which adorn the coffered ceiling of the Envoys' Chamber in the Royal castle at Wawel. Hung here under the ceiling (in the years 1531-35) were represented 194 male and female heads. They were made by the celebrated Cracow wood-carver S. Tauerbach and his assistant Hans Snycerz (identified with Jan Janda)[21]. Such a display of heads, which was certainly valuable, and not busts or portraits was obviously recognised in local understanding as very important. But why should such a setting and severed heads have been the best way to underline the splendour of the castle and the ruler's might? This brings to mind Celtic customs and may constitute a Celtic or a common cultural legacy. Today thirty of these heads have survived and have recently been restored. Obviously the likelihood that something is the remains of a certain cul-

---

[19] M. Lurker, *Słownik obrazów i symboli biblijnych*, Poznań 1989, p. 57.

[20] P. Aries, *Człowiek i Śmierć*, Warszawa 1992, p. 71.

[21] *Encyklopedia powszechna*, ed. J. Barbag, Warszawa 1975, p. 595.

ture increases if it is not the sole isolated example, but rather a part of whole range of phenomena that could have originated from the same cultural source. It is against such a background that we must examine the above phenomenon. We cannot ignore the fact that, besides those traces of old Celtic presence mentioned in the introduction, there exist in Cracow others which are accredited with a Celtic origin.

One trace of Celtic culture may be the legend about Krak who ruled Wawel. In Cracow, as was mentioned earlier, a whole array of archaeological discoveries of Celtic origin have been found as well as Celtic toponyms, and also the myth thread. These weave themselves into a single whole with the so-called Tyniec cycle, of the legend of Walgierz. Undoubtedly the legends were given a stereotyped character in the Middle Ages, but the same threads, in the opinion of researchers, go back to Celtic times and inform us about Celtic moral principles[22].

Historians are of the opinion that certain rites preserved in Cracow are derived from Celtic sources. It is sufficient here to mention the rite of the so called Lajkonik which has its equivalent in the customs of Mari Lwydd and the hobby-horse in Cornwall and Wales. The fundamental figure in the Cracovian custom of the Lajkonik is a wooden horse on which is seated a human figure representing more than likely, as Rosen-Przeworska claims[23], the Celtic Epona-Mother Earth, who in one of her capacities was the guardian of the dead.[24] The element 'laj-' in the name Lajkonik corresponds, according to the same author, to the name of the Celtic deity Lug. With time Lajkonik ritual changed, to a degree, its external character and significance. For example, the form seated on the horse is at present Tatar, commemorating the Tatar invasion of Cracow in the year 1287. According to S. Poniatowski, the Lajkonik ritual has a connection with the spring "All Souls' days" resolving itself into the burning of a straw doll – the symbol of death[25], which is called not only in Cracow, but also in other Polish towns, Lala, Lel or Marzanna (Maia). Our Celtologists are convinced that this custom of burning Lala or Maia may be a preserved form of the Celtic holy rites to Maia regardedby the Celts as both the goddess of the deceased and the guardian of souls[26].

[22] J. Rosen-Przeworska, *Tradycje celtyckie...*, p. 172.

[23] J. Rosen-Przeworska, *op. cit.*, p. 246.

[24] *Ibidem*, p. 220.

[25] S. Poniatowski, *Etnografia Polska*, vol. 3, Warszawa 1931, p. 268-269.

[26] J. Rosen-Przeworska, *Tradycje celtyckie...*, p. 172.

Another custom tied in with the Celtic adstratum or substratum is perhaps the feast of Midsummer day. This feast represented a time of love and was connected, according to certain authors, with sun worship as well as the purification of the human condition with fire and water[27]. In Cracow the feast was held on the shortest night of the year. Its chief attraction was the burning of enormous bonfires around which the whole local population would gather. Around these bonfires merriment went on, songs were sung, and amusing stories told[28]. The young, especially males, would show off their bravery, and would jump through the flames or fight with sticks[29]. Musicians also were to be found around the bonfire and there were large barrels of beer. Some traces of this custom has been preserved up to the present day. Young women still weave wreaths of flowers with a burning candle in the centre and set them afloat on the waters of the Wisła[30], while the young men sail in boats in pursuit of the wreaths. The catching of the wreath foretells forthcoming marriage. A similar custom is to be found in Derbyshire, and at Shorp in Wales[31].

The mounds of Krakus and Wanda are also possibly remains of the Celtic presence in Cracow, J. Kotlarczyk believes that they are astrologically located in such a way in order to serve to mark out the main Celtic holidays. According to his research the mounds are orientated to the date of the Celtic holiday Samhain[32]. One could mention even more examples of Celtic relics, or those considered to be Celtic, in Cracow and the surrounding area.

In the light of the above considerations, and also taking into account that the cradel of Celticity was in Central Europe, one cannot exclude the possibility that the cult of skulls in the rituals of the *Brotherhood of the Good Death* and the Wawel heads are not relics of the Celtic cult of the severed head.

---

[27] J. Adamczewski, *Kraków od A do Z*, Kraków 1978, p. 111.

[28] Z. Kuchowicz, *Z dziejów obyczajów polskich*, Warszawa 1957, p. 236.

[29] *Ibidem*, p. 235.

[30] *Ibidem*, p. 237.

[31] M. Dames, *Mythic Ireland,* London 1992, p. 214.

[32] J. Kotlarczyk, „Celtyckie święta i kopce małopolskie" [in:] *Z otchłani wieków* (1997), no. 2, p. 142-149.

Jolanta Sierakowska-Dyndo
(Warsaw)

Patterns of social order in the Pashtun and Old Celtic cultures

Looking at Celtic society through the prism of the Pashtun society results in spotting many similarities, both in the realm of values and that of social organisation. On the other hand, the picture of the Celts' social structure in the scientific literature is diametrically opposed to the patterns found in the Pashtun societies. Historical accounts of the Celts, written mainly by the Greeks and the Romans, show a picture of a hierarchical, unequal society, dominated by the strong position of the priests. This divergence probably results from adopting another point of view, from perceiving that structure through the prism of one's own experiences and conceptions.

Similarities found in the Celtic and Pashtun traditions prompt us to re-examine the pattern of the order by which the Celts shaped their reality. In our opinion, in tribal communities of both ethne, the most distinct pattern of order was the circle which symbolised a community of equal people. It marked the borders of "their" world in which the notion of order was based upon equality and participation. The circle was a pattern through which they perceived and created both their mutual social relations, and perceived time. The main principle of those relations was a notion of consensus. The council was the main institution and the source of power and decision making on crucial problems which facing community. It guarded the group's interests, while the level of tension within the group was monitored by the norms of customary law.

Under the law of Celts and Pashtuns, the basic ways of achieving justice were compensation and revenge. Hence the law admitted conflict and fighting as means of compensating harm done and achieving a social and political equilibrium. The norms of customary law in both cultures were intended to maintain the state of equilibrium within the community, but were not identical with harmony. There was rather a state which equalised the level of tensions and conflicts.

The world of the Pashtuns and the Celts was above all a world of warriors, where honour was the highest value. All from outside that circle of warriors, "the strangers", i.e. craftsmen, traders, artists, religious men, and philosophers were of client status forming the circle of the dependent people. Their opportunities lay in a new source of power which was found beyond the group's consensus. Only religion and its representatives – druids with the Celts and Muslim clergy with the Pashtuns – could be that source. Through sanctification of tribal power they gradually changed the pattern of order which was petrified in collective imagination and symbolised by the figure of circle.

Wzór ładu społecznego w kulturze pasztuńskiej i kulturach staroceltyckich*

Hipoteza o jedności ludów indoeuropejskich, do których należą zarówno Pasztunowie jak i Celtowie, skłania nas do dokonywania porównań, szukania podobieństw zdolnych wyjaśnić tajemnice ówczesnego świata, a także do weryfikowania dotychczasowej o nim wiedzy. Zachętą do poszukiwania paraleli w kulturze pasztuńskiej i celtyckiej są wyniki dotychczasowych badań prowadzonych przez specjalistów różnych dziedzin nauki (językoznawców, archeologów, genetyków i innych). Dowodzą one, że udział Indoirańczyków w kształtowaniu się etnosu celtyckiego jest prawdopodobnie faktem[1]. W najnowszych badaniach potwierdzają to biolodzy, dowodząc, że pod względem genetycznym Europejczycy są bardzo zbliżeni do ludów irańskich, od dawna zaś piszą o tym językoznawcy. Wśród wielu hipotez są takie, które wskazują, iż pomimo ogromnego rozproszenia Indoeuropejczyków, które dokonywało się na znacznej przestrzeni i w bardzo długim czasie, najliczniejsze podobieństwa w zakresie terminologii dotyczącej kultu, prawa, instytucji są pomiędzy Indoeuropejczykami geograficznie najbardziej odległymi, to znaczy pomiędzy Indoirańczykami z jednej strony, a Italikami i Celtami z drugiej. Można zatem przypuszczać, że ludy

* Pragnę wyrazić moje podziękowanie pani dr hab. J. Pstrusińskiej z Instytutu Filologii Orientalnej UJ za udostępnienie mi materiałów i wyników najnowszych badań dotyczących kultury Celtów. Bez jej pomocy artykuł ten nie mógłby powstać.

[1] Przegląd wyników tych badań zob. J. Pstrusińska, "Why the Celto-Asiatic seminar? I. Celtic versus Indo-Iranian", [w:] *Iranica Cracoviensia. Cracov Iranian Studies in Memory of Władysław Dulęba*, red. A. Krasnowolska, Kraków 1996, s. 195-210.

mówiące bliskimi językami, w których zachowało się tak wiele podobnych terminów musiały mieć i wspólne wyobrażenia, wspólny obraz ładu, wzór porządku, według którego organizowały swoją rzeczywistość. Z tego założenia wychodził Georges Dumézil pisząc, że ludzie, którzy nadawali tę samą nazwę koniowi, tak samo określali króla, złowieszczą chmurę i bogów musieli mieć podobną koncepcję świata, widzialnego, jak i niewidzialnego[2].

Odtworzenie wzoru ich świata, wzoru według którego go postrzegano, wymaga analizy zarówno systemu wartości, jak i rekonstrukcji struktury organizacji społecznej. Pozwala ona określić symbole-archetypy, z których ludzie wyprowadzają swoją istotę i egzystencję.

Symbolami takimi, o niezmiernie szerokim zasięgu, są symbole wyrażające reguły dysponowania władzą – koło i piramida. W kontekście społecznym symbolizują one przeciwstawne pojęcia ładu. Koło wyraża pojęcie ładu opartego na równorzędności i współuczestnictwie, piramida symbolizuje wartości autokratyczne, reguły rządzenia oparte na autorytecie i hierarchii. Odszukanie tych podstawowych wzorów ładu społecznego pozwala na rozpoznanie „logiki kolektywnego działania".

Spojrzenie na społeczeństwo Celtów przez pryzmat społeczeństwa Pasztunów przynosi zaskakująco dużo podobieństw, zarówno w sferze wartości jak i organizacji społecznej. Tymczasem obraz struktury społecznej Celtów jest w literaturze naukowej diametralnie różny od wzorów, jakie odnajdujemy w społecznościach pasztuńskich. W plemiennej społeczności Pasztunów najbardziej czytelnym wzorem ładu był krąg. Symbolizował on wspólnotę ludzi równych. Wyznaczał granice „ich" świata, w którym pojęcie ładu oparte było na równorzędności i współuczestnictwie. Krąg był wzorem, według którego postrzegali i tworzyli wzajemne relacje społeczne. Podstawową zasadą tych relacji była idea konsensusu. Stała ona na straży interesów grupy, poziom zaś napięć występujących w obrębie grupy regulowały normy prawa zwyczajowego, zmierzające ku zachowaniu równowagi w ramach tej społeczności.

Tymczasem przekazy historyczne dotyczące Celtów, głównie kreślone przez Greków i Rzymian pokazują obraz społeczeństwa hierarchicznego, nieegalitarnego, zdominowanego przez silną pozycję kapłanów. Taka rozbieżność może być wynikiem odmiennej interpretacji struktury społecznej Celtów, wynikającej z błędnego odczytania „reguł gry", sensu, jaki nadawali swojemu światu, a także doboru niewłaściwego punktu odniesienia.

---

[2] G. Dumézil, *Mythe et épopée,* t. II-III, Paris 1995, s. 40.

Analiza plemiennej struktury społecznej Pasztunów daje możliwość pełniejszego odtworzenia wzorów ładu, choćby ze względu na większą dostępność materiałów źródłowych, a także żywotność owych wzorów we współczesnym świecie Pasztunów. Podobieństwa, jakie odnajdujemy w tradycji Celtów skłaniają do ponownych rozważań wzoru ładu, według którego organizowali swoją rzeczywistość.

Główną instytucją zapewniającą bezpieczeństwo i zaspokojenie potrzeb grupy i jej członków w obu społeczeństwach był ród (klan), u Pasztunów zwany *chel,* u Celtów *fine*. Spełniał on zarówno funkcje gospodarcze, polityczne, jak i kulturowe. Stanowił także organizację o charakterze wojskowym. Opierając się na więzi krewniaczej grupował kilkadziesiąt małych i wielkich rodzin, które stanowiły najmniejsze, niepodzielne ogniwo w strukturze plemiennej[3]. Grupa rodów wyprowadzająca swoją tożsamość od wspólnego przodka w linii męskiej tworzyła plemię, u Pasztunów zwane *tabar* (także *ghabila, tajfa*), u Celtów określane terminem *tuath* (porównaj walijskie *tud* – plemię, perskie *tude* – naród)[4]. Cezar nazywa je *civitas*, co świadczyłoby o tym, iż postrzegał je jako oddzielne organizmy polityczne[5]. Struktura rodowo-plemienna Pasztunów do dziś jest bardzo żywa. Tworzą ją liczne rody i plemiona, z których największe to Abdali, Ghilzaj i Karlanaj. Natomiast organizacje rodowe w Irlandii i Szkocji w pełni były żywe jeszcze w XVII w. Podobnie w Bretanii ślady takich organizacji utrzymywały się aż do czasów rewolucji francuskiej[6].

Struktura rodowo-plemienna Pasztunów opierała się na zasadzie reprezentacji. Wszystkie grupy miały swojego przedstawiciela, który reprezentował ich interesy na szerszym forum. Na czele najmniejszego ogniwa w strukturze plemiennej, tj. na czele rodziny, stał najstarszy wiekiem bądź pozycją, *meszer*. Był to ojciec lub w wypadku śmierci inny przedstawiciel rodziny w linii męskiej. *Meszer* jako głowa rodziny reprezentował jej interesy, władał jej ziemią i zarządzał tymi, którzy na niej pracowali. Uczestniczył w plemiennych

3 Podstawowym ogniwem rodu celtyckiego była rodzina. Rodziny tworzyły większe grupy krewniacze zwane: *gelfine* – rodzina 3-pokoleniowa, *derbfine* – 4-pokoleniowa, *iarfine* – 5-pokoleniowa, *idfine* – 6-pokoleniowa.

4 P. Russell, *An Introduction to the Celtic languages*, New York 1995, s. 240; Ю. А. Рубинчик, *Персидско-русский словарь*, Москва 1970, т. I, с. 408.

5 T. Champion, "Power, Politics and Status", [w:] *The Celtic World*, red. M. J. Green, London 1995, s. 88.

6 Więcej na ten temat zob. R. Chauviré, *L'historie de l'Irlande*, Paris 1949, s. 35-41.

radach i nawet jeśli nie był starym człowiekiem, miał wszelkie uprawnienia i przywileje należne starszyźnie. Podobna struktura istniała u Celtów. Tam także wszelkie interesy rodziny reprezentował najstarszy z rodu, będący najczęściej głową tegoż rodu.

Najwyższą pozycję w strukturze władzy wykonawczej plemienia bądź rodu Pasztunów zajmował *chan*. Wybierany był spośród najbardziej szanowanych członków plemienia, musiał odznaczać się odwagą, być ambitny i waleczny, żyć zgodnie z zasadami kodeksu *pasztunwali*[7]. Y. W. Anderson twierdzi, że w „idealnym" pasztuńskim rodzie *chan* ani nie był wybierany, ani naznaczany, sam się wynosił na tę funkcję dzięki swoim cechom charakteru i osiągnięciom[8]. Chuszhal Chan Chattak, afgański poeta i chan (1613-1691) pisał:

Ten, kto boi się ryzykować życiem
Lub niechętnie wydaje pieniądze,
Nigdy nie będzie wodzem ani monarchą,
A ziemie podbite nigdy nie będą jego[9].

Pozycja chana była szczególna. Głównym jego zadaniem było jednoczenie wielu spokrewnionych rodów, reprezentowanie ich interesów w kontaktach z obcymi. Raczej wspierał niż rozkazywał. Nie oczekiwano od niego rządzenia, tylko doradzania, perswadowania, wyrażania wspólnych interesów plemienia bądź rodu. Władza chana nie była utożsamiana z przewagą i dominacją, co zwykle idzie w parze z personalizacją autorytetu, lecz raczej z protekcją i opieką. Na nim ciążył obowiązek pomocy ekonomicznej i politycznej, co często sprowadzało się do utrzymywanie wielu współplemieńców. Liczba „rezydentów", których wspierał chan świadczyła o jego znaczeniu i pozycji. W zamian za opiekę obowiązywała lojalność i poparcie.

Ze źródeł antycznych wiemy, że w społeczności Celtów przywódca plemion, zwany był *rí*. Termin ten tłumaczony jest najczęściej jako król. Najnowsze badania nie potwierdzają trafności tego tłumaczenia, sugerują, iż pojęcie

[7] Zasady kodeksu omawiam w książce pt. *Granice wyobraźni politycznej Afgańczyków. Normatywno-aksjologiczne aspekty tradycji afgańskiej*, Warszawa 1998, s. 25-56.

[8] Y. W. Anderson, Khan and Khel: "The Dialectics of Pakhtun Tribalism", [w:] *The Conflict of Tribe and State in Iran and Afghanistan*, red. R. Tapper, London-New York 1983, s. 133.

[9] *Afghan Poetry of the Seventeenth Century: Being a Selections from the Poems of Khush Hal Khan Khattak with Translations and Grammatical Introduction*, red. C. E. Biddulph, London 1890, s. 116.

rí oznaczało protektora, człowieka posiadającego siłę lub charyzmę[10]. Był on wybierany przez zgromadzenie „ludzi wolnych". Każdy członek plemienia mógł być wybrany królem. Musiał wykazywać się takimi cechami, jak mądrość, waleczność, odwaga. Z tradycji prawnej Irlandii wynika, że król mógł kontrolować kilka plemion, nazywany był wówczas „królem wielkich królów"[11]. Zależność, lojalność innych wodzów utrzymywana była poprzez subsydia. Pojęcie głównego, jednego króla jest obce tradycji Irlandii. Żaden król Irlandii nie kontrolował w pełni całego terytorium. Większość z nich sprawowała władzę na małych obszarach, kontrolowała „królestwa" liczące kilka tysięcy ludzi. Król celtycki, podobnie jak pasztuński chan, postrzegany był jako obrońca i protektor społeczności, odpowiedzialny za jej bezpieczeństwo i dobrobyt[12]. Sprawował on funkcję sędziego i wodza w czasie wojny, nie ustanawiał jednak praw. Źródłem prawa była rada.

W obu społecznościach główną instytucją koncentrującą władzę zarówno ustawodawczą, jak i wykonawczą była rada, u Pasztunów zwana *dżirga*, u Celtów *oinach*. Rada była także organem o charakterze sądowo-rozjemczym. O radzie Celtów wiadomo, że oprócz wyboru króla, podejmowała wszystkie postanowienia dotyczące wspólnych interesów, takich jak układy z innymi ludami i plemionami, wojna i pokój, podniesienie podatków itp. Źródła wspominają także o radzie zwanej *aireacht*, w skład której wchodzili najbardziej zasłużeni, liczący się członkowie plemienia. Kompetencje obu rad były różne.

Na temat pasztuńskiej dżirgi zachowały się podobne informacje. W zależności od wagi omawianych spraw i składu osobowego Pasztunowie w okresie przedmuzułmańskim wyróżniali dwie podstawowe formy dżirgi: *sabha dżirga,* zebranie narodu, i *samti dżirga*, zebranie autorytetów. Podobne instytucje spotykamy w dawnych Indiach. Indyjski radża, wódz, swą władzę dzielił częściowo z dwoma ciałami doradczymi, noszącymi niemal identycznie brzmiące nazwy: *sabha dżirga* i *samti dżirga*. Przypuszcza się, że były to rodzaje zgromadzeń. Ich kompetencje nie są do końca jasne. E. Słuszkiewicz po-

---

[10] Por. J. P. Mallory, *In Search of the Indo-Europeans. Language, Archeology and Myth*, London 1989, s. 125.

[11] F. Kelly, *A Guide to Early Irish Law*, Dublin 1983, *Early Irish Law Series*, vol. III, s. 17.

[12] Taki obraz króla zachował się w wielu sagach ludów celtyckich, m.in. w tekstach walijskich. por. A. O. H. Jarman, "The Heroic Ideal in Early Welsh Poetry", [w:] *Beiträge zur Indogermanistik und Keltologie, Innsbrucker Beitrage zur Kulturwissenschaft*, red. W. Meid, Bd. 13, Innsbruck 1967, s. 195.

daje, że *sabha dżirga* prawdopodobnie skupiała wybitne osobistości plemienia, była jakby radą starszych (jak grecka *geruzja*), *samti dżirga* zaś – ogólnym zgromadzeniem wszystkich wolnych lub głów rodzin[13]. W Afganistanie członkami *sabha dżirga* byli zwykli członkowie plemienia, a *samti dżirga* – notable. *Sabha dżirga* zbierała się w celu rozstrzygnięcia wewnętrznych spraw dotyczących jednego rodu bądź wsi. Brali w niej udział wszyscy zainteresowani, w tym także kobiety. Przy tym każdy uczestnik mógł otwarcie zabierać głos i wyrażać swoją opinię. Liczba osób reprezentujących jedną rodzinę nie miała znaczenia, ponieważ nie istniała forma głosowania i większość nie była podstawą do podejmowania decyzji. Debata nad problemem trwała tak długo, aż uczestnicy zostali przekonani do jakiegoś rozwiązania[14]. Jeśli konsensus nie został osiągnięty, problem rozpatrywano na kolejnym zebraniu, bądź pozostawiano nie rozstrzygnięty. Podstawową cechą rady był jej egalitarny charakter. Wyrażał się najwidoczniej w sposobie formowania rady. Członkowie zasiadali w kręgu „tak, aby nikt nie był uprzywilejowany lub silniejszy"[15]. *Dżirga* zbierała się zwykle na otwartej przestrzeni, by można było obserwować z boku jej obrady. Teren ten z biegiem czasu nabierał szczególnego, często sakralnego charakteru.

Problemy wykraczające poza granice rodu lub plemienia rozstrzygała *samti dżirga*. Jej członkami byli ludzie cieszący się autorytetem, znawcy prawa plemiennego *narchijan,* mułłowie bądź pirowie. Nie wybierano przewodniczącego zebrania, by zaznaczyć, że wszyscy członkowie są równi. *Dżirga* mogła wyznaczyć swoich przedstawicieli do rozmów z innymi plemionami lub władzą

[13] E. Słuszkiewicz, *Pradzieje i legendy Indii*, Warszawa 1980, s. 84.

[14] Jednomyślność w podejmowaniu decyzji wymagana była także u plemion słowiańskich. Stosunki panujące u Słowian połabskich w X i XI w. opisuje w swej kronice biskup merseburski Thietmar: „Swoje ważne sprawy rozstrzygają (Wieleci – J. S.-D.) na zgromadzeniu w drodze wspólnej narady i aby jakąś sprawę przywieść do skutku, muszą wszyscy wyrazić zgodę. Jeżeli jakiś tubylec sprzeciwia się na zgromadzeniu już powziętym decyzjom, okładają go kijami, a jeżeli stawia opór jawny poza zgromadzeniem, wówczas albo pozbawiają go majątku, konfiskując go w całości, albo płaci on w ich obecności należną według stanu sumę pieniędzy", zob.: K. Myśliński, „Problemy początku państw i narodów u Słowian Połabskich" [w:] *Geneza i funkcjonowanie wczesnych form państwowości na tle porównawczym*, red. M. Tymowski, M. Ziółkowski, Warszawa 1992, s. 126.

[15] I. M. Atai, *De pasztani ghabilo estelahi ghamus, (hoghughi – dżazai – ta'ameli)*, Kabul 1357 [1978] , s. 73.

centralną, byli oni jednak zobowiązani do działania według jej poleceń zgodnych z obowiązującym prawem.

Instytucja rady rozstrzygająca najważniejsze dla społeczności plemiennej kwestie, regulująca jej funkcjonowanie wynosiła ideę konsensusu grupowego do rangi najważniejszej zasady rządzącej społecznością plemienną. Egalitarny charakter rady, w której zasiadali ludzie równi (zarówno u Pasztunów jak i u Celtów) świadczy o silnym poczuciu równości i jednocześnie dominacji interesu grupowego.

Na straży interesu grupowego stało tradycyjne prawo zwyczajowe. W świecie Pasztunów prawo to zwane *narch* (także *adat*) bardzo precyzyjnie określało miejsce jednostki w społeczeństwie, równoważyło wzajemne stosunki między członkami plemienia, jak również między jednostką a całą grupą. Prawo było podstawowym narzędziem przywrócenia ładu. Główną cechą tego prawa była nadrzędność interesu grupowego nad indywidualnym. Członek plemienia funkcjonował jako część całego systemu społecznego i obrona tego systemu należała do jego podstawowych obowiązków. Obrona interesów grupy widoczna była szczególnie w prawie własności. Władanie danym obszarem przysługiwało bardzo często grupie, a nie jednostce, właścicielem obszaru była bowiem rodzina, grupa lokalna lub klan. Wśród plemion pasztuńskich normy te ujęte zostały w system cyklicznego rozdziału ziemi – *wesz,* który bardzo mocno utrwalał kolektywny charakter własności[16]. Rozdziałowi podlegała zwykle ziemia, wiadomo jednak, że cykliczne zmiany obejmowały także domostwa, a przekazanie dotychczasowych siedzib w dobrym stanie było sprawą honoru[17]. Uczestnictwo w systemie podziału było niezwykle ważne, stanowiło podstawę materialną, system zabezpieczenia, gwarantowało poczucie bezpieczeństwa. Było także formą nobilitacji, wprowadzało w krąg ludzi równych. Z systemu tego wyłączeni byli ludzie spoza plemienia, z innej grupy etnicznej, Pasztunowie skazani na banicję, a także z reguły mułłowie.

---

[16] Obyczaj ten sięga korzeniami bardzo odległych czasów. Wiadomo, że periodycznej zmiany przydziału pól dokonywano na terenach przedaryjskich u Drawidów i u Mundów, zamieszkujących Indie Środkowe, por. E. Słuszkiewicz, *Pradzieje i legendy Indii*, s. 39.

[17] Рейснер И. М., *Развитие феодализма и образование государства у афганцев*, Москва 1954, s. 110; В. М. Массон, В. А. Ромодин, *История Афганистана*, Москва 1965, t. II, s. 123.

Źródła dotyczące Celtów również wspominają o kolektywnej własności ziemi, która podlegała cyklicznym zmianom, szczególnie u zarania historii Celtów, w późnym okresie halsztackim[18] i we wczesnym lateńskim. Wiadomo także, że mimo rozwoju własności prywatnej w późniejszym okresie, własność wspólna nadal istniała jeszcze przez długi czas. Z walijskich praw średniowiecznych wynika, że mieszkańcy wsi w Anglii posiadali wspólne pola. Także w Irlandii, nawet w czasie panowania angielskiego, klany dysponowały wspólną ziemią, która w określonej porze roku podlegała ponownemu rozdziałowi. F. Schlette przytacza interesującą opinię F. Engelsa, który podczas wizyty w Irlandii zauważył, że „w świadomości chłopów właściciel gruntów ciągle jest jeszcze swego rodzaju przywódcą klanu, którego obowiązuje zarządzanie ziemią w interesie wszystkich, od którego w razie potrzeby można otrzymać także pomoc”[19].

Priorytetowa pozycja grupy widoczna była także w normach prawa karnego, bardzo precyzyjnie określającego kary za dokonane krzywdy oraz formy zadośćuczynienia. W świetle zasad prawa zwyczajowego Pasztunów, krzywdy zadane jednostce odbierane były jak krzywdy zadane całej grupie. Przysłowie pasztuńskie mówi: „Od jednego uderzenia w policzek sto twarzy doznaje uszczerbku”[20]. Toteż nierzadko lokalne konflikty urastały do rangi konfliktów rodowych czy plemiennych. Prawo zwyczajowe przewidywało, że każdy członek plemienia lub grupy społecznej był odpowiedzialny za tę grupę, w zamian otrzymywał od niej pomoc natury ekonomicznej i prawnej. W praktyce oznaczało to zbiorową odpowiedzialność grupy.

Prawo, *narch,* oparte było na idei zadośćuczynienia wyrządzonym krzywdom, precyzyjnie określało zarówno rodzaje krzywd, jak i sposób ich zadośćuczynienia. Prawo to uznawało zemstę (rewanż) i rekompensatę za podstawowe sposoby dochodzenia sprawiedliwości. Rekompensata najczęściej wnoszona była w formie pieniężnej. Jeśli dotyczyła zabójstwa, zwana była *chun* (pers. krew). Inne przestępstwa, jak kradzież, krzywoprzysięstwo, podpalenie domu,

---

[18] Okres halsztacki (nazwany tak od wykopalisk w austriackim miasteczku Hallstatt) datowany jest od końca VIII w. p.n.e. do połowy V w. p.n.e., po nim następuje okres lateński, który trwał do początków nowej ery.

[19] Por. F. Schlette, *Celtowie*, (tłum. S. Lisiecka, B. Wierzbicka), Łódź 1987, s. 119. Więcej na temat kolektywnej własności ziemi i jej cyklicznego rozdziału u Celtów zob.: С. В. Шкунаев, *Община и общество западных Кельтов*, Москва 1989, s. 87-103.

[20] *Paszto mataluna*, Kabul 1357 (1979), s. 152.

nawadnianie pola poza kolejnością itp., także miały swoją cenę określaną w zależności od kategorii czynu. *Tawan* było karą płaconą za zranienie, *nagha* – za wycięcie drzew, kradzież, itp., *szarm* – za odmowę udzielenia gościny, obrazę członka rady plemiennej i. in. Prawo precyzyjnie określało cenę krwi należną poszkodowanej rodzinie. Cena ta stanowiła punkt odniesienia przy wymierzaniu wysokości innych kar, przede wszystkim kary *tawan*. Jej wysokość zróżnicowana była w zależności od miejsca zranienia, wieku, płci i pozycji zranionej osoby. I tak np. za wybicie jednego oka rekompensata wynosiła połowę ceny krwi *chun*, za dwoje – jeden *chun*, za wybicie każdego zęba – 1/10 *chun*[21]. Wysokość ceny wzrastała, jeśli poszkodowanym był przywódca rodu lub osoba znana i ceniona. Cenę krwi bardzo wysoką, wynoszącą siedmiokrotny *chun* płacono także za porwanie cudzej żony, choć w wielu plemionach czyn ten wymagał pomszczenia. Wysokość *chun* określali biegli w prawie zwyczajowym *narchijan* na specjalnych posiedzeniach zwanych *maraka* (w latach 30-tych wahała się ona od siedmiu do jedenastu tysięcy afghani). W jej skład wchodzili członkowie plemienia cieszący się szacunkiem i poważaniem, (także jeśli byli młodzi) oraz znawcy prawa. Wszystkich obejmował immunitet, naruszenie ich godności i bezpieczeństwa pociągało za sobą kary. Kwestie sporne rozstrzygane były bądź po wcześniejszym wysłuchaniu świadków, bądź decyzją członków *maraka*. Procedura taka była na tyle istotna, że utrwaliła się w przysłowiu pasztuńskim, które mówi: „Najpierw mnie osądź, dopiero potem zabij"[22]. Decyzje *maraka* bądź *dżirga*, zwoływanej w sprawie rozstrzygnięcia poważnych konfliktów, musiały być bezwzględnie przestrzegane. W przypadku niewykonania lub ich naruszenia winnemu groziło spalenie domu, często też wykluczenie z plemienia.

Zapłata ceny krwi była jedną z podstawowych form zadośćuczynienia za wyrządzone krzywdy. Prawo zwyczajowe przewidywało jednak szereg przypadków, których nie można było odkupić rekompensatą pieniężną. Przyjęcie w tym wypadku zapłaty okrywało całą rodzinę, a tym samym cały ród czy klan, hańbą. Prawo zwyczajowe przewidywało zemstę *badal* jako jedyną możliwą rekompensatę za czyny pozbawiające czci i honoru. Do takich należało m.in. morderstwo, porwanie żony, zhańbienie niezamężnej dziewczyny. Niedopełniona zemsta okrywała hańbą wszystkich członków grupy. I. M. Atai pisze: „Na

---

[21] Por. M. J. Atai, *De pasztani ghabilo estelahi ghamus*, s. 112

[22] *Paszto mataluna*, s. 105.

[23] M. I. Atai, *op. cit.*, s. 18.

swój rewanż, *badal*, można długo czekać. Dla Pasztuna jest hańbą odstąpienie od rewanżu. W niektórych plemionach *badal* jest dokonywany tylko przez rodzinę, w innych pomaga w tym cały ród lub plemię"[23]. Prawo zemsty respektowane przez większość pasztuńskich plemion nie ulegało przedawnieniu, obowiązywało dopóty, dopóki nie zostało dokonane. Nierzadko przechodziło z pokolenia na pokolenie, aż zostało zrealizowane. Utrwaliło się w przysłowiu, które mówi: „Pasztun po stu latach dokonał zemsty i jeszcze powiedział, że się spieszył"[24]. Szacunek dla zmarłych nakładał na kolejne pokolenia obowiązek pomszczenia krzywdy. *Badal* jako norma prawa zwyczajowego nie była zatem legalizacją prywatnej zemsty, choć taka interpretacja wydaje się najbardziej powszechna, lecz postrzegano ją przede wszystkim jako formę zadośćuczynienia.

Podobny system prawny funkcjonował wśród Celtów. Celtyckie normy moralne i prawne były ujęte w skomplikowany system, przekazany nam tylko częściowo przez pisarzy starożytnych, w większej części zaś zachowany w staroirlandzkich, walijskich, bretońskich źródłach pisanych. Zachowane traktaty prawne dają nam obszerny obraz tego systemu i są dowodem, iż jego korzenie wywodzą się z tradycji indoeuropejskiej. Prawo to wprowadza pojęcie ceny honoru przeliczanej na tzw. *cumale*[25]. Honor, zarówno u Celtów jak i Pasztunów, był najwyższą wartością, bardziej cenioną niż życie. Aby utrzymać swoją cenę honoru należało przestrzegać zasad określonych w prawie zwyczajowym. Obowiązywały one zarówno króla, jak i pozostałych członków społeczności Celtów. I tak np. aby nie utracić swojej ceny honoru nie można było spożywać jedzenia, które pochodziło z kradzieży, nie udzielić gościny, i inne. Pozycja króla, wyceniona znacznie wyżej w kategorii ceny honoru, wymagała od niego przestrzegania dodatkowych zasad, związanych przede wszystkim z pojęciem sprawiedliwości. Wszystko, co naruszało prestiż i godność (np. prace wykonywane przy użyciu siekiery czy łopaty, niegodne wodza) powodowało utratę ceny honoru, zarówno honoru króla, jak i każdego wolnego członka grupy społecznej[26]. Niesprawiedliwe działanie w stosunku do ludzi zależnych zmniejszało wartość ceny honoru, jaką posiadał zarówno król, jak i wojownik. Prawo precyzyjnie określało działania i czyny niegodne króla i innych członków plemienia.

[24] *Paszto mataluna*, s. 108.

[25] Jeden *cumal* szacowano na trzy mleczne krowy, por. F. Kelly, *A Guide to Early Irish Law*, s. 17.

[26] Zob. M. Dillon, N. K. Chadwick, *The Celtic Realms*, London 1973, s. 139.

Prawo przewidywało wiele kategorii pośrednich pomiędzy najwyższą ceną honoru, jaką posiadał król i najniższą dotyczącą każdego wolnego członka społeczności plemiennej. Każdy postępując wbrew obowiązującemu prawu tracił swój honor, tym samym zmniejszał niejako swoją wartość, co w konsekwencji łączyło się z obniżaniem ewentualnych kwot zadośćuczynienia. Prawo przewidywało bowiem wypłacanie poszkodowanym, bądź rodzinie, rekompensat pieniężnych, *cró*, jako formy zadośćuczynienia za określone przewinienia np. zranienie, zabójstwo i inne.

Prawo Celtów, które dla jednych badaczy było potwierdzeniem hierarchicznej struktury społeczności, dla nas jest przede wszystkim skutecznym narzędziem utrzymywania równowagi, wyrównywania szans. Precyzja w określaniu ceny honoru u Celtów, czy ceny krwi u Pasztunów, wynikała z ogólnie obowiązującej w prawie zwyczajowym zasady wzajemności, która tutaj przybierała negatywną formę, w literaturze przedmiotu zwaną *talion*[27]. Zgodnie z tą zasadą jeśli jedna ze stron poniosła stratę, to musi to zostać odwzajemnione przez równoważną stratę u drugiej strony. W myśl tego, zabójstwo prowadzi do krwawej zemsty, rana winna być pomszczona zadaniem takiej samej rany, lub wypłatą odpowiedniej rekompensaty. Normy te nie są w istocie postrzegane jako sankcje, kary za przewinienia. Ich podłożem były potrzeby ekonomiczne, konieczność wyrównania strat poniesionych przez grupę. Życie jednostki jest bowiem w społecznościach plemiennych dobrem całej grupy, a obrona jednostki jest jednocześnie obroną interesów tejże grupy. Podstawową wartością, której broniło prawo zwyczajowe, był stan równowagi, pojmowany jako wyrównywanie poziomu napięć i konfliktów. Prawo wyrównując szanse obu stron, przywracało równowagę, chroniło w ten sposób istniejący ład społeczny, oparty na zasadzie zrównoważenia i konsensusu.

Egalitaryzm plemion nie wykluczał jednak istnienia hierarchii. Opierały się na niej stosunki panujące w rodzinie pasztuńskiej, relacje między poszczególnymi rodami, układy pomiędzy chanem i członkami plemienia. Hierarchia była jednak pojmowana jako reprezentacja, była strukturą oddolną, działającą w obrębie systemu opartego na idei równości. Można przypuszczać zatem, iż Celtowie, u których obowiązywały podobne prawa i struktura społeczna, tak samo pojmowali hierarchię. Stąd silna potrzeba rywalizacji, zabiegania o prestiż i uznanie. Decydowały one o statusie społecznym, który w dużym stopniu,

[27] Zob. J. Kurczewski, *Prawo prymitywne. Zjawiska prawne w społeczeństwach przedpaństwowych*, Warszawa 1973, s. 24.

zarówno u Pasztunów jak i u Celtów (potwierdzają to Irlandzkie traktaty prawne) zależał od indywidualnych zasług[28]. Silne poczucie równości nie wykluczało zróżnicowania społecznego, wybicia się ponad wszystkich. W tradycji *pasztunwali* istnieje termin *asil* oznaczający człowieka szczególnie szlachetnego, dotrzymującego danego słowa. Dzięki swoim czynom i postawie Pasztun mógł stać się *asil*, co oznaczało, że zyskał wśród członków plemienia szczególną pozycję. „Ci, którzy uważają siebie za *asil*, nie uznają innych za równych sobie"[29]. Termin ten odnosił się także do całego plemienia, które mogło być uznane za *asil*, najczęściej dzięki zwycięstwom na polu walki, bądź innym zasługom. *Asilwali,* czyli bycie *asil*, było dziedziczne. Godność ta jednak zobowiązywała do ciągłego jej potwierdzania odpowiednią postawą i czynami. W przypadku zachowań i czynów niezgodnych z pojęciem *asil* społeczność plemienna Pasztunów cofała swoje uznanie. U Celtów oznaczało to pomniejszenie ceny honoru.

Zarówno w kulturze Pasztunów jak i Celtów dominował ethos wojownika, roszczącego sobie prawo do miejsca na najwyższym szczeblu drabiny społecznej. Kult odwagi, heroizmu i samopoświęcenia przenikał tradycję tych ludów. Honor, wolność i religia były najwyższymi wartościami, których bronili. Na uwagę zasługuje fakt, że obie grupy uznawały swój język za nośnik najwyższych wartości, w tym wartości religijnych. Celtowie zawsze byli przekonani, że ich języki były językami Niebios, mową Ogrodów Edenu. Jak podaje A. Ross, w Szkocji do dziś żyją jeszcze ludzie, którzy wierzą, że brak znajomości galijskiego utrudni porozumienie się ze Świętym Piotrem u bram Niebios[30]. Z kolei wśród Pasztunów język paszto utożsamiany jest z islamem. Potwierdzeniem tego może być relacja, jaką przytacza w swojej książce Rasa Said Rasul. Autor wspomina historię swojej matki, prostej pasztuńskiej wieśniaczki, która po raz pierwszy pojechała do Delhi. Nie usłyszawszy tam na ulicach języka paszto, doszła do wniosku, że w mieście w ogóle nie ma muzułmanów, gdyż dla niej być muzułmaninem oznaczało mówić w paszto[31]. Język paszto funkcjonował zatem w świadomości Pasztunów jako wykładnia świata, definiował rzeczywistość przez pryzmat wartości, które symbolizował. Dla Pasztuna nazwa-

[28] T. Champion, *Power, Politics and Status*, s. 92.

[29] M. I. Atai, *op. cit.*, s. 181.

[30] A. Ross, "Material Culture, Myth and Folk Memory", [w:] *The Celtic Consciousness*, red. R. O'Driscoll, New York 1982, s. 203.

[31] Rasa Said Rasul, *De Chuszchal-chan uslami kirdar*, Kabul 1966, s. 132-139.

nie go terminem *bi-paszto* (bez paszto) jest wielką obrazą, która wymaga pomszczenia[32]. Dowodzi to, iż w obu tradycjach podział na „swoich" i „obcych" był bardzo głęboki, a zasady równości, współuczestnictwa odnosiły się do grupy uważanej za własną. Kształtowało to postawy wyższości w stosunku do innych, obcych grup. W relacjach na temat Celtów nierzadko spotyka się opinie, iż wynosili siebie ponad innych uważali za wyjątkowych, „często przesadzali w wychwalaniu siebie"[33]. Podobnie Pasztunowie uznawali siebie za naród wybrany, szczególnie uprzywilejowany przez Boga. Według *pasztunwali* żaden Pasztun na świecie nie uzna nikogo za lepszego od siebie, a nawet za równego. Zatem wzór ładu, którego symbolem był krąg, wyrażający ideę równości i współuczestnictwa odnosił się tylko do ładu w ramach własnej grupy społecznej. Mogła nią być grupa etniczna, plemię, ród. Stosunki z innymi, „obcymi" miały już inny charakter, układały się na zasadzie klientelizmu. System ten oparty na wzajemnej zależności patrona i klienta nakładał na obie strony określone obowiązki. Klientela zapewniała patronowi odpowiednią pozycję materialną, a tym samym społeczną. Patron zobowiązany był do protekcji, chronienia klientów przed gwałtem czy wymuszeniem. Pozostawanie poza zasięgiem czyjejś opieki było ryzykowne.

W Afganistanie podobny rodzaj nieformalnych stosunków zwany był *hamsaja*. Pojęcie to dosłownie oznaczające „tego, który dzieli ten sam cień" odnosiło się do każdego „obcego", zarówno do plemienia, które było sojusznikiem innego, silniejszego, jak i do Pasztuna, który opuścił swoje plemię i znalazł miejsce wśród innej społeczności plemiennej. *Hamsaja* to także Pasztun oddający się pod opiekę bogatego i silnego członka plemienia i wreszcie terminem tym określano wszystkich ludzi spoza danego plemienia, będących w zależności od niego. Zależność ta wyrażała się w konieczności płacenia renty, świadczenia różnych usług. Każdy obcy, także ten, który otrzymał ziemię za służbę wojskową, *mlatar*, był określany tym terminem. Znaczną część *hamsaja* stanowili tubylcy, zamieszkujący tereny Afganistanu jeszcze przed ekspansją Pasztunów, a ich liczebność niekiedy znacznie przewyższała liczbę członków plemienia sprawującego kontrolę.

Cała rzesza ludzi zależnych, *hamsaja*, stanowiła grupę bardzo niejednolitą, a ich pozycja była zdecydowanie niższa niż członków plemienia. Świad-

---

[32] M. I. Atai, *op. cit.*, s. 41.

[33] J. J. Tierney, "The Celtic Ethnography of Posidonius", [w:] *Proceedings of the Royal Irish Academy*, 60 (1960), s. 251.

czy o tym choćby wysokość „ceny krwi", jaką określało prawo zwyczajowe w stosunku do *hamsaja.* Zwykle była ona cztery razy niższa od tej, jaką należało wypłacić za współplemieńca. W zależności od rejonu i plemienia, pozycja *hamsaja* była różna. Niekiedy mógł on swobodnie wybierać swojego patrona, w innym wypadku przypisanie do plemienia było bardzo silne. Do grupy *hamsaja* należeli zarówno zubożali Pasztunowie, którzy oddawali się pod opiekę silnego plemienia, rzemieślnicy, najczęściej należący do innych grup etnicznych (Tadżycy, Hindusi), czy chłopi z terenów podbitych. Wszyscy oni postrzegani byli jako obcy, którym nie przysługiwały przywileje członków plemienia. W ich sprawie nie zwoływano *dżirga*, nie mogli też w niej uczestniczyć, wykluczeni byli zwykle z systemu *wesz*[34]. Ich udział w strukturze władzy był bardzo ograniczony, a funkcje miały charakter usługowy, oparty na dwustronnej umowie. Często występowali w roli najemników, *gholam.* Tadżycy, Hindusi, „wolni" Pasztunowie stanowili trzon drużyny chana, *laszkar.* W zamian za służbę uczestniczyli w podziale łupów i nadaniach ziemi.

Klientelizm funkcjonował w Afganistanie jawnie i uświęcony był przez tradycję. System polegający na nierównym statusie obu stron, zobowiązywał plemiona, występujące w roli patrona do wzięcia odpowiedzialności za podporządkowanych im *hamsaja.* Obowiązek ten bardzo jasno sprecyzowany został w *Chajjat-e Afghani*: „Jeśli *dżirga* uznała za swego *hamsaja* Pasztuna, który musiał opuścić swoje plemię (ze względu na kradzież, zabójstwo itp.), oznacza to, że czyniąc go swym *hamsaja,* rozdziela tym samym jego winę, pomiędzy członków plemienia, którzy stają się współuczestnikami jego wstydu"[35]. Plemiona silniejsze miały obowiązek bronić interesów słabszych, jeśli te stanowiły ich *hamsaja.* Wiadomo też, że rzemieślnicy mieszkający na ziemiach plemion, otrzymywali od nich niewielkie przydziały ziemi, które nie były włączone w system *wesz.* System klientelizmu był dość elastyczny, a zawierane układy miały często charakter tymczasowości, były rozwiązaniami doraźnymi. Niemałe znaczenie dla ich trwałości miał tu prestiż i pozycja patrona. Te zaś z kolei zależały między innymi od wielkości rozdzielonych dóbr. Hojność patrona była miarą jego siły. Często sprowadzało się to do utrzymywania wielu współplemieńców. W jednym z wierszy pasztuński poeta Chuszhal Chan Chattak wspomina:

Cały swój majątek wydałem na armię
albo na żywienie moich gości.

---

[34] M. I. Atai, *op. cit.*, s. 50, 68.

[35] Mohammad Chajjat, *Chajjat-e Afghani*, Lahore 1874, s. 359.

Miałem ich setki w swoim domu,
Tysiące przychodziły na zabawy i zawody[36].

Liczba „rezydentów", których wspierał patron, w tym wypadku chan, świadczyła o jego znaczeniu i pozycji. W zamian za opiekę obowiązywała lojalność i poparcie.

Podobny system funkcjonował w społeczności Celtów. Potwierdzają to zarówno źródła klasyczne, jak i irlandzkie traktaty prawne[37]. Patron gwarantował swoim klientom opiekę, bezpieczeństwo, udział w łupach i darach. Zapewniał niezbędne narzędzia do uprawy oraz bydło, czasem też ziemię. W zamian klient zobowiązywał się do płacenia określonej kwoty renty, udzielania poparcia politycznego, pełnienia różnych usług na rzecz patrona oraz do pełnienia służby wojskowej. Pisze o tym Cezar: „Im bardziej wpływowy jest rycerz dzięki pochodzeniu i majątkowi, tym więcej wasali (celtyckie *ambakt*) i klientów ma w swojej drużynie. Jest to jedyny rodzaj wpływu i władzy, jaki znają"[38]. Układ ten opierał się na zasadzie umowy społecznej i stanowił podstawę stosunków społecznych Celtów, przenikał wszystkie jej poziomy. W roli klienta mógł funkcjonować nie tylko wolny członek plemienia bądź obcy, klientem mógł być także król wobec innego silniejszego króla plemion celtyckich. Odrębną kategorię klientów, oddających się pod opiekę wojowników, stanowili „ludzie sztuki" – poeci, znawcy prawa, lekarze, rzemieślnicy. Prawo irlandzkie wyróżnia dwie kategorie klientów: *céile* (podstawowy, poddany) i *sóerchéile* (wolny). W obu kategoriach umowa zawarta między obu stronami mogła być rozwiązana, a wynikające z tego tytułu straty rekompensowane przez odpowiednią, zrywającą umowę stronę. Zasady te ściśle regulowało prawo.

Podobnie jak u Pasztunów status celtyckiego patrona mierzony był liczbą jego klientów oraz hojnością. Posejdoniusz pisze że król Arwernów, Luernios w czasie przejazdu przez tereny swego plemienia kazał „oznaczyć kołkami dużą powierzchnię i ustawić tam beczki z najlepszym piwem oraz taką ilością jadła, że każdy, kto tylko miał ochotę, mógł przyjść i spożywać gotowe pożywienie, przy czym wszystkich bez przerwy obsługiwano"[39]. Ucztowanie i wspólne biesiadowanie patronów i ich klientów było normą zarówno u Pasztunów jak i u Celtów, świadczyło bowiem o statusie i zamożności. W poematach walijskich opie-

[36] *Afghan Poetry of the Seventeenth Century*, s. 66.
[37] Por. F. Kelly, *A Guide to Early Irish Law*, s. 29-33.
[38] Cyt za F. Schlette, *Celtowie*, s. 112.
[39] *Ibidem*, s. 107.

wających ethos wojownika są liczne wzmianki o wspólnych ucztach, niekiedy trwających cały rok[40]. W zamian za szczodrość patrona obowiązywała lojalność i poparcie, przede wszystkim udział w walkach. W poemacie *Gododdin*[41] poeta stwierdza:

Wojownicy Myndoga[42]*, sławni w bitwie*
płacili swoim życiem za ich miodowe uczty.

Tradycje biesiad opiewanych w poezji Celtów, potwierdzają także grobowce celtyckie, w których zwykle znajdowano ceramiczne naczynie, symbolizujące „kocioł obfitości i dobrobytu" oraz głowę lub udziec dzika, wołu i drób. W tradycji celtyckiej na kocioł przysięgano, składano przysięgę małżeńską, jak również towarzyszył on aktom pobratymstwa i przymierza[43]. Podobną funkcję pełnił on w tradycji Pasztunów. W kodeksie Pasztunwali zwyczaj wspólnego spożywania posiłków nosił nazwę *atam*. Atai podaje, iż termin ten zawierał w sobie pojęcie świętości. W dawnych przedmuzułmańskich czasach garnek z jedzeniem, wnoszony wysoko nad głową na pole bitwy, oznaczał rozejm, przerwanie bitwy między dwoma plemionami[44].

W strukturach obu ludów na czoło hierarchii społecznej wysuwa się wojownik. Wojownik jest postacią dominującą, toteż jego wizja ładu, nadawała sens ówczesnej rzeczywistości. Ład ten zamykał się w figurze koła i opierał się na zasadzie konsensusu, idei równości i współuczestnictwa, oraz ideale równowagi. Poza kręgiem wojowników znaleźli się „obcy", w tym także celtyccy druidzi, podobnie jak duchowni muzułmańscy (w większości związani z bractwem sufich). W społeczności Pasztunów duchowni zwykle nie uczestniczyli w podziale ziemi, u Celtów zwolnieni byli z wszelkich powinności, nie brali udziału w działaniach wojennych. Można przypuszczać, iż ich wysoka pozycja społeczna wynikała z faktu „uświęcania" władzy – władza ta jednak pozostawała w kręgu wojowników.

Toteż mimo iż tradycyjna struktura plemienna stopniowo ulegała przemianom, krąg bardzo długo pozostawał najbardziej czytelnym wzorem władzy w świado-

[40] A. O. H. Jarman, *The Heroic Ideal in Early Welsh Poetry*, s. 199.

[41] Poemat *Gododdin*, którego twórcą jest Aneirin żyjący w VI w. n. e., należy do klasyki poezji walijskiej.

[42] Myndog Mwynfawr wódz plemienia z Gododdin, królestwa w północnej Brytanii.

[43] Por. J. Rosen-Przeworska, *Tradycje celtyckie w obrzędowości protosłowian*, Wrocław 1964, s. 171.

[44] M. I. Atai, *De pasztani ghabilo estelahi ghamus*, s. 80.

mości Pasztunów i, sądząc po zaskakująco licznych podobieństwach, także u Celtów. Figura ta określała ramy wyobraźni czasowej jak i przestrzennej. Wśród plemion pasztuńskich i celtyckich wyobrażenie czasu jako koła, nie zaś ruchu liniowego, zdaje się być podstawowe. Cykliczność była m. in. zasadą regulującą dysponowanie ziemią. W figurze tej zamykał się czas stale powracający, odradzający się. Jest to koncepcja bardzo stara, podstawowa dla wyobraźni mitycznej. Od wieków znana była tradycji indoirańskiej w Indiach, podobnie jak w Chinach. Czas mityczny toczył się koliście zgodnie z ruchem ciał niebieskich, powracających stale do tych samych punktów w przestrzeni. Stanowił model ludzkiego życia, w którym kolejne pokolenia w cyklicznym kręgu odtwarzają te same role i zdarzenia, w jakich uczestniczyli ich przodkowie. Na takiej podstawie tworzyły się koncepcje porządku, w którym człowiek, poddany jednolitym prawom natury, miał swoje skromne miejsce we wszechświecie. Według takich samych praw krążyły ciała niebieskie, odradzała się przyroda i ludzkie pokolenia.

W figurze koła znalazły wyraz także rytuały i zwyczaje. W kręgu Pasztunowie zasiadali, by rozstrzygać wszelkie kwestie sporne i podejmować decyzje, w kręgu tańczyli taniec wojowników, *atan*.

Krąg był pojęciem mocno zakorzenionym w tradycji Irlandii. Jak podaje P. B. Ellis, w dawnej Irlandii wszechświat postrzegano jako coś okrągłego, ślady takiego myślenia zachowały się w języku. Staroirlandzkie słowa *criunne* i *roth* oznaczały zarówno świat, jak i krąg[45]. Naśladowanie ruchu słońca przez zataczanie kręgów wokól domu miało gwarantować pomyślność. W Szkocji jeszcze w XVIII w., aby zapewnić sobie powodzenie, obnoszono ogień zataczając krąg wokół domu, gospodarstwa, pola, bydła i ludzi. Kobiety po urodzeniu dziecka zataczały wokół niego krąg przed udzieleniem zgody na sakrament chrztu[46].

Zdaniem Mirandy J. Green, pojęcie cykliczności jest podstawową ideą w wierzeniach i praktykach celtyckich druidów, a symbol kręgu, wyrażający całość i wieczność, przenika całkowicie ich sposób myślenia. Życie jest postrzegane jako krąg, jest nieskończenie powtarzającym się cyklem: życia, śmierci, odrodzenia i ponownych narodzin. Toteż w kręgach najczęściej kamiennych, ale także wyznaczanych przez drzewa bądź ludzi, odbywały się ceremonie celtyckich druidów[47].

[45] P. B. Ellis, *Druidzi*, Warszawa 1999, s. 118.

[46] *Ibidem*.

[47] Por. M. J. Green, *Exploring the World of the Druids*, London 1997, s. 177.

U Celtów symbol ten przetrwał także w architekturze. Ich grobowce budowane z bloków skalnych nakrytych okrągłym kopcem, zdobione spiralami i kołami, wznoszono na planie okręgu[48]. Odzwierciedlały one być może ideę porządku, która nadawała sens ich wyobrażeniom społecznym. Idea ta, utrwalona w symbolu koła i przechowana w tradycji, stanowi źródło inspiracji we współczesnej sztuce i architekturze Irlandii[49]. Być może źródła tych wzorców sięgnęły także tradycji architektonicznych ludów irańskich, których budowle i miasta oparte były na planie okręgu. W ten sposób budowano achemenidzkie cytadele, partyjskie i sasanidzkie miasta. Wykopaliska prowadzone w północnym Afganistanie odkryły wiele takich „kolistych" miast, m. in. w Altin Diljar Tepe czy Emszi Tepe. Ufortyfikowane, z potężnymi cytadelami otoczonymi murami, stanowiły od wieków typ zabudowań charakterystyczny dla architektury Azji Środkowej[50].

---

[48] Więcej na ten temat zob. G. Eogan, "The Prehistoric Foundations of the Celtic West: Passage Tombs and Early Settled Life in Western Europe" [w:] *The Celtic Consciousnes*, red. R. O'Driscoll, s. 95-117.

[49] Zob. R. Varia, "The Permanence of the Spiritual: Celtic Art And Modern Art: Brancusi, Damian" [w:]*The Celtic Consciousnes*, red. R. O'Driscoll, s. 573-578.

[50] Zob. Maurizio Taddei, "Afghanistan: Prehistoric architecture" [w:] *Dictionary of Art*, red. J. Turner , t. I, N. York 1996, s. 190.

Piotr Stalmaszczyk
(Lodz)

Bibliography of Celtic studies in Poland. Part one: culture and history

Introduction

Celtic Studies are concerned with the languages, literature, culture, mythology, religion, art, history, and the archaeology of historical and contemporary Celtic countries, and traces of Celtic influences elsewhere[1]. The historical Celtic countries include Gaul, Galatia, Celtiberia, Britain, and Ireland, whereas the modern Celtic territories are limited to Ireland, Scotland, Wales, the Isle of Man, Cornwall, and Brittany. It has to be stressed that Celtic Studies are not identical with Irish (or Scottish, Welsh, Breton) Studies, though they are, for obvious reasons, closely connected.

The present bibliography of Celtic Studies in Poland is composed of two parts. Part One includes publications relevant to Celtic literature, tradition, history, mythology, religion, and the most important publications on archaeological findings. The second part covers Celtic languages and linguistics (a preliminary version of such a bibliography has appeared in *Bulletin de la Société Polonaise de Linguistique* LIII, 1997), translations into Polish of books relevant to Celtic Studies, and further additions.

The Bibliography lists books and articles published by Polish scholars in Poland and abroad. Though works devoted to various aspects of Celtic philology and history appeared in Poland already at the turn of the century, it is Stefan Czarnowski who deserves to be called the forerunner of Celtic studies in Poland. Stefan Czarnowski (1879–1937), the author of numerous studies on sociology, religion, history and theory of culture, also published several articles

[1] I am fully aware of the approximate character of this definition. For the most recent contribution to the debate on 'Celticity', see: D. Ellis Evans 'Celticity, Celtic awareness and Celtic Studies', *Zeitschrift für celtische Philologie* (1997), Band 49-50, 1-27.

devoted to Celtic issues, especially literature and religion (listed in the Bibliography), and translations of specimens of Celtic literatures (to be listed in the second part of the Bibliography). However, his most important achievement in the field of Celtology was ***Le culte des héros et ses conditions sociales. Saint-Patrick, Héros national de l'Irlande*** (Paris 1919), an historical and sociological study of St. Patrick and mediaeval Ireland, in which he followed the methodological assumptions worked out by Émile Durkheim. Though published almost seventy years ago, this study has lost very little of its value and importance, and still deserves to be closely analysed. Unfortunately, it is not well-known and as a result references to it are rare[2].

Today, research pertinent to Celtic Studies is conducted by several Polish scholars and institutions. The Bibliography provides an account of the achievements of these scholars. As far as institutions are concerned, two need to be mentioned here. First of all, the Chair of Celtic Studies at the Catholic University of Lublin (Professor Edmund Gussmann); the only place in Poland where regular courses in modern Irish and Welsh are offered, and where vigorous research in the phonology of the Celtic languages is conducted (details will be provided in the second part of the Bibliography). Secondly, the 'Celto-Asiatic Seminar' at the Institute of Oriental Philology at the Jagiellonian University (organised by Professor Jadwiga Pstrusińska) devoted to interdisciplinary comparative research, as best attested by the contents of the present volume.

Also other universities offer more or less regular courses and seminars, such as the 'Introduction to Celtic Studies Seminar' at the Institute of English Studies at Łódź University (conducted by Piotr Stalmaszczyk). Hopefully, the future will see more such initiatives.

It has already been mentioned that Celtic studies form a separate discipline from Irish studies, Scottish studies, or Welsh studies. For this reason the Bibliography does not include, for example, a biography of the Irish poet and playwright W. B. Yeats, whereas it does include an article on the presence of Celtic elements in Yeats' drama.

This bibliography is far from complete in such fields as mythology, religion or art. As far as archaeology is concerned, the reader is referred to the

[2] Translating Czarnowski's study into English would be a demanding and ambitious challenge, however, the task of publishing a second edition of the French original could be accomplished relatively easily.

studies by Janina Rosen-Przeworska, Zenon Woźniak and Zygmunt Krzak, and the comprehensive bibliographical notes therein. I do not consider myself an expert in the above mentioned fields, however, I hope that the present publication will prompt scholars working in the above mentioned fields to provide comprehensive additions. Any form of co-operation is more than welcome.

The bibliography is not annotated, only in the case where the title is not clear enough a short explanation is added.

Bibliography

Bieńkowski, P. 1928. ***Les Celtes dans les arts mineurs gréco-romaine avec recherches iconographiques sur quelques autres peuples barbares***, Kraków.

Bladowska, E. 1987. 'Monastycyzm celtycki' [Celtic Monasticism], *Zeszyty Naukowe Uniwersytetu Jagiellońskiego 833, Studia Religiologica* 18, 7-20.

Bober, A. 1967. 'Patrystyka iroszkocka i anglosaska' [Irish and Anglo-Saxon Patristics], in: A. Bober, ***Studia i teksty patrystyczne*** [Patristic studies and texts], Kraków: Wydawnictwa Apostolstwa Modlitwy, 17-142.

Bober, A. 1991. ***Anglia, Szkocja, Irlandia – Teksty źródłowe do historii Kościoła i patrystyki I-IX w.*** [England, Scotland, Ireland – sources for the history of the Church and patristics in I-IX c.], Lublin: Towarzystwo Naukowe Katolickiego Uniwersytetu Lubelskiego.

Bolz, B. 1972. 'Irlandzkie zapiski marginesowe w gnieźnieńskim kodeksie MS 1' [Irish marginalia in the Gnesnen Codex MS 1], *Studia Źródłoznawcze* 17, 51-66.

Celtowie i ich mennictwo [The Celts and their mints], Materiały z sesji naukowej, Warszawa, 26 April 1985, Warszawa 1986: Polskie Towarzystwo Archeologiczne i Numizmatyczne, Komisja Numizmatyczna.

Czarnowski, S. 1914. 'Dawna literatura irlandzka' [Old Irish literature], *Tygodnik Polski* 2, 347-348, 365-366, 380-383. (Reprinted in Czarnowski, 1956, vol. 3, 11-21).

Czarnowski, S. 1919. ***Le culte des héros et ses conditions sociales. Saint-Patrick, Héros national de l'Irlande***. Paris: Travaux de l'Année Sociologiques publiés sous la direction de N. E. Durkheim, Libraire Félix Alcan. (Published in Polish as Czarnowski 1956, vol. 4).

Czarnowski, S. 1925a. 'Herkules Galijski' [Heracles of Gaul], *Przegląd Historyczny* vol. V, 238-260. (Reprinted in Czarnowski, 1956, vol. 3, 139-160).

Czarnowski, S. 1925b. 'L'arbre d'Esus, taureau aux trois grues et le culte de voies fluviales en Gaule', *Revue Celtique*, vol. XLII, nos. 1-2, 1-57 (Polish translation in Czarnowski, 1956, vol. 3, 173-214).

Czarnowski, S. 1929. 'La biens féminins en droit celtique', *La revue historique de droit français et étranger* 1, 649-651 (Polish translation in Czarnowski, 1956, vol. 3, 134-135).

Czarnowski, S. 1930a. 'Literatury celtyckie' [Celtic literatures], in: ***Wielka Literatura Powszechna Ilustrowana***, Warszawa: Trzaska, Evert i Michalski, vol. 3, 3-66. (Reprinted in Czarnowski, 1956, vol. 3, 22-96).

Czarnowski, S. 1930b. 'Le sanglier mythique des Gaulois et des Bretons insulaires', abstract of conference paper in *Actes du V-e Congres International d'Histoire des Religions a Lund 1929*, Lund 1930 (Polish translation in Czarnowski, 1956, vol. 3, 217-218).

Czarnowski, S. 1956. ***Studia z dziejów kultury celtyckiej. Studia z dziejów religii. Dzieła Tom III*** [Studies on Celtic culture. Studies on history of religion. Works, vol. 3]. (Includes Czarnowski's papers on Celtic literatures, religion and mythology, and translations). Warszawa: Państwowe Wydawnictwo Naukowe.

Czarnowski, S. 1956. ***Kult bohaterów i jego społeczne podłoże. Święty Patryk bohater narodowy Irlandii. Dzieła Tom IV*** [The cult of hero and its social background. St. Patrick, the national hero of Ireland. Works, vol 4] Warszawa: Państwowe Wydawnictwo Naukowe. (Polish translation, by A. Glinczanka, of Czarnowski 1919)

Czekanowski, J. 1961. 'Celto-słowiańska teoria' [Celtic-Slavonic (Anthropological) Theory], ***Słownik Satrożytności Słowiańskich***, vol. 1, part 2, 221-223.

Doyle, A. 1997. 'Irlandia: literatura' [Ireland: literature], ***Encyklopedia Katolicka***, vol. VII, Lublin: Wydawnictwo KUL, 479-483.

Dreger, W. 1983. 'Pierwowzory historyczne króla Artura od czasów najdawniejszych do czasów Galfreda z Monmouth' [Historical prototypes of King Arthur, from the oldest times to Geoffrey of Monmouth], *Studia Źródłoznawcze* 27, 113-145.

Gąssowski, J. 1973. ***Irlandia i Brytania w początkach średniowiecza w świetle badań archeologicznych*** [Ireland and Britain at the begining of Middle Ages from the point of archaeology], Warszawa: Wydawnictwa Uniwersytetu Warszawskiego.

Gąssowski, J. 1979. ***Mitologia Celtów*** [The mythology of Celts], Warszawa: Wydawnictwa Artystyczne i Filmowe.

Gierek, B. 1998. ***Celtowie*** [The Celts], Kraków: Wydawnictwo Znak.

Goraj, M. and E. Bryll, 1977. 'Czy można pisać poezję w umierającym języku?' [Is writing poetry in a dying language possible?], *Literatura na Świecie* 11, 178-191.

Goraj, M. and E. Bryll, 1991. 'Pisać poezję w umierającym języku?' [Writing poetry in a dying language], in: *'Harfa i Orzeł' Z dziejów związków polsko-irlandzkich*, [The Harp and the Eagle – from the history of Polish-Irish Relations] Warszawa: Towarszystwo Polsko-Irlandzkie, 9-16.

Grzybowski, S. 1977. ***Historia Irlandii*** [The history of Ireland], Wrocław: Ossolineum (second edition, 1998).

Jabłoński, W. 1956. 'Irlandia wczesnego średniowiecza' [Ireland in the early Middle Ages], in: S. Czarnowski 1956, vol. 4, Warszawa: PWN, 237-243.

Kempiński, A. M. 1993. ***Słownik mitologii ludów indoeuropejskich*** [A Dictionary of the Mythology of the Indo-European Peoples], Poznań: Kantor Wydawniczy SAWW. (Includes more than 90 entries devoted to Celtic mythology)

Kokowski, A., 1989. 'Pendeloque de Krusz Zamkowa (Pologne)', *Études Celtiques* 28, 209-218.

Kostrzewski, J. 1961. 'Celtyckie elementy w kulturze słowiańskiej' [Celtic elements in Slavonic culture], ***Słownik starożytności słowiańskich***, vol. 1, part 2, 228-229.

Krzak, Z. 1984. 'Siedziba boga Dagdy' [The seat of the Dagda], *Z otchłani wieków* 2, 90-99.

Krzak, Z. 1994. ***Megality Europy*** [The Megaliths of Europe], Warszawa: Wydawnictwo Naukowe PWN.

Lipoński, W. 1995. ***Narodziny cywilizacji Wysp Brytyjskich*** [The birth of civilization in the British Isles], Poznań: Kantor Wydawniczy SAWW (second edition: Poznań: Bene Nati, 1996).

Majewicz, A. and E. Majewicz, 1991. 'Literackie dziedzictwo Celtów' [Celtic literary heritage], in: ***Dzieje literatur europejskich*** [The history of European literatures]. Vol. 3 part 2, Warszawa: Państwowe Wydawnictwo Naukowe, 647-768.

Makiewicz, T., 1989. 'L'interpretation de la signification des autels-foyers celtiques dans le contexte europeen' *Études Celtiques* 28, 273-281.

Mikołajczyk, A., 1986. 'Problemy napływu monet celtyckich i geto-dackich na ziemie Polski i Ukrainy zachodniej' [Celtic and Geto-Dacian coins in Poland and the Western Ukraine], in: ***Celtowie i ich mennictwo***, 34-40.

Morawiecki, L. 1986a. ***Mennictwo celtyckie*** [Celtic coins and mints], Kraków: Wydawnictwa Polskiego Towarzystwa Archeologicznego i Numizmatycznego.

Morawiecki, L. 1986b. 'Mennictwo celtyckie Europy Środkowej' [Celtic coinage in Central Europe], in: ***Celtowie i ich mennictwo***, 41-68.

Parczewski, A. 1902. 'Początki chrystianizmu w Polsce i Misja irlandzka' [Beginnings of Christianity in Poland and the Irish Mission], *Rocznik Towarzystwa Przyjaciół Nauk*, Poznań, vol. XXIX.

Pstrusińska, J. 1995. 'Kultura staroceltycka a kultury Hindukuszu' [Ancient Celtic culture and the cultures of the Hindukush], *Sprawozdania z Posiedzeń Komisji Naukowych*, Polska Akademia Nauk, Oddział w Krakowie, vol. XXXIX/1, 101-102.

Pstrusińska, J. 1997. 'Why the Celto-Asiatic seminar? 1. Celtic versus Indo-Iranian' in: ***Iranica Cracoviensia. Cracow Iranian Studies in memory of Władysław Dulęba***, Kraków: Cornelius Publishing House, 195-215.

Pstrusińska, J. 1998. 'An attempt at an interpretation – from the Iranologistic perspective – of Celtic ethnic names'. *Sprawozdania z Posiedzeń Komisji Naukowych*, Polska Akademia Nauk, Oddział w Krakowie, vol. XLII/1,

Rosen-Przeworska, J. 1948. 'Zabytki celtyckie na ziemiach Polski' [Celtic antiquities in Poland], *Światowit* 19, 179-322.

Rosen-Przeworska, J. 1961a. 'Zagadnienia celtyckie w pracach Stefana Czarnowskiego' [Celtic issues in the work of Stefan Czarnowski], *Archeologia Polski* 6:2, 273-312.

Rosen-Przeworska, J. 1961b. 'Z problematyki kontaktów celto-scytyjskich' [Some remarks on contacts between the Celts and Scythians], *Archeologia Polski* 6, 65-97.

Rosen-Przeworska, J. 1961c. 'Les sculptures de Ślęza, et le probleme celtique en Pologne', Conferences de l'Academie Polonaise des sciences ... Paris, Fasc. 25. Warszawa.

Rosen-Przeworska, J. 1962a. 'Les recherches sur la civilisation celtique en Pologne (I)', *Revue Archéologique* (Presses Universitaries de France), II, 2, 125-164.

Rosen-Przeworska, J. 1962b. 'Les recherches sur la civilisation celtique en Pologne (II)', *Revue Archéologique* (Presses Universitaries de France), III, 1, 37-77.

Rosen-Przeworska, J. 1964. ***Tradycje celtyckie w obrzędowości Protosłowian*** [Celtic traditions in Proto-Slavonic customs], Wrocław-Warszawa-Kraków: Ossolineum.

Rosen-Przeworska, J. 1971. ***Religie Celtów*** [The Religions of the Celts], Warszawa: Książka i Wiedza.

Rosen-Przeworska, J. 1979. ***Spadek po Celtach*** [The Celtic heritage], Wrocław: Ossolineum.

Rosen-Przeworska, J. 1981. 'Celtycka geneza niektórych wątków wierzeniowych i ikonograficznych u Słowian zachodnich' [The Celtic origin of some beliefs and iconographical motifs of the western Slavs], in: J. Strzelczyk, ed., ***Słowiańszczyzna Połabska między Niemcami a Polską. Materiały z konferencji naukowej zorganizowanej przez Instytut Historii UAM w dniach 28-29 IV 1980***, Poznań: UAM.

Sadowska, E. 1984. 'Druidzi w świetle przekazów autorów starożytnych' [The Druids in the Light of Classical Records], *Meander* 1984:7-8, 305-315.

Sadowska, E. 1986. 'Wyspa na rubieży czyli o dawnej Irlandii' [The Island at the Fringe: on the Literature of Early Ireland], *Literatura na Świecie* 1 (174), 311-322.

Sadowska, E. 1988. 'Stefan Czarnowski: a Polish forerunner of Celtic studies', *Hemispheres* 3, 171-194.

Sadowska, E. 1991. 'Rola symboliki psa i wilka w systemie inicjacji militarnej Irlandii 'epoki heroicznej'' [The Symbolic Role of Dog and Wolf in the System of Martial Training in 'Heroic' Ireland], *Etnografia Polska* 1991, 35:1.

Sadowska, E. 1992. 'Martial Training in 'Heroic-Age' Ireland', *Hemispheres* 1992, 7.

Sadowska, E. 1994a. '*Immrama* – Atlantic Navigation in Early Irish Voyage-Tales', ***Proceedings of the International Symposium, Frombork 1992: 'Time and Astronomy at the Meeting of Two Worlds'***, Warsaw 1994, 460-475.

Sadowska, E. 1994b. 'The Military nature of the Raiding Campaign in *Táin Bó Cúailnge*', ***Ulidia. Proceedings of the First International Conference on the Ulster Cycle of Tales***, Belfast 1994, 243-250.

Sadowski, P. 1991. 'Stefan Czarnowski – prekursor studiów celtyckich w Polsce' [Stefan Czarnowski – a Precursor of Celtic Studies in Poland], in: '*Harfa i Orzeł' Z dziejów związków polsko-irlandzkich*, [The Harp and the Eagle – from the history of Polish-Irish Relations] Warszawa: Towarzystwo Polsko-Irlandzkie, 17-19.

Stalmaszczyk, P. 1992. 'Place-names in Celtic Poetry: Problems with Translation and Interpretation', in: B. Lewandowska-Tomaszczyk and M.

Thelen, eds., ***Translation and Meaning, Part 2***, Maastricht: Rijkshogeschool Maastricht, Faculty of Translation and Interpretring, 425-431.

Stalmaszczyk, P. 1994a. 'Geographical Names in Gaelic Poetry: Function and Problems with Translation', ***AINM*** *Bulletin of the Ulster Place-Name Society*, vol V, Belfast 1991-1993, 71-81.

Stalmaszczyk, P. 1994b. 'Modern Scottish Poets: Influences & Themes', *The Celtic Pen* 1:4, Belfast, 3-5.

Stalmaszczyk, P. 1994c. 'Modern Scottish Poets: Part Two', *The Celtic Pen* 2:1, Belfast, 21-24.

Stalmaszczyk, P. 1994d. 'A Note on the Function of Geographical Names in Gaelic Poetry', *Folia Litteraria 36, Acta Universitatis Lodziensis*, 123-127.

Stalmaszczyk, P. 1994e. 'Sorley MacLean and Modern Gaelic Poetry', in: I. Janicka-Świderska (ed.) ***Studies in Literature and Language. In Honour of Adela Styczyńska***, University of Łódź, 157-161. (reprinted as Stalmaszczyk 1996)

Stalmaszczyk, P. 1995. 'Early Scottish Literature from 1093 until 1751', *The Celtic Pen* 8, Belfast, 24-25.

Stalmaszczyk, P. 1996. 'Somhairle MacGill-Eain – Alba's major voice', *The Celtic Pen* 10, Belfast 1996, 8-11 (= Stalmaszczyk 1994e).

Stalmaszczyk, P. 1997. 'Dinnshenchas – Irish Placename Lore', *The Celtic Pen* 12, Belfast, 20-21.

Strzelczyk, J. 1968. 'Początki misji iryjskich i anglosaskich wśród Słowian' [The beginnings of Irish and Anglo-Saxon missions among the Slavs], *Roczniki Historyczne* 34.

Strzelczyk, J. 1984a. 'Iroszkoci w Europie średniowiecznej', [The Irish in the culture of Medieaval Europe] *Nasza Przeszłość* 61, 5-43.

Strzelczyk, J. 1984b. 'Seduliusz Szkot (Iroszkocki poeta karolińskiego odrodzenia)' [Sedulius Scottus (An Irish poet of the Carolingian Renaissance)], *Meander* 1984:5, 213-227.

Strzelczyk, J. 1987. ***Iroszkoci w kulturze średniowiecznej Europy*** [The Irish in Medieaval Europe], Warszawa: Państwowy Instytut Wydawniczy.

Strzelczyk, J. 1995a. 'Światła z Zachodu. Iryjczycy i Anglo-Sasi w kulturze wczesnośredniowiecznej Europy', [The lights from the West. The Irish and Anglo-Saxons in the culture of early medieaval Europe], *Mówią Wieki* 8 (435), 6-10.

Strzelczyk, J. 1995b. 'Duchowość monastycyzmu iroszkockiego' [Spirituality of Celtic monasticism] in: M. Starowiejski (ed.) ***Duchowość starożytnego monastycyzmu***, Kraków: Tyniec Wydawnictwo Benedyktynów, 131-152.

Węgrzyniak, R. 1997. 'Yeats: Celtyckie mity i labirynt symboli' [Yeats: Celtic myths and the maze of symbols], *Dialog* 5, 135-141.

Witczak, K. T. 1997. 'Śląsk w epoce antycznej: kult Alków (Tacyt, *Germania* 43) i jego celtycka geneza' [Ancient Silesia: The cult of the Alci (Tacitus, *Germania* 43) and its Celtic origin], in: ***Tradycje kultury antycznej na Śląsku***, Opole: Uniwersytet Opolski, 43-56.

Woźniak, Z. 1970. ***Osadnictwo celtyckie w Polsce*** [Celtic settlements in Poland], Wrocław-Warszawa-Kraków: Ossolineum.

Woźniak, Z. 1974. ***Wschodnie pogranicze kultury lateńskiej*** [The Eastern borders of La Tène culture], Wrocław.

Zabieglik, S. 1993. ***Zarys historii Szkocji*** [An outline of Scottish history], Gdańsk: Wydział Zarządzania i Ekonomii Politechniki Gdańskiej.

Zawadzki, T., and J. Potocki, 1961. 'Celtowie' [The Celts], in: ***Słownik starożytności słowiańskich***, vol. 1, part 2, 223-228.

Lidia Sudyka
(Cracow)

Possible traces of the Indo-Aryan presence in the prehistoric homeland of the Celts

The parallels between the Celtic world and India have been, and still are, stressed by many scholars dealing with different subjects.

Learned books on Celtic art never forget to mention the Gundestrup cauldron and figures on it are described in such terms as: "a horned figure in a tantric yogic pose" or without the epithet "tantric", "the types of the goddess Sri Lakshmi", "the universal ruler Chakravartin". It turns out that only in India can one find the proper words to describe certain phenomena of the Celtic world. Authors discussing Old Celtic law never fail to quote the corresponding passages from Hindu law treatises. The social stratification of ancient Celtic society has also been a matter of comparison. Some links between Celtic and Indian mythology have created a frequent subject of fierce debates. As early as 1896 Paul Kretschmer noticed that Indo-Iranian on the one hand, and Italo-Celtic on the other, had a group of words in common. These observations have been further developed and analysed by generations of scholars.

It was the general opinion that all these resemblances were so striking as to be more than fortuitous. In subsequent years researchers have tried to give a convincing explanation for this fact. The first explanation was based on the kinship of languages which led to the conclusion that the peoples speaking Indo-European languages were descendants of the ancient Indo-European folk sharing not only a language, but a common culture as well. Nowadays this seems too hasty a conclusion, and even this hypothesis cannot provide a sufficient explanation as to why two these particular nations, although geographically remote, are so close to each other.

After the publication of the *Atlas linguistique de la France* (1902-10) edited by J. Gilliéron and E. Edmont, and the studies based on it, a new method of research known as linguistic geography came into existence. Since that time, as M. Dillon writes, "Linguists came to think in terms of central areas, lateral areas, and isolated areas, of which the first are sources of innovation and the other two are refuges of archaism"[1]. The same idea of central and isolated areas was soon applied not only in the field of linguistics but also in the field of comparative religion and mythology as well. No wonder, that India and Ireland, located at the opposite ends of Indo-European world, seemed to be the ideal pair that should be, and were studied carefully. The conception of "cultural links between two cultures situated on the fringes of the Indo-European world" was very tempting and was taken up with enthusiasm by many scholars. Eagerly and happily they discovered new resemblances and similarities.

Needless to say, there are numerous weak points in this approach. First of all, one should always bear in mind that some of these resemblances may be fortuitous, others are the result of parallel developmental processes, and others again perhaps very general structural similarities of the kind discussed by Lévi-Strauss on a global level (but we are still, of course, left with a considerable number of striking parallels). Another salient point is that the cradle of what we can call Celticity was in central Europe and it was not until comparativly late that the Celts reached their "peripheral position" to preserve their Indo-European heritage. In N. K. Chadwick's opinion, the date of the first Celtic settlement in Ireland is uncertain, but may go back to the Bronze Age around 1000 B.C. According to C. Renfrew, the first immigration to Britain took place at the turn of eighth and seventh century.

The problem of the coming of the Aryans to India is still under discussion. There are even scholars who claim that the Aryans did not come to India from outside but have always been there.

To sum up: "the peripheral theory" has also turned out to be unsatisfactory in our case.

However, there is one more possibility which has hardly been considered – that close territorial contacts between the Celts and some Indo-Aryan groups could have contributed to the development of distinctive Celtic features. The presence of an Iranian or Indo-Iranian element in the area of the possible Celtic prehistoric homeland has been stressed much more often. Links between the Celts and the Scythians of Indo-Iranian descent have been the subject of numerous books and articles.

---

1 M. Dillon, *Celts and Aryans, survivals of Indo-European speech and society,* Simla 1975, p. 17.

On the basis of archaeological data it is also known that around 700 B.C. the Cimmerians (a people of Iranian origin, according to most scholars) were located in the vicinity of Hallstatt. Various other groups infiltrated into the framework of the Cimmerian and later Scythian migrations to central Europe.

Let us quote a passage from the *Argonautica* of Apollonius of Rhodes, the Royal Librarian at Alexandria under Ptolemy II during the middle years of the third century B.C.:

> In the meadows the shepherds of the countryside left their vast flocks in terror at the ships, believing that what they saw were beasts emerging from the sea which teemed with monsters. For they had never before seen ships on the water – neither the Scythians who mingled with the Thracians, nor the Sigunnoi, nor the Traukenioi, nor the Sindoi who already lived around the great desert plain of Laurion[2].

The author informs us that the Scythians mixed with the Thracians, the Sigynnians, the Traukenians, and the Sindoi people who all lived around the plain of Laurion. Apollonius constructs the voyage in such a way as to encompass as much as possible of the world known to him. What we know about the Argonautic voyage and its route allows us to equate the lowland of Laurion with the Hungarian Plain and it seems that the order of settlement from east to west of the peoples mentioned above corresponds to the order in which they are listed by Apollonius. There have been some attempts to put them in a different order, but none of them has been successful.

To discuss the origin of the Scythians mixed with the Thracians or the Traukenians is beyond the scope of this article.

Now I would like to take two other groups into consideration, namely: the Sigynnoi or Sigunnoi and Sindoi.

Herodotus writes about the Sigynnians:

> Of the country north of Thrace, and of who lives in it, there is no precise information; but it would seem that beyond the Danube lies a boundless tract of uninhabited land. One people only have I been able to hear of on the other side of the Danube: these are the Sigynnae, who dress, it is said, in the Median fashion, and have little, snub-nosed, shaggy horses, with hair about four inches long all over their bodies. These horses cannot carry a man, but are very fast in harness, with the result that driving is here the rule. The borders of this country reach almost to the Veneti

2 Apollonius of Rhodes, *Jason and the Golden Fleece. (The Argonautica)*, Oxford 1995; 4, 300-339; p. 106.

> on the Adriatic. The Sigynnae claim to be colonists from Media, but how that can be so I cannot myself imagine – though anything can happen in the course of time[3].

More information about the origin and cultural identification of the Sigynnians is given in the work of the Polish archaeologist J. Chochorowski entitled *Ekspansja kimmeryjska na tereny Europy Środkowej*. He stated that the Sigynnae and Sindoi were undoubtedly of eastern origin and at least for some time they were able to preserve their ethnic identity.

If they were immigrants in the lands where the Greeks described their life and activities where did they come from? – the question could be posed.

Once again we have to refer to the Greek sources. Scylax, Herodotus, Strabo testify that these tribes were settled in the Caucasus region. The Sindoi occupied the area of the Kuban river estuary. What Herodotus wrote about the localisation of their country is:

> The sea freezes over, and the whole of the Cimmerian Bosphorus; and the Scythians, who live outside the trench which I mentioned previously, make war upon the ice, and drive waggons across it to the country of the Sindoi[4].

As far as the Sigynnians are concerned it seems that they were scattered southward from the Caucasus, which gives an impression that these were their secondary settlements.

Interesting information can be found among the Orphean writings, in fragments preserved from one of the versions of the *Argonautica* which dates from 400/500 B.C. While the route of the Argonauts to Colchis is being described, the inhospitable Sigynnae tribe is mentioned as living on the south-eastern coast of the Black Sea and near the south-western coast of the Caspian Sea. No doubt, both the Sigynnae and Sindoi were in a very unstable zone, lying in the main stream of migrations. Perhaps, because of the Cimmerian and Scythian movements, the Sigynnians were dispersed and some groups of them together with the Sindoi infiltrated into the Laurion lowland where they created an enclave easily distinguished among their neighbours because of their specific attire, customs etc., as was pointed out by Herodotus.

Strabo (68 B.C.-c.20 A.D.) in his *Geography* mentioned the Sigynnians and Sindoi only as peoples dwelling in the region of Caucasus. That means that

---

[3] Herodotus, *The Histories*; 5,9.

[4] *Ibidem*; 4,28.

they were no longer present in the Hungarian Plain in Strabo's time, as he was very well acquainted with the ethnic situation of the valley of Danube.
We do not know what happened to the Sigynnians and Sindoi. They could in time have mingled with their neighbours, or with newcomers, or just have moved somewhere else.

One can make an attempt to find traces of them in other regions of Europe. In the *Corpus Inscriptionum Latinarum* there is an inscription from the La Turbie monument which was erected as a memorial to the subordination of the Alpine tribes to Rome. Among the Alpine tribes the Sindunnis are mentioned as a people living in the territory which is nowadays a border area of Switzerland, Italy, and Austria.

It cannot be excluded that our Sindoi, Sindi or Sindu people, as they were called, moved into this area. Perhaps it is not accidental that the two ethnonyms are almost identical.
The Sindunnis are also mentioned by Pliny, and in the edict of Claudius dated 46 A.D.

Now what we know about the Sindoi is as follows:

1. The Sindoi were well established in the lower Kuban area around the fifth century B.C. or even earlier.
2. Around the fourth century B.C. a tribe bearing exactly the same name arrived in the Danube valley.
3. In the first century A.D. the people called Sindunnis, which one can consider a Latinised version of the Greek ethnonym, emerged near Trento; however we have no information whether they were considered strangers there.

It is not very much. A lot of questions still remain.

An interesting hint to the origin of the Sindoi was supplied by Paul Kretschmer who devoted almost thirty years of his life to reconstructing the route of advance of the Indo-Aryans. Kretschmer studied the hydronyms, toponyms, and ethnonyms, and on that basis he demonstrated their route, pointing out that some of the names in the vicinity of the Black Sea and Caspian Sea had an Indo-Aryan etymology. This proves that Indo-Aryan peoples were present there and that the Sindoi themselves were of Indo-Aryan origin.
In Sanskrit *sindhu* means 'river' in general or a particular river – the Sindhu i.e. Indus; or its plural form *sindhavaḥ* can designate the inhabitants of the country situated on a river, or on the bank of the river Indus.
According to many sources the Sindoi were established in the area of the river Kuban.

What is more, Kretschmer connects the name Kuban (in Greek documents *Kuphis*) with Sanskrit *Kubhā* which appears in the *Ṛgveda* as the name of the river Kabul in Afghanistan.

The Caspian tribe called Daš he equates with the Sanskrit ethnonym Dāsa, Dasyu. The name of the Caucasus itself (in early manuscripts: *Croucasis, Croucasim or Groucasim*) he has also derived from Sanskrit root *kaś* which means 'to shine, glitter'. This latter derivation is in agreement with the explanation given by Pliny – *candidus.*

According to Kretschmer one group of the Indo-Aryans, namely the Dāsas[5], can be found on the coasts of the Caspian Sea. Traces of their presence have survived in the name Daser iranianised to Daher and finally to Dahistan. To find the next traces of an Indo-Aryan presence one has to move eastwards and here we come across the name Sindes[6] which signifies 'river'.

Another group of Indo-Aryans, according to Kretschmer, moved southwards from the Caucasus, in the direction of Mesopotamia and became the ruling élite in the Mitanni kingdom. This, in the opinion of Kretschmer, who postulated "die kleinasiatische Herkunft der Götternamen Indra und Varuṇa", gave the Indians their gods Indra and Varuṇa.

From the Mitanni kingdom the Aryans went to India through Gedrosia. This route is testified by the name of the Gedrosian town Pura. In Sanskrit *pura* means 'town'. In 1960 Eilers and Mayrhofer in their article "Namenkundliche Zeugnisse der indischen Wanderung?"[7] criticised Kretschmer's theory severely.

Of course, with the flow of time (he published his work in 1943) some of Kretschmer's remarks had been invalidated by new findings, but Eilers and Mayerhofer questioned almost every single detail.

However, since 1960 the scope of our knowledge has also been widened. New evidence has been found, and new articles published. In 1977, for example, Trubačev presented a list of names from the same region with possible Indo-Aryan etymologies.

---

5 As far as this ethnonym is concerned the writers give different forms starting with Greek Dáai, Daai, Dáoi, Dasai to Latin Dahae.

6 Modern Tejend.

7 W. Eilers, M. Mayrhofer, 'Namenkundliche Zeugnisse der indischen Wanderung? Eine Nachprüfung', *Die Sprache* 6 (1960), p. 107-134.

In a recently published book, *Indo-European and the Indo-Europeans. A Reconstruction and Historical Analysis of a Proto-Language and a Proto-Culture* (1995), T. V. Gamkrelidze and V. V. Ivanov state:

> Traces of Aryan tribes and names are also found in the northern Black Sea area in the Kuban region as well as in the vicinity of the Caspian. These Aryan words, more archaic than the later Iranian forms...". Here Kretschmer's examples are given, with the reference: "However, see Eilers and Mayrhofer (1960) for objections to Kretschmer's comparisons"[8].

Some of Kretschmer's ideas are supported by the hypothesis of Asko Parpola presented in his work *The Coming of the Aryans to Iran and India and the Cultural and Ethnic Identity of the Dāsas*[9].

I would like to stress that Parpola uses not only linguistic evidence, but also textual sources, namely: the *R̥gveda*, the Avesta, the Mitanni oath, and the text on horse training and chariotry, and archaeological data (for example the findings of Roman Ghirshman, an expert on the movements of the Aryans), integrating them. The different sources usually provide complementary information and their integration is always valuable as it can shed new light on the debate.

The main difference between Parpola and Kretschmer concerns the Mitanni Aryans, i.e. the direction of movement of the Aryans. Parpola's theory is that the Mitanni Aryans were the descendants of the Sauma Aryans mixed with the Dāsas. However, for Parpola as well as for Kretschmer the Dāsas were an Aryan people.

According to Parpola, the first contact between the Aryans coming from the northern steppes, the worshippers of Soma, and the Dāsas who worshipped the fire took place in Bactria and Margiana around 1800 B.C.
The R̥gvedic hymns prove that their creators knew this area very well. They mention the Kubha river (at present the Kabul river), the Gomati river (modern Gumal), the Krumu river, now Kurram.

Some groups of Dāsas stayed in Bactria while others entered the Indian subcontinent introducing into India for the first time around 2000 B.C. an Aryan

---

[8] T. Gamkrelidze, V. Ivanov, *Indo-European and the Indo-Europeans. A Reconstruction and Historical Analysis of a Proto-Language and a Proto-Culture*, 1995, p. 811.

[9] A. Parpola, "The Coming of the Aryans to Iran and India and the Cultural and Ethnic Identity of the Dāsas", *Studia Orientalia*, vol. 64, Helsinki 1988, p. 195-302.

language, the proto-form of Magadhi Prakrit, the basis of the future classical Sanskrit. The Sauma Aryans met the Dāsas in Bactria where the first hymns of the *Ṛgveda* were composed. The later hymns were created on Indian soil where the Ṛgvedic Aryans once again encountered the Dāsas who had settled there earlier. The language of these younger hymns is very different. It is no longer a pure Vedic language as it has been changed under the influence of the language of the Dāsas and Dravidians.

According to Parpola, the Ṛgvedic Aryans were trying to subordinate the Dāsas not only by means of weapons, but also by incorporating their god Varuṇa into their own pantheon. In fact this method has been quite popular among conquerors all over the world: to accept some religious beliefs or deities of the other group which one wants to dominate. It can be of great use in securing the loyalty of future subjects. Parpola quotes some hymns to prove from a textual basis that the amalgamation of the Sauma Aryans and the Dāsas really took place. He offers also correlation with archaeological data. It is stated in the *Ṛgveda* that the Aryans or their god Indra had destroyed the forts of the Dāsas and these forts were called *tripura.* The exact meaning of the word is 'the triple fort' and such fortified sites with the three concentric walls (notably Dashly-3 in northern Afghanistan) were found in the territory of ancient Bactria.

Parpola writes:

> The Vedic texts leave no doubt about burning of Dāsa forts by the Sauma Aryans. Perhaps future excavations will discover evidence of this. Actually, the above quoted statement is not quite exact, because there is the "Burnt Building" of Hissar IIIB, even if the fire is said to have been limited. Nearby Yarim Tepe is said to have been destroyed at the same time.[11]

In 1987 Viktor Sarianidi described a newly discovered temple in the Togolok oasis, which belongs to the last phase of the Bronze Age culture of Margiana. Though it looks as if the place was more important as a Soma temple, both Soma and fire sacrifices were held there. Parpola points out that Togolok-21 is fortified with three concentric walls which was the characteristic mark of the forts of Dāsas. All the evidence enables this culture (called by archaeologist Ghalegay IV of Swat valley) to be identified as Proto-Ṛgvedic where the fusion of two religious cults took place: the cult of Soma with the Ṛgvedic Aryans as

[10] The oath appears in the treaty (c. 1380 B.C.) between the Hittite king Šuppiluliuma I and the Mitanni king Sativaja.

[11] A. Parpola, *op. cit.*, p. 230.

its carriers, and the fire cult of the Dāsas, who were also an Aryan people who had arrived in the lands earlier.

Perhaps it was here that the Ṛgvedic Aryans added the god Varuṇa to their own pantheon. The presence of both Indra and Varuna among the Mitanni oath[10] deities "suggests that the Mitanni Aryans stem from a fusion of the Dāsas (i.e. Namazga V related Bactrians with forts) worshipping Varuṇa and of the Sauma Aryans (i.e. foreign invaders) worshipping Indra.....That the Mitanni Aryans probably came from Bactria and Margiana and in any case maintained a close connection with these regions during Mitanni period (via Gurgan or Khorasan) is suggested by the presence of the Bactrian camel and of possible peacocks in the Mitanni seals....." (Parpola, p. 233).

It is very likely that not all of the carriers of the Proto-Ṛgvedic culture proceeded towards India, but that some of them expanded westwards reaching the Mitanni kingdom; the rest stayed in the regions of Bactria and Margiana becoming with time more and more Iranianised.

It is worth remembering that according to Herodotus (7,62) the Medians were earlier called *Arioi*. Perhaps they stem from this latter group. We cannot reject such a possibility. The Ṛgvedic Aryans called themselves *Arya.*
Interestingly enough the Sigynnians are described by Herodotus as colonists from Media.

Strabo (11,9,2) again, informs us that among Da(h)as there was a group called Párnoi. Perhaps it is not by chance that in the *Ṛgveda* the tribe Paṇi[12], is mentioned as belonging to the Dāsas.
Strabo says that the Párnoi previously lived in Margiana:

> Then Arsakes, a Scythian man, who had (in his command) some men of the Da(h)as, namely nomads called Parnoi, who were living along the river Ochos (modern Tejend[13]), invaded Parthia and conquered it.

Parpola comments on this event as follows:

> Due to this movement from the east to west, the Dahae came to live on the east coast of the Caspian Sea, north of Hyrcania (Gurgan), where a district called Dahistan, known since medieval times still exists (Parpola, 223-224).

---

[12] Parpola gives: "The Greek form of the name, **Párnos** < (from Iranian ***Parna**), corresponds to Sanskrit **Paṇi-**, if it is assumed to be a 'Prakritic' development of the reduced grade from ***Pṛṇi-**"(Parpola, 224).

[13] The river Ochos, modern Tejend, was identified by Kretschmer as the river Sindes.

One can find another interesting detail in *The Cambrian Popular Antiquities*: commenting on Julius Caesar's remark (*De Bello Gallico* 6.18.1) that "the Gauls claim all to be descended from Father Dis, declaring that this is the tradition preserved by the Druids"[14], the author contends that "Dis, or Pluto, is said to have reigned over the infernal regions, which Homer places in the country of the Cimmerians. The meaning of the tradition then is, that the Gauls, according to the Druidical tradition, came from the country to the north of the Black Sea, and were descendants of the ancient Cimmerians"[15].

Is this merely a piece of inspired guesswork by an early antiquarian? The name *Dis* sounds very similar to *Dāsa, Dāsai*[16]. Of course it would be too risky to build even a hypothesis on such an unstable ground with the convergence of the names, which may be purely coincidental, as the only proof. However, the idea is tempting, especially if one recalls the name of the king or chieftain mentioned in the *R̥gveda* (6,18,8), Dāsa Cumuri whose castle was destroyed. Was he a predecessor of the tribe later called Cimmerians (Greek: *Kimmerioi,* Assyrian: *Gimirrai,* Hebrew: *Gomer*, Latin: *Cimmeri*)? Unfortunately, we know too little to answer such a question. What we know about the Cimmerians for certain, is that at the beginning of the first millennium B.C. they were living in the Caucasus and Black Sea area, while later we find them reaching Europe and being identified with the discoveries in Hallstatt. One should also bear in mind that even if the Cimmerians stemmed from the Dāsas they would come from the group which had stayed in Bactria and was therefore exposed to Iranian influence. If we are looking for an Indo-Aryan people, we have to come back to the Sindois or Sindis. They may be an offshoot of the group which went to the Mitanni kingdom or an earlier wave of Indo-Aryans. On archaeological and linguistic grounds it is known that even earlier one branch of Indo-Aryans could have penetrated to the north Caucasian steppe via the Caucasus and the route from the steppes to the Hungarian Plain is not very long or difficult for horsemen.

In Trubačev's opinion, "Already in the first millennium B.C., the Right Bank Ukraine was part (periphery) of the Ancient Slavic linguistic and ethnic

---

[14] Caesar, *The Conquest of Gaul,* trans. by S. A. Handford, rev. edn. Harmondsworth: Penguin Books, 1982, p. 142.

[15] P. Roberts, *The Cambrian Popular Antiquities or, An Account of some Traditions, Customs, and Superstitions, of Wales with Observations as to their Origin,* London 1815, p. 21.

[16] The connection between Dis and Dyaus, Zeus, Jupiter cannot be also excluded.

area. As the complexity of the ancient ethnogeography of Scythia becomes progressively clearer, and there is more factual evidence of the preservation in some parts of its territory, of an Indo-Aryan (Old Indic) component or its remnants, besides of Iranian (Scythian), a question arises about actual Slavic-Indo-Aryan contacts as well, approximately in the Scythian period [169,170]. In spite of all the discussion that it has produced or will produce, the statement of such contacts founded upon systematic arguments and facts can move our knowledge forward on this question by shedding new light on known facts and discovering new ones"[17].

That is why the presence of the Indo-Aryan peoples in Europe should be taken into consideration when we are talking about similarities and parallels between old Celtic and Indian cultural phenomena. Links between Celtic and Indo-Iranian languages cannot be only a matter of the remote past (as remote as the Indo-European period).

To sum up:

Around 400 B.C. (or earlier) peoples of eastern origin settled again in the Hungarian Plain. At least one of these groups in all probability was Indo-Aryan. As far as we know, the Celts were well established in the lower Danube region during the reign of Alexander. In the early fourth century B.C. they began to move eastward into Transylvania and north-eastward where they crossed the Prut and Dniester.

The valley of the Danube seems to be the probable meeting place of the Celts and the Sindoi.

The fact that the Sindoi, the people well established in the Kuban area, were Indo-Aryans is still a hypothesis, however there is some evidence to support it. Even the information that they appeared around the Laurion lowland in the company of the Sigynnians is an important clue, if we remember that they were also neighbours in the Kuban region. It seems that they were all pushed by some wave and it is very likely that the Cimmerians were responsible for this.

Thus if many scholars agree that the Sindoi of the Kuban region could be Indo-Aryans, the same should apply to the people dwelling in the Danube valley around 400 B.C.

---

[17] O. N. Trubačev, *Linguistics and Ethnogenesis of the Slavs: The Ancient Slavs as Evidenced by Etymology and Onomastics*, *The Journal of Indo-European Studies*, 1985, vol. 13, No 1-2, p. 242.

I am aware that there are many dangers in such a reconstruction. Nevertheless, we should try to connect certain facts discovered by specialists in different fields. Of course, as Parpola writes:

> Quite apart from possible omissions, misunderstandings and logical errors, no such higher level reconstruction can ever claim finality. New excavations and analyses are constantly refining our understanding of archaeological cultures, and similar changes in our knowledge are being brought about by newly discovered texts, languages, etymologies, and so forth.(Parpola, 195).

The latest research in the field of history and geography of human genes may also add some vital pieces of information to make the picture more complete.

I wish to thank Prof. J. L. Brockington and Mrs. M. Brockington for their valuable remarks and checking my English.

Bibliography

Apollonius of Rhodes, *Jason and the Golden Fleece. (The Argonautica)*, Oxford 1995

T. Aufrecht, *Die Hymnen des Rigveda,* Bonn 1877

L. Bednarczuk, "Języki celtyckie", [in:] *Języki indoeuropejskie*, vol. II, Warszawa 1988

Caesar, *The Conquest of Gaul,* trans. by S. A. Handford, rev. edn. Harmondsworth 1982

J. Chochorowski, *Ekspansja kimmeryjska na tereny Europy Środkowej*, Kraków 1993

The Oxford Illustrated Prehistory of Europe, ed. B. Cunliffe, Oxford 1995

M. Dillon, *Celts and Aryans, survivals of Indo-European speech and society,* Simla 1975

W. Eilers, M. Mayrhofer, "Namenkundliche Zeugnisse der indischen Wanderung? Eine Nachprüfung", *Die Sprache*, 6 (1960)

R. W. Elsie, *The Position of Brittonic. A Synchronic and Diachronic Analysis of Genetic Relationships in the Basic Vocabulary of Brittonic Celtic*, Bonn 1979

T. V. Gamkrelidze, V. V. Ivanov, *Indo-European and the Indo-Europeans. A Reconstruction and Historical Analysis of a Proto-Language and a Proto-Culture*, 1995

K. F. Geldner, *Der Rig-Veda*, Cambridge Mass. 1951-1957, *Harvard Oriental Series* 33-36

Herodotus, *The Histories*, trans. Aubrey de Sélincourt, revised ed. 1996

K. Kretschmer, "Sindoi", *Paulys Realencyclopädie der Classischen Altertum-wissenschaft*, II/5

P. Kretschmer, "Inder am Kuban", *Anzeiger der Akademie der Wissenschaft in Wien* 80 (1943)

M. Monier-Williams, *A Sanskrit-English Dictionary,* Oxford 1899

A. Parpola, "The Coming of the Aryans to Iran and India and the Cultural and Ethnic Identity of the Dasas", *Studia Orientalia*, vol. 64, Helsinki 1988

J. Pstrusińska, "Why the Celto-Asiatic seminar? I. Celtic versus Indo-Iranian", [in:] ed. A. Krasnowolska, *Iranica Cracoviensia*, Cracow 1996

C. Renfrew, *Archeology and Language, the Puzzle of Indo-European Origins,* London 1987

C. Renfrew, review of A. Parpola, "The Coming of the Aryans to Iran and India and the Cultural and Ethnic Identity of the Dasas", *Journal of the Royal Asiatic Society*, vol. 1, part 1, April 1991

P. Roberts, *The Cambrian Popular Antiquities or, An Account of Some Traditions, Customs, and Superstitions, of Wales with Observations as to Their Origin,* London 1815

Strabo, *The Geography,* Cambridge 1930

O. N. Trubačev, "Linguistics and Ethnogenesis of the Slavs:The Ancient Slavs as Evidenced by Etymology and Onomastics", *The Journal of Indo-European Studies,* vol. 13, nos. 1&2, 1985

Interdysciplinary Celto-Asiatic Seminar

Academic year 1995/96

Jadwiga Pstrusińska: *Why a Celto-Asiatic Seminar?*

Bożena Gierek: *The religion of the ancient Celts.*

Jadwiga Pstrusińska: *The parallels between the religious terminology of the ancient Celts and the religious terminology of the Hindukush region.*

Leszek Bednarczuk: *On Celtic languages.*

Jan Chochorowski: *The Celts and the Cimmerians.*

Piotr Kłodkowski: *The world of Indian and Irish mythology – a comparative study.*

Tomasz Bochnak, Cezary Galewicz, Jadwiga Pstrusińska, Zygmunt Pucko: *The cult of severed heads – a discussion.*

Tomasz Marszewski: *The problem of origin and diffussion of some East Iranian names of hemp – an example of the interdisciplinary method in ethnohistorical research.*

Academic year 1996/97

Tomasz Gacek: *A comparative study of Celtic and Asian music.*

Andrew Fear: *The interactions between the Macedonian settlers of Bactria and the native population.*

Jan Chochorowski: *The kurgans of Eurasia.*

Bożena Gierek: *Contemporary druidism.*

Tadeusz Majda: *Celto-Asiatic parallels in literature and art.*

Piotr Stalmaszczyk: *The mystery of the Picts and their language.*

Lidia Sudyka: *The Sindoi – European Indo-Aryan people?*

Marzenna Czerniak-Drożdżowicz: *Celto-Indian parallels in art.*

Algis Uždavinys: *Deliberations on the spiritual hermeneutics of myth (based on Iranian, Celtic and Baltic parallels).*

Academic year 1997/98

Anna Poleska: *The Celts of the Polish territories (the state of research).*
Tomasz Gacek: *On some archaic versyfication systems of the Celto-Asiatic area.*
Lidia Sudyka: *A comparative study of woman in Old Celtic and Old Iranian culture.*
Barbara Mękarska: *Some remarks on the Celtic etymology.*
Jadwiga Pstrusińska: *The old Celtic torque and pectoral in the light of Old Iranian culture.*
Marek Olbrycht: *The problem of the Cimmerians presence in Europe.*
Piotr Stalmaszczyk: *Celtic influences on the English language.*
Jolanta Sierakowska-Dyndo: *The patterns of social order in Pashtun and Old Celtic cultures.*
Asko Parpola: *Formation of the Aryan branch of the Indo-European (c. 3000-1000 B.C.) in the light of linguistic and archaeological evidence.*
Tadeusz Majda: *The parallels between Asian and Old Celtic rites and mythology.*
Iwona Milewska: *Sandhi in Sanskrit and Old Celtic languages.*

Academic year 1998/99

Piotr Stalmaszczyk: *Who were the druids?*
Jadwiga Pstrusińska: *Celto-Iranian parallels of the semantic development of the ethnonym 'Gaul'.*
Jacek Szymura: *Man's past as recorded in genes.*
Lidia Sudyka: *On 'Mabinogion'.*
Katarzyna Kulikowska: *Celtic and Scythian military accessories.*
Anna Krasnowolska: *The Celtic calendar.*
Marek Olbrycht: *On Iranian peoples in Europe (from historical perspective).*
Jolanta Sierakowska-Dyndo: *The social status of the bard.*

Druk i oprawa: ZAKŁAD POLIGRAFICZNY UNIWERSYTETU JAGIELLOŃSKIEGO
KRAKÓW UL. KOPERNIKA 31